Jean Espagne

An essay of the wonders of God,

In the harmony of the times, generations, and most illustrious events therein

enclosed : from the original of ages, to the close of the New Testament

Jean Espagne

An essay of the wonders of God,
In the harmony of the times, generations, and most illustrious events therein enclosed : from the original of ages, to the close of the New Testament

ISBN/EAN: 9783337793333

Printed in Europe, USA, Canada, Australia, Japan

Cover: Foto ©Lupo / pixelio.de

More available books at **www.hansebooks.com**

Johannes Despagne S.ti Evangely Minister
Doctrinâ Singulari
Studio indefess:
Morum Suavitate
Adversorum tolerantiâ.

AN ESSAY
OF
The Wonders of GOD,
IN

The Harmony of the Times, Generations, and most Illustrious Events therein enclosed.

From the Original of Ages, to the close of the New Testament.

Written in *French* by JOHN D'ESPAGNE, Minister of the Holy Gospel.

Both Parts published in *English* by his Executor.

LONDON,
Printed by *William Godbid* for *Henry Herringman*, at the Sign of the *Anchor* in the *Lower Walk* of the *New-Exchange*. M.DC.LXII.

The Subject and Division of this Treatise.

I Regard not those that copy other mens writings, and impudently make them their own: As there are beggars that steal the children of good families, yea, and also maim them, to repair their low condition; so, many that have nothing of their own to write, expose other mens, and say, they are the Authors thereof: What's more common then this kind of rapine? But I hope it shall appear, that I am far from this. If I say any thing hath been already writ, which may fall out unknown to me, 'tis as little as nothing; yea, I have abstained from setting down here the observations I have seen in some Writers, that come but near to the subject I now treat of. I avoid as much as possible I can such helps, and would be asham'd to crave them.

Now that I write of at this time, is not a simple Chronology, as may be imagin'd at first sight; the world is full of Chronologers, and their endeavours is but to reckon, how many years, or how long time is past since the Creation, or since Christ, or since some other famous event; this is all their Arithmetick. But we must have another, where there is more skill, without which, all Chronology is but a matter without form.

All the times since the beginning have run by certain measures and proportions, wherein lies one of the rarest secrets of History. This admirable symetry of Ages and Years, spread abroad and ranked

ranked with so much order, and so artificially compass'd about by the hand of the Antient of days, produceth reflections, which makes his incomparable wisdom appear.

And not onely the times, but the generations and successions, as well of Kingdoms as of Families, yea, and of persons too, are measur'd and proportion'd. And 'tis to be observed, that each Generation, each Family, and each Person, is marked with a certain number, and with a particular character. We know, that numbers are not the causes of that which falls out, but they are marks or seals that God impresseth on his works, to the end we may distinguish them by the difference of their cyphers.

The Septenary is very frequent and general, as being the number of the compleat Creation. The tenth, twelfth, the fortieth, and some other numbers, are by turns, for several significations. Could it be said, that the holy Ghost was pleased to note out an Empire, that afterwards caused so many troubles, and with three numeral Letters marked out the name of a man, which signifies 666?

But 'twill be said, The Scripture expresseth not these numbers but very seldom, and less the proportions we speak of: Also it tells not how many Kings the Kingdom of *Juda* hath had before the Captivity, but onely gives the Catalogue of them from the first to the last. The Scripture speaks to those who know how to reckon. Moreover, God would have it, that the secrets of these measures, correspondencies, oppositions, and distributions of times,

times, and what is enclosed in them, should be wrapt up with covers, to the end we might bring our industry to unfold them. And truly, although the study thereof be troublesome at first, yet we shall find very sweet flowers there, and also the fruits of the Tree of life.

But here's the great brunt, this the great opposition made to me, That Chronology that serves for the basis of my work is disputable in some points, and therefore I lay many disputable observations thereon. To which I answer, 1 That I have many good warrants for this Chronology, and that 'tis born before me. 2 That I can maintain and resolve the difficulties therein. 3 That in the disagreement of the Chronologers, we must always prefer the supputation, where some mysterious point meets, which results from the circumstance of the time. What! shall the variety of our opinions, that come from imperfection, annihilate the wonders of God?

Moreover, the things I produce cannot be denyed, without giving the lie to the Scripture; nor the Harmonies I have met with, without renouncing the skill of numbring; nor to hold them for casual, without denying the providence of God; nor saying they have their causes, without blaspheming them against his wisdom.

The beginning of times shall be in the beginning of this work. Now in the first Antiquity, and also since, many things have occurr'd, that the ignorant take to be very inconsiderable. But we must know, that the first times, and what past therein, is a

very

very necessary Alphabet for the most learned: All the highest matters that are, have need of an *A B C* to express them; as the eloquentest Language that is cannot be pronounc'd, but with the sound of the Alphabetical Letters.

And forasmuch as the Sun had the principal Office of marking and measuring out the times, wee'le begin with him, and 'twill appear, that himself was marked out and measured by the times.

Afterwards we shall see the general measures of times past since the production of the first *Adam*, to the Ascension of the Second; yea, to the destruction of the second Temple: And after that, divers parcels of time of the Old Testament, and the matters therein contained. Then wee'le make a pause, till we come to the particular measures of the New Testament, which shall make the second part of this Treatise.

One day telleth another, and one night certifieth another; how much more one Generation another, and one Age another Age? Then how much more science results from the agreement and concert of all the Ages together, and of all the Generations, which highly correspond one with another? In the diversity also of their tones, measures, and cadencies, we shall hear an excellent and most divine Harmony.

A Monsieur DESPAGNE
Ministre de la parole de Dieu
en l'Eglise Francoise de
Westminster, recueillie
en la Chappele de
Sommerset.

Sur son livre de l'Harmonie des Temps.

ODE.

BELLE lumiere des Pasteurs,
Ornement du Siecle où nous sommes,
Qui trouves des admirateurs,
Par tout où il y a des hommes.
Guide fameux de nos esprits,
Dont les discours & les escrits,
Charment avec tant de puissance :
Permets que d'un trait de pinceau,
Je peigne ma recognoissance,
Au front d'un ouvrage si beau.
 Je scay que par cet attentat,
La majesté de ton Volume,
Ne peut rehausser son estat,
De la foiblesse de ma plume.
Mais puisque tes illustres soings,
Desquels nous sommes les tesmoings,
       Chassants

Chassants l'ignorance & le vice,
Tendent à te rendre immortel :
Mes vers seront un sacrifice,
Qui sera propre à ton Autel.
 De vray quand on void les ressorts,
Que ta discretion pratique,
Pour faire ajuster les accords,
De cette divine musique,
Et que d'un zele imitateur,
Je poursuy d'en loüer l'Auteur ;
Je suis trompé si aucun nie,
Qui soit deux arguments divers ;
L'un plus beau que ton Harmonie,
L'autre que celuy de mes Vers.
 Tant d'ouvrages laborieux,
Fidelles tesmoings de ta peine,
Monstroient assez aux curieux,
La fertilité de ta veine.
Qu'estoit-il doncques de besoing,
Avec un incroyable soing,
D'en donner de nouvelle preuve ?
Sinon pour monstrer aux sçavans
Que ton esprit est à l'espreuve,
Du soing, du travail & des ans.
 Il me semble qu'aux doux accens,
De cette Divine Harmonie,
Les peuples vont s'entrepressans,
Pour faire hommage a ton Genie,
François, Allemans, Hollandois,
Suisses, Danois, & Suedois,
Et cette Nation deslite,
De qui l'appuy nous est si doux,

        Et

Et dont le Souvenir merite
De ne mourir qu' avecques nous.
　Parmi toutes ces Nations,
On n'en trouvera point qui sõüille,
La blancheur de tes actions,
Si ce n'est des testes de Hoüille.
Mais ces esprits mal façonnez,
Meritent d' estre pardonnez,
Car ta doctrine (cher Despagne)
Les perce de mille aiguillons,
La voyant sur une montagne
Et la leur dedans les Valons

THEOPHILE DE GARENCIERES
Docteur en Medecine.

Viro

Viro undequaque ornatissimo

JOANNI DESPAGNE Verbi divini præconi in Ecclesia Gallo-Westmonasteriensi.

In suam temporum Harmoniam, Hyeme typis excusam.

EPIGRAMMA.

Unde tibi (venerande Senex) hic suppetit ardor,
   Quo, medio brumæ tempore vena calet?
Quo, tantam fundunt lucem, simul atque calorem
   Scripta, sub Arctoi sydere nata poli?
An natale solum, quæ quondam semina jecit,
   Frigore sub tanto multiplicata tument?
An quantò minor es, tanto tibi spiritus ingens;
   Et brevis immensas ipse recondis opes?
An potius monstras, divino afflatus amore,
   Quantum est ingenii cum pietate jubar?

Nam

Nam tua congeries rerum dum se obvia
    pandit,
   Quivis inexhaustum te putat esse penu.
Si legit auratas libri Brittannia Voces,
    Tunc putat in Thamesim surripuisse
    Tagum.
Si tua divinis spectetur gloria rebus:
   Tale sub alterutro non datur axe caput.
Macte animo (venerande Senex) sic de-
    nique fiet;
   Ut quo plus vivas, hoc moriare minùs.

          Theophilus de Garencieres
          Doctor Medicus.

Πρὸς τ̀ ἐπίσημον ἄνδρα
ΙΩΑΝΝΕΝ ΙΣΠΑΝΟΝ,
τῦ θεῖυ λόγυ κηρυκτὼ

εἰς τὼ ἑαυτῦ χρόνων ἁρμονίαν

ΕΠΙΓΡΑΜΜΑ.

Εὐπαίδευτε γέρων θῆκες ὅταν ἄδης ἀριθμὸς,
  πρὸς τὼ Ἁρμονίαν ἔρχεται πᾶσα Ψυχή.
Ἄνθρωποι φθονεροὶ ὀγκεῦντ' ὡς Τίγριδες ὀργῆ
  ἀλλ' ἀπὸ παιδ'ίτων, αἶνον ἔχεις κὶ χάριν.
Εἶτ' ἔπεται μοσίον τῦτυ μὲ δ'ἄιτερον ἔργυ,
  Τοῖς φθονερῦς δάιαι σοι πολὺς ὅσαι βί·

Ὁ φίλος ζῦ,

Θεόφιλος Γαρυκίερς
Ἰατρὸς.

The First Part of the HARMONY of the TIMES, &c.

The Day wherein the Sun stood still, and was to him as a Sabbath-day, hapned after the Sun was Created in the Year seven times three hundred sixty and five, a Number that answereth the three hundred sixty and five days of the Annual Course of the Sun, as the Number Seven doth that of the Sabbath.

THE History in the Tenth of *Joshua*, quotes the year of that miracle, but it is easie to find it. The *Israelites* who came out of the Wilderness, entered into the Land of *Canaan* in the year

year of the Creation 2553. between which time, and that wherein the Sun stood still, many occurrences interven'd, as, their passage through *Jordan*, seven days spent to encompass *Jericho*, the siege and sacking of *Ai*, the Conspiration of divers Kings of *Canaan*, the arming and mustering of sundry Nations to oppose *Israel*, the affair of the *Gibbeonites*, the five Kings who assaulted them, the besieging of *Gibeon*; the succour brought by *Joshua* unto them, the battel that was fought there, and other particulars. So many atchievments and exploits which succeeded one another, and were before the standing still of the Sun, were the work of more than one year; if we count them to be two, as all apparences do oblige us, we shall find, that it was in the year of the Creation 2555. when the Sun stood still. Now these 2555 are seven times 365, or 365 weeks of years.

And grant that this Miracle should have fallen out a little sooner, to wit, in the year 2554, it was nevertheless towards the end of the last 365 weeks of years, which answers the days of the annual course of the Sun.

When we say 365 days, we implicitly understand the five hours and the minutes which are above the 365 days; for Antiquity

tiquity had also her intercalcations of days, and her embolisms or interjections of months; and the Scripture presupposeth them, when it makes mention of numbers of years. But we onely express 365 days, to avoid the frequent repetition of the hours and minutes, which are supernumerary. So we also understand, that every one of these years containeth 365 days, 5 hours, and about 49 minutes.

But as for that great wonder, which is now under our consideration, the circumstance of the time wherein it fell out, doth yet render it more illustrious. Truly 'tis not wonderful, that the Sun being about to finish the 365 weeks of the years of his course, hath had a day of Rest: Man was commanded to rest himself on the seventh day, the ground doth rest on the seventh year, and the Sun going about to finish seven times as many years as he employeth days to perfect a year, hath had a command to rest for the space of one day.

This measure, which containeth 365 years, may be called a year of years as 365 days do make up an ordinary year, which is a year of days, so 365 years do make up a year of years. We do give it this name, although it be not textual, nor expressed in the Scriptures, or in the ordinary Chronology. Words are indifferent,

rent, provided they be intelligible. And thus the Sun going about to finish his seventh year of years, stood still to rest himself.

Certainly, the wisdom of God was so pleased that this miracle should be at such a time rather then at any other. His intent in commanding the Sun to make an halt, was chiefly, that the *Israelites* might have light, whereby they might the better be enabled to pursue their enemies. But this reason, although expressed alone, excludeth not those which accompany it. In so many other occasions, where the *Isranlites* had need of the standing still of the Sun, God was never pleased at all to work this wonder. And to demonstrate, that God had a further aime herein, than onely the compleating the victory of *Joshua*, we ought to consider, what is easie to observe, that all the earth hath felt this prodigy; for whilst one part of the world beheld this long day, the other part had as long a night. What then hath been the cause of this strange interruption of the course of the Sun? The greatest part of the world adored that flaming body as a Deity, the ceasing of its motion tended to declare, that there was a Superior who could stop his course, and inhibit and suspend his operations.

This Miracle, moreover, did fall out most

most conveniently at that time; the *Israelites* were newly entred into the Land of *Canaan*, full of Idolaters, and encompass'd with Nations that ador'd the Sun, the Moon, and all the Host of Heaven; God, by this, advertis'd his people, that they should not suffer themselves to be drawn away to such abominations, *Deut.* 17. 2, 3. And to confute them by a visible and irrefragible argument, caused both the Sun and the Moon to stand still at the word of a man.

But there is yet a more special reason why this miracle fell out at the time we have mentioned. The Septenary number of Times, Days, Years, and Ages, and of their periods and Revolutions, is a character whereby we know God hath marked most of his works. 'Tis remember'd of the Rest God took the seventh day, having finish'd the Creation: For this cause he would have the Sun, who is the measure of days and years, should rest one day in his seventh year of years, even then when he had accomplish'd his 365 weeks of years, or seven times 365 years; seven times as many years as he had run days in one year. Finally, as every seventh year was a year of Sabbath, the Sun observed a Sabbath in the seventh year of his 365 weeks of years, which was a year of Sabbath.

How much light meeteth in this wonderful Sabbath of the Sun! that Luminary which giveth light to all the rest of the world, was it self enlightned on that day. *He knoweth the time of his going down*, *Psal.* 104. 19. but did not know till then there should be a day wherein his setting should be later than ordinary. The Sun did never give so much light to our eyes, as these considerations do bestow on our spirits.

Behold then an admirable concurrence; 365 annual days, 365 years answering thereunto; 365 weeks of years, or seven times 365 years expired when the Sun stood still; then did his cipher meet with that of the Sabbath, the number of three hundred and sixty five being measured by sevens.

But let us behold another miracle which he hath shewed us in Heaven.

In the Tenth Year of the Tenth Year of Years, expired since the Creation, the Sun went back Ten Degrees, Isa. 38. 8.

BEhold yet a wonder that parallels or surpasses the former, it fell out, the Sun being 3295 years old. Let

Let us calculate, as above; the term of 365 is a year of years, for 3285 years are nine times 365. ten years after, which was in the year 3285, hapned the going back of that great Luminary. These ten years were then the first of the tenth year of years expired since the Creation. So that when the Sun did go back, he was come to the tenth year of his tenth year of years: and the ten degrees of his Retrogradation did seem clearly to signifie it. In short, in the tenth year of the tenth year of years, the Sun went back by ten degrees. What man is so stupid, that's not ravished in admiration of so celestial an Harmony.

Add to this, that in this Interval of ten years, which ended in the retrogradation of the Sun, hapned the transmigration of the Ten Tribes of *Israel*, that were carried away into *Assyria*.

The History of the Old Testament is of Ten Prophetical Years; and from the ending of it unto the death of Christ, there is the space of another Prophetical Year.

IN the Language of the Prophets, one day is often taken for a year, and the Prophetical year is of 360 solary years. For Example, *Revel.* 12. 6, 14. *One thousand two hundred and sixty days are a time, and times, and half a time*; that is to say, three Prophetical years and a half, three hundred and sixty Solary years being taken for one Prophetical year.

Now, why God accounts 360 ordinary years for one onely year Prophetical, we might find a conjecture in the Analogy of a natural revolution, which hapned within such a term. For at the end of 360 years, and no sooner, the measure of the Lunary year, according to Astronomers, doth meet with that of the Sun. But there is a nearer, and more manifest reason thereof: Amongst the Hebrews, the year which they called Civil, was onely of 360 days; as for the five supernumerary days,

days, they were to be found in every sixth year, adding to it a month, which was called Embolismical. And as for the hours that are above the 365 annual days, there was yet another Embolism, or addition to supply them, at the end of one hundred and twenty years; or from time to time they interserted one or more days: as then the ordinary year was of 360 days, the Prophetical year was of 365 natural years. So from the Creation to the year 3600, there are ten Prophetick years, or ten times 365 Solary years. Now the History of the Old Testament doth end with the tenth Prophetical year. For according to the order of the times, whereof the question is now, and not according to the order wherein the Books are ranked, the last Date of the History of the Old Testament is of the Reign of *Darius Codomannus*, the last King of *Persia*, *Nehem.* 12. 22. This Prince Reigned but six years, and was overcome by *Alexander* in the year of the world 3600, which was the last year of the tenth Prophetical year, there being ten times 360 years complete. And there the History of the Old Testament endeth.

From thence to the death of Christ, in the year of the Creation 3960, there precisely passed another Prophetical year; For from the year 3600, where at the
tenth

tenth Prophetical year expired, to the year 3960, there are 360 years, which are yet one Prophetical year, which is the interval that is found between the ending of the Old Testament, and the exhibition of the New, when Christ seal'd it with his Blood.

Thus the Holy History having begun from the original of Times, did go on till it came to the end of the ten Prophetical years; there it rested, and became silent for the space of another Prophetical year, which ended at the death of Christ, and was followed by the writing of the New Testament. This measure of time was as a Tenth of years proportionated and substituted to all those that went before. And thus as Christ was drawing near to shut up the Prophecies, the which he did by his Death, and his Exaltation, the Pen of the Prophets rested during the space of one Prophetical year.

Admirable

Admirable conformities. Since Adam, be therein included, two and twenty Patriarchs, until the Church began to become a Body National. Two and twenty Generations of High Priests, from the Institution of the Priesthood, to the intermission of the Sacrifices, which hapned at the destruction of the first Temple. Two and twenty Governors, as well lawful as tyrannical, from the entring of Israel into the Land of Promise, under the conduct of Joshua, to the first King, who was Saul. Two and twenty Kings, beginning at Saul, until the ruine of the first Temple, where Royalty and Kingship was extinguished. Two and twenty Generations in the Race of our Saviour, from the Captivity of Babylon to Christ the Prince.

The two and twenty Patriarchs.

1 *Adam*
2 *Seth*
3 *Enos.*
4 *Kenan*
5 *Mahalaleel*
6 *Jared*
7 *Henoc*
8 *Methuselah*
9 *Lamech*
10 *Noe*
11 *Sem*

12 *Arphaxad*
13 *Scelah*
14 *Heber*
15 *Peleg*
16 *Rehu*
17 *Serug*
18 *Nahor*
19 *Terah*
20 *Abraham*
21 *Isaac*
22 *Jacob*

Whilst

Whilst the Church consisted onely in some Families, which was until the death of *Jacob*, it was governed by these Patriarchs; afterwards it became a Nation.

The two and twenty Generations of High-Priests.

1 *Aaron*
2 *Eleazar*
3 *Phineas*
4 *Abishuah*
5 *Bukki*
6 *Huzi*
7 *Zerajah*
8 *Merajoth*
9 *Amaria*
10 *Ahitub*
11 *Tsadok*
12 *Ahimaaz*
13 *Hazaria*
14 *Johanan*
15 *Hazaria*
16 *Amazia*
17 *Ahitub*
18 *Tsadok*
19 *Scallum*
20 *Hilkia*
21 *Hazaria*
22 *Zeraja*

All these are named in the First Book of the *Chronicles*, chap. 6. 'Tis observable, that the High Priesthood was sometimes exercised by some, who were descended from *Aaron* by *Ithamar* his youngest son: but those in this Catalogue, descended from *Aaron* by *Eleazar*, were the true Branch, to whom the High Priesthood appeartained. The last of all, viz. *Zeraja*, was put to death after the burning of
the

the first Temple, and then there was an intermission of the Sacrifices.

The two and twenty Governors, otherwise called Judges.

Beginning with *Joshua*, who was the first, and ending with *Samuel*, who was the last of the Judges; and therein comprehending the Tyrants and Pagans, who from time to time, by severall Intervals, oppressed *Israel*, we do find successively twenty two Governors.

1 *Joshua*
2 *Hothniel*
3 *Ehud*
4 *Shamgar*
5 *Debora*, assisted by *Barak*
6 *Gedeon*
7 *Abimeleck*
8 *Tolah*
9 *Jair*
10 *Jeptha*
11 *Ibtzan*
12 *Elon*
13 *Habdon*
14 *Samson*
15 *Eli*
16 *Samuel*

Add hereunto the Oppressors, who oftentimes interrupted the liberty of *Israel*, and possessed the Government thereof, viz.

1 *Cuzan*

[14]

1. Cusan King of Mesopotamia
2. Moab
3. Jabin, one of the Kings of Canaan.
4. Midian
5. Ammon
6. The Philistines

These six Goverments intervened between those sixteen we have named first, and altogether do amount to two and twenty. The holy History computing the time when these Oppressors domineered over Israel, doth comprehend them also under the name of Judges, Act. 13. 19, 20.

The two and twenty Kings.

We will not mention those who reigned over the ten Revolted Tribes, but

1. Saul
2. David
3. Solomon
4. Roboam
5. Abia
6. Asa
7. Jehosaphat
8. Joram
9. Ahazia
10. Joas
11. Amazia
12. Hozias
13. Jotham
14. Ahaz
15. Hezekias
16. Manasses
17. Amon
18. Josias
19. Jehoahaz
20. Joakim
21. Jechonias
22. Zedekia

Amongst

[15]

Amongst the lawful Kings *Athalia* is not mentioned, who for a time usurped the Kingdom, which belonged to the children of *Abazia*.

The two and twenty Generations from the Captivity, inclusively, unto Christ.

They are to be found in the Genealogy set down in the third Chapter of St. *Luke*, who representeth it in one respect as St. *Matthew* had represented it in another; from whence ariseth the diversity of supputations between these two Evangelists; St. *Luke* goes backward, and this is the number of the degrees.

1 *CHRIST*
2 *Joseph*, the Husband of the *Virgin*
3 *Heli*, Father of the *Virgin*
4 *Matthat*
5 *Levi*
6 *Melchi*
7 *Janna*
8 *Joseph*
9 *Matathias*
10 *Amos*
11 *Naum*
12 *Hesli*
13 *Nagge*
14 *Maath*
15 *Matathias*
16 *Semei*
17 *Joseph*
18 *Juda*
19 *Joanna*
20 *Rhesa*
21 *Zorobabel*
22 *Salathiel*, who was in the Captivity of *Babylon*.

True

True it is, that the History of the Old Testament, 1 *Chron.* 3. 19. doth name *Pedaia* the father of *Zorobabel* in stead of *Salathiel*, who was his uncle; nevertheless 'tis manifest, that in numbring upwards from Christ to the Captivity, wherein was the father of *Zorobabel*, there are precisely two and twenty Generations.

Thus, further to recapitulate all the parts of this Divine Oeconomy, we do therein observe,

Before the Church became a Nation, 22 Patriarchs.

From the Institution of the Priesthood untill the destruction of the first Temple, 22 Generations in the High Priesthood.

From the entrance of *Israel* into *Canaan* unto the first King, 22 Judges or Governors.

Since the beginning of Kingship to the suppression of it, 22 Kings.

Since the Captivity of *Babylon* unto Christ, 22 Generations.

This is also very remarkable: In the two and twenty Generations of the world, God renewed the Promise touching the Seed of the woman. For *Jacob*, who was the two and twentieth Patriarch, did speak of *Shilo*, the Seed of the woman, who was to come. And the two and twentieth Generation, after that the Ancestors of *Shilo* were transported to *Babylon*, where the

the Promise seemed to be annihilated, was *Shiloh* himself. The first twenty two Generations had in their beginning the Promise touching the Son of the Virgin, and concluded with a second Promise touching the Son of the Virgin, and the last two and twenty Generations, ended by the exhibition of the Son of the Virgin.

All the Generations of Christ; even comprehending therein that which is from the days of Eternity, are 77, ranked and distinguished from seven to seven.

THe Genealogy of our Saviour (which is here treated of) doth go up a degree higher, and is infinitely higher than any other which we read of in the Scripture. For all others begin with *Adam*, as they are recapitulated in the first of the *Chronicles*; but that of our Saviour doth begin with God himself, and endeth in the Son of God. St. *Luke* begins it with the Son of God, and goeth even to God himself, who is included in that Genealogy, because it is the Genealogy of

C   his

his Son. If we begin where the Evangelist ends (which is indifferent) we shall find, that the seventy seven Generations of the Son of God are divided into sevens, whereof every one, for the most part, beginneth with some mysterious point, relating to the Person of Christ. This is the order of the Degrees.

The first Septenary, 1 *GOD*, 2 *Adam*, 3 *Seth*, 4 *Enos*, 5 *Cainan*, 6 *Mahalaleel*, 7 *Jared*.

The second Septenary, 1 *Enoch*, 2 *Methusala*, 3 *Lamech*, 4 *Noe*, 5 *Sem*, 6 *Arphaxad*, 7 *Sala*. We do not in this place make mention of any other *Cainan*, whom the inadvertency of some Translations, or of the Copy written, have introduced after *Arphaxad*, *Luk.* 3. 39.

The third Septenary, 1 *Heber*, 2 *Phaleg*, 3 *Ragu*, 4 *Saruch*, 5 *Nahor*, 6 *Terah*, 7 *Abraham*.

The fourth Septenary, 1 *Isaac*, 2 *Jacob*, 3 *Juda*, 4 *Pharez*, 5 *Esrom*, 6 *Aram*, 7 *Aminadab*.

The fifth Septenary, 1 *Nassaon*, 2 *Salmon*, 3 *Boaz*, 4 *Obed*, 5 *Jesse*, 6 *David*, 7 *Nathan*.

The sixth Septenary, 1 *Mattatha*, 2 *Menan*, 3 *Melea*, 4 *Eliakim*, 5 *Jonan*, 6 *Joseph*, 7 *Juda*.

The seventh Septenary, 1 *Simeon*, 2 *Levi*, 3 *Matthat*, 4 *Joram*, 5 *Eliezer*, 6 *Jose*, 7 *Er*.

The eighth Septenary, 1 *Elmodam*, 2 *Cosam*, 3 *Addi*, 4 *Melchi*, 5 *Neri*, 6 *Salathiel*, 7 *Pedaia*, not mentioned by St. *Luke*, but in 1 *Chron*. 3. 12.

The ninth Septenary, 1 *Zorobabel*, 2 *Rhesa*, 3 *Joanna*, 4 *Jude*, 5 *Joseph*, 6 *Semei*, 7 *Matthias*.

The tenth Septenary, 1 *Maath*, 2 *Nagge*, 3 *Esli*, 4 *Naum*, 5 *Amos*, 6 *Matthias*, 7 *Joseph*.

The eleventh and last Septinary, 1 *Janna*, 2 *Melchi*, 3 *Levi*, 4 *Maath*, 5 *Heli*, 6 *Joseph*, 7 *JESUS* the *CHRIST*.

Most of these Septenaries do begin by some illustrious mark of the Person of Christ, who was to close the Genealogies.

The first doth begin in God himself, to show the Generation of his Son.

The second doth begin with *Enoc*, the seventh man from *Adam*, the third who went out of the world, and the first that in his body went up into Heaven; Christ the third who went up bodily into heaven, was the seventh after *Adam* inclusively.

The third doth begin with *Heber*; in the time of his life hapned the confusion of the Tongues in *Babel*. Christ, after his Ascension into heaven, did work a quite contrary wonder, bestowing the gift of Tongues.

The fourth doth begin with *Isaac*, the first who was miraculously conceived, as the fore-runner of a greater wonder hapned since, *viz.* the Conception of the *Messias*.

The fifth doth begin with the coming out of *Egypt*, and the celebrating of the first Passeover, a figure of Christ sacrific'd for us; at that time lived *Naasson*, the chief of the Tribe of *Juda*.

The sixth, seventh, and eighth have their beginning, where the old Testament ceased to prosecute the Genealogy of our Lord. For the Old Testament having mentioned one of the sons of *David*, to wit, *Nathan*, from whom Christ is descended, it doth not give an account of those that came from him, but of two or three onely, and those remote from him by many degrees. Therefore the New Testament beginneth the Catalogue where the Old began to be silent; to wit, at the entrance of the seventh Septenary.

The ninth, the tenth, and the last, have their beginning at the return from the Captivity of *Babylon*, under the conduct of *Zorobabel*; a Deliverance hapned by vertue of the Alliance, since written with Chrifts own blood, *Zech.* 9 11.

Amongst the wonderful particulars included in this Genealogy, this may be observed;

observed; we know the Scripture marketh the time of the coming out of *Egypt* as a period, in diverse respects most considerable; 1 *King.* 6. 1. if then we do number the Generations onely from the coming out of *Egypt* unto Christ, we find forty nine Generations, which are seven times seven; a very significant number, and fit to represent the fulness of the Generations which end in Christ: Let us also see it further in the fulness of Times in the following Observation.

Since the Promise touching the Seed of the Woman unto the accomplishment, when the Virgin conceived, there passed seven years, or a week of years, seven times seventy years, seventy weeks of years, and yet seven times seventy weeks of years.

HE that knoweth the style of God, and how he doth set the times in order, will not find this Arithmetick to be strange. In divers places, as well of the New as the Old Testament (*Dan.* 7. 25. *Rev.* 12. 14.) he nameth the measure of a *time, and times, and half a time*; all which doth amount unto three years and a half.

But why did he not express it more briefly by the total sum, and not by such parcels and broken numbers? There are many weighty reasons for it, which we will touch in the due place. So likewise, why doth it suffice to speak the total number of the years which hath passed since the Creation, without dividing them into unequal parts? The bare view of the total doth not shew the proportions and gradations from one unto the other; and from their inequality there doth a melody result.

It is a phrase which seemeth to have been proverbial, even since the beginning of the world, to exaggerate, or to amplifie a matter, by putting one seven followed by seventy times seven; *Cain shall be avenged seven-fold, but Lamech seventy and seven-fold, Gen.* 4. 24. And our Lord commandeth to forgive, *not onely seven times, but seventy times seven*, *Matth.* 18. 22. The like multiplication may be observed in the most of God's works, especially in the œconomy of Times; and that for the causes above mentioned. As for the present subject, we do set the nativity

tivity of Christ in the year of the world 3928. a little after the beginning of the said year. If we abate the months of Christ's being in his mothers womb, it will follow, that he was conceived in the year 3927. Then the Virgin conceived, according to the Promise; then *was the Word made flesh*.

Now this number of 3927 is altogether compounded of Septenaries, the first is single, the second is multiply'd by the first, and the third by the second. You have then here seven years, seven times seventy years, and seven times seventy weeks of years, from the Promise to the Effect thereof.

It must be enough for us to contemplate this rare Geometry, if I may speak improperly of the times which preceded the Incarnation of the Son of God. As to the reason of the conjunctions, divisions, order, and ranking of the Septenaries that make up those times, I could give some conjectures of them; but it must be enough for me to admire, that those gradations so diversly proportionated, ended, when God sent his Son made of a woman, a term which the Apostle doth call, *The fulness of times*, *Gal.* 4.

From the Fall of the first Adam, to the Ascension of the Second (which was in the 33 year of the abode of Christ upon Earth) there passed three and thirty times one hundred years.

THe term of 120 years is famous in the Scriptures; it was the number of the years of *Moses*, it is the third part of a Prophetical year, *viz.* of 360 years; it was the fourth part of the time which passed since the coming out of *Egypt*, to the foundation of the Temple of *Solomon*, *viz.* of 480 years; it was the eighth part of the time which passed since the finishing of the first Temple, unto the time of the rending of the vail of the Temple at the death of Christ, *viz.* of 960 years; it was the term prefixed by God to the world, before he sent the Deluge; so long a time Christ preached by his Spirit to those in prison, 1 *Pet.* 3. 19. and by that Spirit did he preach to men from the beginning of the world unto the accomplishment of our Redemption, by the space of three and thirty times one hundred and twenty

twenty years. For from the Creation to the three and thirtieth and the last year of Chrifts abode on earth, we reckon 3960 years, which are three and thirty times one hundred and twenty, all that time doth then contain as many parcels, as were the years of Jefus Chrift in this world. God, for the time of our Redemption, hath multiplyed one hundred and twenty years three and thirty times, which expired upon the three and thirtieth year of Chrift, being the year of his Death and of his Afcenfion.

This, by diverfe meafures of time, as by fo many feveral lines meeting in one and the fame Centre, the Antient of days hath conducted men to the moment wherein the fufferings and the glories of Chrift were to happen, 1 *Pet.* 1. 11, 12.

Since

Since the Creation to the time of the Jews coming out of Babylon, *to build the Second Temple, seven times seventy weeks of years, and forty years; and since their coming out of* Babylon *to the ruine of the Second Temple, seventy weeks of years and forty years, which began at the death of Christ.*

AT the year of the world 3430 ended seven times seventy weeks of years, or seven times 490 years; the year whereat they do end meeteth with the thirtieth of the Babylonish Captivity, which continued seventy years; so that to the end of the Captivity there were seven times seventy weeks of years, and forty years. From thence to the destruction of the Temple, there were seventy weeks of years (which expired at the death of Christ) and forty years.

The first forty was a time of preparation for the deliverance of the Jews, who were

were to return to their own Country, and there to build again the Temple; the second forty years was a term of time prefixed for their Repentance, to the duration of the Temple, and the abode of that Nation in their own Country; as their fathers had entred thereinto, after they dad dwelt forty years in the wilderness.

Adam *lived thirty years, and thirty times thirty years, (in all nine hundred and thirty). Christ did begin his Ministery at the thirtieth year. Since the Revolt of Adam to the Revolting of the Ten Tribes, when they abandoned the Temple, which was the Figure of Christ, there were* 3030 *years. And from the death of Adam to the death of Christ, who was the second Adam, there were* 3030

3030 years. And from the Revolt of the Ten Tribes to the death of Christ thirty years, and thirty times thirty years, which was the age of the first Adam.

ALL these number of years would not seem much considerable, were it not for the admirable reflections, whereby they do meet upon subjects answering one the other. The first *Adam*, the second, who is Christ, and the Temple, which represented Christ, have some mutual relations, in several respects, and particularly in these circumstances.

There are then thirty years of the age of Christ, when he began his Ministery: thirty years, and thirty times thirty years of the life of *Adam*. From the death of *Adam*, until the time of *Israel*'s renouncing the Temple, (which was a figure of the second *Adam*) 3030 years. From the death of the first *Adam* to the death of the second 3030 years. From *Israel*'s renouncing the Temple, unto the time of the destruction of the true Temple, and of his raising again the third day, thirty years, and thirty times thirty years,

years, being since the creation of *Adam* 3960 years.

Four men, each of them being the seventh in order within some remarkable Period, and illustrious for Miracles; an excellent Gradation from one to the other.

THe seventh from the Creation, *viz.* *Enoc*: in his person the first Miracle that ever was, was wrought, for he was transported without seeing death; nevertheless he himself did never work any miracle at all.

The seventh from *Abraham*, who miraculously had *Isaac*, was *Moses*, the first man that wrought miracles; nevertheless he never raised any from the dead.

The seventh and last who wrought miracles, under the Old Testament, and who even raised some from the dead, was the Prophet *Elisha*; but he was not raised from the dead himself.

The seventh raised from the dead, is the first who wrought miracles, under the New Testament, the first raised in
Glory,

Glory, and who alone did raise himself from the dead, is Chriſt; in him is perfection: He is the ſeventy ſeventh in the Genealogy, which beginneth in God himſelf, *Luk*. 3.

Theſe enumerations are without diſpute. As *Enoc* was the ſeventh after *Adam* inclusively, ſo was *Moſes* the ſeventh after *Abraham*, the Genealogies do demonſtrate it. As for the others, in all the extent of the Old Teſtament, there were never but ſeven men who had the gift of miracles; 1 *Moſes*, 2 *Aaron* his brother, 3 *Joſhua*, who commanded the Son to ſtand ſtill; 4 *Samuel*, who changed the whole face of the aire; 5 the Prophet that was ſent to *Jeroboam*, 1 *King*. 13. 6 *Eliah*, 7 *Eliſha*. Every one knows, that there hath been three raiſed from the dead under the Old Teſtament, and three under the New, before Jeſus Chriſt died and roſe again; ſo that he is the ſeventh, in the Catalogue of thoſe that have been raiſed from the dead, but with the aforeſaid preheminences.

As many years as Enoc *lived in this world, so many days the world continued under the waters of the Deluge.*

THis Patriarch sojourned 365 years upon the earth, and was afterwards bodily translated into heaven. The continuation of the Deluge was of twelve Lunary months and ten days, which make up one Solary year, *viz.* 365 days, answerable to the 365 years of *Enoc*'s life.

The miraculous translation of this great man hapned at such a time, when men had forgotten that there was another life after this, tends to put them in mind of it by so express an example. But the world having for a long time sleighted that wonder, God condemns it since to be drowned.

We know, and there are many examples of it in Scripture, that the Justice of God doth sometimes prefix a term of years for as many days, and sometimes a term of days for as many years, *Numb.* 14. 34. *Ezek.* 4. 5, 6. And so men having not considered the translation of *Enoc*, nor lifted up their thoughts to heaven, God ordained, that they should continue buried under

under the Deluge as many days, as *Enoc* had lived years on the earth, 365 days for 365 years.

Several measures of the Time, which the patience of God doth give unto sinners, before he punisheth them.

TO the whole world he gave three times forty years, before he sent the Deluge; there were the 120 years which God did mark out unto them; but unto the *Amorites* he gave ten times forty years, till their iniquity was fulfilled, *Gen.* 15. 16. To the Nation of the *Jews*, after they had procured the death of the Lord of Glory, he gave forty years before he ruined their estate. To *Nebuchadnezzar* he allowed one year before he deprived him of his sense, *Dan.* 4. But to a City, *viz. Ninive*, he allotted onely forty days, within which they were to repent.

Such measures, and their variety, have their various causes, unknown to us; that we might speak of them, we should be informed of the quality of the crimes committed, of their number,

ber, of their degrees, of their complication, and of their continuance, &c. Moreover we should know the number and the quality of the offendors, the measure of the light they had, the proportions of their number, and of their offences, with the number of the godly, and of their virtues, and other circumstances, which I have touched on the Second Commandement of the Decalogue.

A remarkable Period of seven times as much time as God had prefixed to the World, when he denounced the Deluge.

THis term (as we have seen) consisted of 120 years, *Gen.* 6. 3. now the years of the *Israelites* dwelling in the land of *Canaan*, after the conquest of it, till they came out of it to go to *Babylon*, were precisely 7 times 120 years; for from the year wherein they made an end of subduing that Country, (which was the sixth of the government of *Joshua*) to the first year of the Captivity of *Babylon*, we do find just 840 years, which

which are seven times 120, seven times as much time as God had given to the men of the old world, when he threatned the Deluge.

But that time from the Conquest to the Captivity, doth yet include other proportions, which will come in their order.

An Analogy of the Eight Persons that were saved in the Ark: Of the Eight Generations that passed since the distinction made between the Sons of God and the Sons of Men: And of the Eighth Part of the greatest Age of the Men of that Time.

After the nativity of *Enos*, the son of *Seth*, the son of *Adam*, they did begin to call on the Name of the Lord, *Gen.* 4. 26. it was a mark of Profession which distinguished the children of God from the children of corrupted men. But not long after the children of God joyned themselves by marriages to the daughters of of men; this mixture, and the corruption which proceeded from thence, continued to the time of *Noah*, who was the eight Generation from *Enoch* inclusively.

It is also to be observed, that 960 years was then the greatest measure of the days of man, there were never but two that exceeded that age, and none other attained thereunto; so that 120 years were largely the eighth part of the greatest age of men at that time.

Thus, before the denouncing of the Deluge, the patience of God stayed till eight generations should be over, since the distinction made between the children of God and the children of men; and according to the number of these Generations, he saved eight persons in the Ark; and denouncing the Deluge, he further staid the eight part of the age of man.

All this Oeconomy hath been of Octonaries of Generations, of Years, and of Persons.

D 2

A Consideration of the Age of Noah, *when he was commanded to build the Ark.*

HE had already lived 480 years, which are four times 120 years; to this number God added 120 years more, which ended at the Deluge. This term, which God prefixed to the world, kept this just and exact proportion, answerable to the years of that Patriarch. The years of a man are but the parcels of time of the duration of the world; but then, the 120 years of the duration of the world, before it perished by the Deluge, were but a parcel of the years of a man.

Of Lamech *the Father of* Noah, *the seventh in several respects, and dying in the* 777th *year of his age.*

THus *Lamech* prophesied touching his son *Noah*, He shall give us rest, (or, shall comfort us) concerning our work *and toil*

toil of our hands; this was the cause why he called him *Noah*, that is to say, *Who comforteth in giving rest*.

As this Patriarch foretold Rest, so he himself was altogether made up of Septenaries, which is the number of Rest. As *Enoc*, who was bodily translated into eternal Rest, was the seventh man after *Adam*; so *Lamech* was the seventh who went out of the world after *Enoc*, the seventh who died after *Adam*, having lived 777 years.

For after *Enoc*, *Lamech* was the seventh Patriarch who departed out of this world. But if we reckon not *Enoch*, because he departed without seeing death, *Lamech* was the seventh who died after *Adam* inclusively. All this is manifest to any, who knows how to order the years, and the Genealogy contained in *Gen.* 5.

D 3 *Fourteen*

Fourteen Generations for the Unity of the Language of Adam amongst Men; and yet three times fourteen Generations for the Unity of the same Language amongst the children of God: The first and the last fourteens.

Saint *Matthew*, chap. 1. ordereth the Generations from *Abraham* to CHRIST, dividing them into three fourteens; something like unto this is discovered in the Languages. The Language of *Adam* continued alone in the world, there being none other, for the space of fourteen Generations; this unity continued to the nativity of *Phaleg* the son of *Heber*. Now *Heber* was the fourteenth Generation after the beginning of the world, after the birth of his first son, the plurality of Languages hapned in *Babel*.

Nevertheless the primitive Tongue, although not alone then in the world, continued yet alone in the Church for the space of three times fourteen Generations, which were fulfilled at the return from

from the Babylonish Captivity: for the *Jews* having then corrupted their Language in *Babel*, and learn'd the Tongues of other Nations, brought them into *Judea* with them, *Nehem.* 13. 23, &c. Now this hapned in the days of *Zorobabel*, who was the forty second Generation after *Heber*, as we may see in the Genealogy of our Lord above related.

In his Genealogy, if we do reckon onely the first Generations, and the last, we may see, That as from *Adam* to the Confusion of tongues in *Babel* there were fourteen Generations, so from the carrying away the *Jews* into *Babel*, where they corrupted also their language, unto Christ, who conferred the gift of Tongues, there were fourteen Generations: This last fourteenth is according to the account of St. *Matthew*.

SINCE

Since the Flood, to the Promise given to the Patriarch Abraham, *61 weeks of years. Since the foundation of the first Temple to its ruine 61 weeks of years. Since the foundation of the second Temple was interrupted, to the final ruine of the Empire of the* Grecians, *who so long persecuted the Church of the* Jews, *61 weeks of years.*

FRom the Flood in the year of the world 1656, to the Promise, in the year 2083. there were 427 years; this term, long after, was also the measure of the continuance of the first Temple, for from its foundation, in the year 2993, until its destruction by the *Babylonians*, in the year 3420, we see also 427 years. The like number of years ran, since the foundation of the second Temple was interrupted, in the third year of *Cyrus*, (*Dan.* 10. 1.) till the Monarchy of the *Persians*, and that of the *Grecians*, who

succeeded

succeeded them, were utterly overthrown. For the intermission of the work of the second Temple, whose foundation was laid, did begin in the year 3473. And the Domination of the *Grecians* expired when *Augustus* incorporated *Egypt* to the *Roman* Empire, in the year 3900. Thus that interval hath been also of 427 years, which are 61 weeks of years.

The years of Noah after the Flood being double the years of Abraham.

NOah lived after the Flood 350 years; his death by two years preceded the nativity of *Abraham*, who lived in all but 175 years, half so many years as *Noah* had lived since the Flood began.

When, and by how many degrees the life of men have been shortned from time to time, and by what proportions, we have seen on the fifth Commandment of the Decalogue. Here we do onely consider, amongst the diverse measures whereby God compasseth times, that even in shortning the life of man he worketh by certain proportions from

man

man to man, in a wonderful manner, though but seldome perceived: Thus *Abraham* had just half as much time as *Noah* had, after he set foot in the Ark. Let us add this following Example.

Enoc sojourned less time in this world than any of the Patriarchs who were before the Flood, and his son Methuselah *lived seven years longer than any man ever lived.*

Ared lived 962 years, no other did ever come to so great an age, *Methuselah* excepted, who went beyond him by seven years, for he lived 969 years. The days of his father *Enoc* were short in this world, in respect of the other Fathers of that time. He was in this world one year of years, 365 years. But his son had one week of years more, then ever any other man. The seventh and last year of that week, which God gave him by way of priviledge; the year of his Eternal Rest was also the last year of the old world. For that Patriarch went to rest in heaven a few days before the Flood. Here is a greater depth in it than seemeth at first sight.

Ten times forty years expired at the departure out of Egypt. The tenth and last forty years ended when Moses was twice forty years of age. Another forty years in the Wilderness ending with the last forty years of Moses.

IT is known, that the number of forty, whether it be of years or of days, is often a term of affliction. God marked out one of four hundred years, or ten times forty years, to the posterity of *Abraham*, Gen. 15. 13. These years expired at the coming out of *Egypt*; when *Moses* was ending the second forty years of his life; for he was forty years of age when he fled into *Midian*, and forty years after he led the people out of *Egypt*. And thus the two last forties of the ten times

forty

forty years, foretold to *Abraham* the Patriarch, were the two first forty years of the age of *Moses*.

These ten times forty years were followed by another forty years which the *Israelites* fulfilled in the wilderness, and which also ended the last forty of the years of *Moses*.

Such and so exact have been the proportions of the days of that great man, in the total sum of the years, which God a long time before had marked out unto him; and so many concurrences are marvellous in our eyes.

Two Miracles of a contrary effect, the one in the seventh Generation after Adam, *and the other in the fourteenth Generation after the seventh.*

IN the seventh Generation after *Adam*, *Enoc* was translated: And in the fourteenth Generation after *Enoc*, the wife of *Lot* was turned into a Statue. Two contrary effects in two humane bodies, the one exalted to heaven, the other fastned and riveted to the earth:

The

The punishment answereth the offence, the wife of *Lot* staid in the way, contrary to the order she had of God, and God makes her altogether unmoveable.

These two Examples have been as so many warnings to men. And the interval of the Generations between those two wonders is worthy to be considered. The second hapned in the time of *Abraham*, who was twice the seventh Generation after *Enoc* inclusively, as *Enoc* was the seventh after *Adam*.

A Concurrence of several Septenaries in Jacob, and in his son Joseph.

Iacob in the seventieth year of his age, went to *Laban*, served him seven years, was married being seventy seven years of age, and lived seven times one and twenty years, which make up 147 years.

Joseph was born in the fourteenth year of *Jacob*'s abode with *Laban*; he foretold to *Pharaoh* seven years of abundance, and seven years of famine; he lived seventy years after the entring of his father *Jacob* into *Egypt*: And fourteen Generations (twice seven) passed from the time

of

of *Jacob* till the race of *Joseph*, the Tribe of *Ephraim* headed the revolt of the ten Tribes under one of the line of *Joseph*, viz. *Jeroboam*; this hapned at the beginning of the Reign of *Rehoboam*, who was the fourteenth Generation after *Jacob inclusively*, as may be computed in the first of St. *Matthew*.

Sometimes the Events of the Fathers and of the Children are marked with the same numeral character, though appliable to a diverse and contrary success.

Arphaxad the *first* man born *after* the *Flood*, was the twelfth Generation after Adam *inclusively*. The twelve Patriarchs, *the sons* of Jacob, *were the twelfth Generation after* Arphaxad *inclusively*. The Union of the twelve Tribes continued after Juda, himself therein comprehended, for the space of twelve Generations. And

And since the division of the Tribes, till the ten Tribes were carried into Assyria, there were twelve Generations.

Brethren, though many in number, are yet accounted but for one generation, because all in one and the same degree of descent. And thus the twelve Patriarchs, from whom the twelve Tribes descended, were the twelfth generation after the Flood; this is their order, *Arphaxad, Sala, Heber, Phaleg, Ragau, Saruc, Nahor, Terah, Abraham, Isaac, Jacob, Juda,* and the other Patriarchs his brethren. In *Arphaxad* the Church began to be peopled after the Flood.

From *Juda*, he therein included, before the breach or revolt of the ten Tribes, there passed twelve Generations; *Juda, Pharez, Esrom, Aram, Aminadab, Naason, Salmon, Boaz, Obed, Jesse, David, Solomon.*

Since the Apostacy of the ten Tribes, hapning at the beginning of the Reign of *Roboam, Solomons* Successor, till the transmigration of *Assyria*, there passed twelve Generations, who were successively

sively, so many Kings of *Juda*, named in the Story of the Old Testament: 1 *Reboboam*, 2 *Abia*, 3 *Asa*, 4 *Jehosophat*, 5 *Joram*, 6 *Ahazia*, 7 *Joas*, 8 *Amazia*, 9 *Hazaria*, 10 *Jotham*, 11 *Ahaz*, 12 *Hezekia*: In his time was the transmigration of the ten Tribes, and the twelve Tribes were reduced to two.

But in the New Testament we again find them twelve Tribunals, to judge them, and twelve Gates in the heavenly *Jerusalem*, &c.

Now, as many notable Revolutions have hapned from twelve to twelve Generations, according to the number of the twelve Tribes of *Israel*, we shall yet see the same number in many periods of years.

From the comming out of Egypt, to the foundation of the first Temple, twelve times forty years. From the foundation of the first Temple, to the foundation of the second, twelve times forty years. From the foundation of the

second

second Temple, to the begining of the week of years, ending at the death of Christ, wherein he rent the veil of the Temple, twelve times forty years. From the finishing of the second Temple to the ruine thereof, twelve times forty years.

From the coming out of *Egypt* unto the time *Solomon* laid the foundation of the Temple, there were 480 years; which are twelve times forty, 1 *King.* 6.-1. and you are to observe, that the first of these twelve forty years were spent in the wildernefs.

From the foundation of the first Temple to the foundation of the second, under the Reign of *Cyrus*, there were also twelve times forty years; for the first Temple was founded in the year of the Creation 2993. and the foundation of the second Temple was interrupted (as they were still building of it) in the year 3473. the interval is of 480 years, which are yet twelve times forty.

And again, From the foundation of the second

second Temple, to the beginning of the last week of years of the abode of Christ on earth, there were twelve times forty years, for they do end at the year of the world 3953. which was seven years, or one week of years, before the death of Christ: In the last half of which week he accomplished the work of Redemption, and anulled by his death, all the Sacrifices of the Temple. This is the time which is marked in *Dan.* 9. 27.

And finally, since the second Temple was finished, in the year 3519. till the time of its destruction, which was in the year 4000. there were twelve times forty years complete.

Since the finishing of the Conquest of Canaan *by the Israelites, to the time they were carried away to* Babylon, *twelve times seventy years; and from the time of their transportation into* Babylon, *till they return'd into* Canaan *seventy years; and from*

from their return to Canaan *till they procur'd the Death of Christ seven times seventy years.*

THe Conquest ended at the sixth year of the government of *Joshua*, and of the entrance of the *Israelites* into *Canaan*; In the seventh year they became peacable possessors of it, they had six years of war, and in the seventh they rested. Now from the end of the Conquest to the beginning of the Captivity of *Babylon*, there were precisely 840 years, which are twelve times seventy, as many Septenaries of years, as there were portions when they divided the Countrey amongst themselves, according to the number of the twelve Tribes. True it is, that the ten Tribes went out of *Canaan* before the Captivity, but the Tribe of *Juda* and part of *Benjamin* fulfilled their twelve times seventy years. These twelve septenaries of years were followed by seventy years of Captivity, which are one twelfth above the time the Jews possessed the Land of Promise. And the seventy years of the Captivity were followed by seven times seventy years, which are the seventy weeks of *Daniel*,

and

and ended when Christ continued all the seventh day in the grave.

So the number of the years of the twelve Tribes hath been measured by the Septenarie, twelve times seventy years before the Captivity, seventy years for the Captivity, and seven times seventy years from the Captivity to the Redemption.

In Joseph's Dream, thirteen Luminaries did homage to him, presaging his Promotion to come; and thirteen years he was a slave, before the thirteen Persons, represented by the thirteen Luminaries, did homage indeed unto him.

THe Sun, the Moon, and the eleven Stars prostrated themselves before him, this was since fulfilled, when *Jacob* and his family took shelter under the shadow of *Joseph*. But before this came to pass, *Joseph* underwent a thraldom of thirteen

thirteen years. Who would have thought a Dream of thirteen Luminaries, that were to do homage to him, should have included a servitude of thirteen years. *Joseph* being seventen years of age had this dream, which did promise him a Domination over all his brethren; presently after he was sold, and continued a slave till he was thirty years of age, at what time he interpreted *Pharaoh*'s Dreams. Here are thirteen years, during which he was a slave, after the Dream which had promised to him a Superiority over the thirteen chiefest persons of his family.

A thing doth often lie concealed in its contrary; the thirteen Luminaries seemed to prognosticate nothing but prosperity unto *Joseph*; but before he came to have dominion over the thirteen Luminaries, he must be a slave as many years as he had seen Luminaries doing homage to him.

The Dead doing homage to the Living.

IN *Joseph*'s Dream, the Moon, that did homage to him, signifi'd his mother, as *Jacob* did interpret it, *Gen.* 37. it could not be *Rachel*, for she was dead before

fore this Dream hapned; nor *Leah*, for she died before *Jacob* went to *Joseph* into *Egypt*, *Gen.* 49. 31. How then, being dead, did she Homage unto *Joseph?* In the persons of her children. *Lea*, who held the place of a mother to *Joseph* when this dream hapned, and who died before the fulfilling of it, did yet nevertheless serve to fulfil it; although she was dead, she bowed before *Joseph*, she spake, she prayed him to give her food; the submissions and requests which her children made to *Joseph*, were of *Leah* her self represented in her children. So *Rachel's* being dead many ages before, did bewail her children, even those who were born 1660 years after her death, *Matth.* 2.

From the time Jacob, *his Wife, and his Sons (represented by the Sun, the Moon, and the eleven Stars) did homage unto* Joseph, *untill the time the Sun and the Moon did really do homage to one of the*
De-

Descendants of Joseph, *there passed 257 years.*

And since the Posterity of Joseph forsook the Service of God, becoming the Ringleaders in the Revolt of the Ten Tribes, until they were carried away into Assyria, *after the Sun had gone back ten Degrees, there passed also 257 years.*

Of the eight Generations before the standing still of the Sun, and of the eight years that followed his going back.

Iacob and his family went to put themselves under the protection of *Joseph*, in the year of the Creation 2298. And in the year 2555. *Joshua*, who descended from *Joseph*, commanded the Sun and the Moon to stand still in their course. That which hapned onely to *Joseph* in a Dream, hapned really to *Joshua*. Now since the fulfilling of that Dream, when

when *Jacob* and his children did humble themselves before *Joseph*, untill the Sun and the Moon stood still at the command of *Joshua*, that is to say, from the year 2298, to the year 2555, we see that 257 years passed.

A long time after, *viz.* in the year 3030. one of the offspring of *Joseph*, *Jeroboam* by name, did set up the Idolatry of the golden Calves, and drew away the ten Tribes of *Israel*: That impiety continued till the year 3287, whereat hapned the transmigration of *Assyria*, which was then the interval of 257 years.

As many years as the glory of *Joseph* lasted, after homage of those represented to him by the Luminaries of heaven, to the time of the very same Luminaries doing obeysance to one descended from him; so many years the reproach of *Joseph* continued in the land of *Israel*, since one of his line made the greatest part of the Tribes to fall into Apostasie, till they were thrown out of their own Country.

And whereas in the eighth generation after *Joseph* inclusively, the Sun stood still, to assure them of their settlement in the land of *Canaan*, in the eight year after the going back of the Sun, during the reign of *Hezekia*, they were driven out of the land of *Canaan*; for their transmigration hapned in the year 3287. and the Sun went

went back in the year 3295. As for *Joshua*, who commanded the Sun to stand still, he was the eighth after *Joseph*, *Joseph* being included in that number, 2 *Chron.* 7.

Of the twelve Sons of Jacob, *two onely were without blemish.*

Of the twelve Spies that went unto Canaan, *two onely were faithful to God.*

Of the twelve Tribes, two onely adhered to God, and to the House of David.

ALL the sons of *Jacob*, *Joseph* and *Benjamin* onely excepted, were guilty; *Ruben* and *Juda* were incestuous, the eight others plotted the death of *Ioseph*, and at last sold him. All the Spies sent from the Wilderness to the land of *Canaan*, *Caleb* and *Ioshua* onely excepted, return'd a bad report thereof, caused the people to murmur, and provoked God's anger. All the Tribes, two excepted, forsook the Temple and the true Religion under the Reign of *Ieroboam*.

Some

Some are of opinion, that all the Christians in the world, all that profess the Name of Christ, are hardly the sixth part of Mankind, two of twelve. But who knoweth how many sub-divisions can be made? Of ten Lepers made clean, where are the nine? one onely of ten had the spirit of gratitude.

Of the ten Children of Job, *and of the ten Righteous who might have hindred the destruction of* Sodom: *A great Question upon the Comparison of these two Examples.*

FOr the sake of ten righteous (had they been found in *Sodom*) God would have spared that City, that was so abominable; but the ten children of *Job* were not spared, but perished under the ruines of one house: If they were righteous, as the History doth not tax them of any enormity, 'tis strange that God, having offered to spare a whole City of abominable sinners, and that for the want of ten righteous, he should cause ten righteous men to perish in one Family alone: If we

say

say that the children of *Job* were sinners, as *Bildad* seemeth to imply, *Job* 8, 4. we know he said as much of *Job* himself, though falsly. But suppose *Job's* children were wicked, could not ten wicked ones be spared for the life of one righteous man, especially since he was their father, as well as a thousand, or may be ten thousand wicked ones in *Sodom*, could be spared for the sake of ten righteous? To the house of *Job*, where the head of the Family was righteous, God did not keep so favourable a proportion as he would have done to *Sodom*, had she had as many righteous as *Job* had children.

The reasons of this difference are above us, nevertheless we may say thereupon, that we ought not find strange, if the corrections of those whom death transmit to heaven, are sometime sharper than the temporal punishments of those, who notwithstanding go afterwards to everlasting fire, as those of *Sodom*, *Jud.* 7.

Job *and* Jeremy *have cursed the day of their Nativity, but have not made mention what year or month it was.*

Since they spake of blotting out the memory of that day, and of taking it out of the Kalender, we must not wonder they do suppress the date.

But I have observed else-where (in my observations on the Creed) that the Scripture never saith upon what day a man is born, it never quoteth the birth-day of any one; it doth not so much as express that day wherein *Jesus Christ* was born. What thereupon I have observed, needeth not be repeated again.

Job'*s Sons have no names in the Scripture, and yet his Daughters are named therein.*

Job 42. 13, 14, 15. The three daughters of *Job* have every one of them a name, and besides a glorious Epithet, their

their beauty is also mentioned; but as for the seven sons he had, not one of them is named. It is against the custom of the Scripture, which in the Genealogies doth rather express the names of the males, except when they fail in a race. Shall we say, that *Job* had forgot, or made slight to impose names on his children? or were they less worthy than their sisters? It is a glory to a pious man to have his name read in the holy History; but the names of all the sons of *Job* are buried in the same grave with them, without an Epitaph, when his daughters are therein mentioned with honor. Should we know the successes, either good or bad, of the posterity of *Job*, we would see the causes of that difference. But the chief aime of the Scripture being the Genealogy of the Son of God, it doth shorten the Genealogy of all those, of whom Christ is not descended according to the flesh, although illustrious in other respects.

From *the division of Tongues in Babel, to the death of Heber, who was the Father of the Hebrews,* 430 *years. From the Promise made to Abraham, to the Law,* 430 *years. From the Law, till David was annointed in Bethlehem,* 430 *years complete.*

THe first of these Parallels is manifest in *Gen.* 10. 25. and 11. 17. the division of Tongues hapned at the nativity of *Phaleg* the son of *Heber*; after which, *Heber* lived yet 430 years, and even out-lived *Abraham*. This Patriarch *Heber* had seen the time when the holy Tongue was alone on the earth, and saw the beginning of the diversity of Languages; but he himself and his posterity kept the Language of their Ancestors, and from *Heber* were called *Hebrews*. It was expedient that he who was antienter then all the Languages of *Babel*, should yet live a long time after their original, that

that the Primitive Tongue might be received in the families of all the sons of God. Therefore that term was of 430 years.

The like number of years passed from the Promise to the Law, presently after the coming out of the Land of *Egypt*, *Gal.* 3. 17.

Again, the like number of years was from the Law, given in the year 2513, to the annointing of *David*, by *Samuel*, in *Bethlehem*, at the end of the year 2943, or at the beginning of the year following.

The Promise, the Law, and the Kingship of *David*, from whom came Christ, have been dispensed by equal intervals of time.

The Waters of Egypt *remained blood for seven days. The day of the Sabbath forbidden to the* Egyptians. *A secret virtue of the Septinary number towards the waters, acknowledg'd knowledged by the Naturalists.*

The waters of *Egypt*, turned into blood, or rather the blood which before was water, did continue in that place seven whole days; one of the seven was to be a day of Sabbath, according to the antient Ordinance of God. But he was not pleased, that in all that week the *Egyptians* should have one day of rest. For the necessity occasioned by that prodigious blood, which had taken the place of the water, forced them to dig the ground to find drink; that labour continued seven whole days, so that there was no Sabbath for them, *Exod.* 7. 24, 25. Besides, the Sabbath was a day of rejoycing, but that whole week was sad to the *Egyptians*: They had taken from the *Hebrews* the liberty of the Sabbath, compelling them to work without intermission or distinction of days; God, for one week, paid them in the same coyn. And had they been men of judgment, they might have acknowledg'd, that God would not permit them to observe the Sabbath day, because they caused it to be violated.

But as for the seven days of that corruption of waters, although it was supernatural,

natural, it doth also bring into our remembrance the natural cause of an effect which the Naturalists do observe. The water, say they, which hath been seven times corrupted, and seven times purifi'd, doth never putrefie again. Wonderfull is that revolution, which being come to the seventh time, doth ever afterwards rest, as if arrived to its Sabbath. Not that the number of seven hath this vertue, but so it is, that God hath so ordained, that such a revolution should cease when it should come to that number. And even this also is a memorial of the seventh day, wherein all the works of God were completed.

The sixth Prophetical Year expired seventy seven years after the Promise made to Abraham; and the seventh Prophetical year expired in the seventh year of the wandring of the Israelites *in the Wildernesss.*

WE have already said, that the Prophetical year is of 360 solary

Solary years; now six times 360 years make up 2160 years: so the year of the Creation 2160 ended the sixth Prophetical year. But the Promise was given in the year 2083. which was 77 years before the Prophetical year expired; when that ended, the Promise was 77 years of date. This term of time, otherwise considerable, meeting at the end of such a Prophetical period, did shew to that Patriarch a notable concurrence of time.

There was another at the end of the seventh Prophetical year, for it ended with the year 2520, as 'tis easie to be computed. Now the year 2520 was the seventh after the coming out of *Egypt*; for the *Israelites* came out of it to go into the Wilderness in the year 2513, so the seventh year of their abode in the Wilderness, was the last of the seventh Prophetical year. Therefore, as the sixth Prophetical year expired in the 77 year since the Promise, so the seventh Prophetical year ended in the 7 year after the coming out from *Egypt*.

The

The distinction of the Tribes hath sometimes served to chastise the Israelites.

GOD, who was the Founder of their State, and the Author of their Policy, was pleased, that the Tribes should be distinguished, more eminently the Royal Tribe of *Juda*, and the Sacerdotal of *Levi*. That distinction was necessary for many weighty reasons, yet many times it hath been the occasion of emulation and division. The *Ephramites* thinking themselves sleighted by *Jeptha*, pitched Battel with him; The *Benjamites*, to countenance some lewd persons of their Tribe, made war with all the other *Israelites*; We know the war betwixt *Juda* and the other Tribes for the Kingship, after the death of *Saul*, and yet the dispute betwixt them about bringing back *David* after the defeat of *Absolom*: Finally, the ten Tribes forsook the Tribe of *Juda*, and made a State and a Religion apart.

When the *Israelites* sinned against God, the distinction of the Tribes hath often turned into division, and division into ruine. The same came to pass when they offered to confound the Rights and Privileges

Privileges of one Tribe, to make them common, as the Priesthood, and the Kingship, whereof there are some Examples.

An Analogy of the seventh day, wherein no Manna fell, and of the seventh day of the hunger of a Man.

Upon the Eve of the Sabbath God had ordained *Manna* to be gathered for the next day, because none fell on the seventh day; the manifest reason of that intermission was the holiness of the day of Rest, inconsistent with the manual work required for gathering of *Manna*. But it seems there is yet another secret in that cessation on the seventh day.

'Tis certain, and there are many examples in the Scripture, that several divine Mysteries are inclosed in some natural secret reflecting upon them. Now 'tis the common opinion, that naturally a man cannot endure hunger above seven days, *viz.* untill there be no more chylous or nourishing humour in his stomach, or in his intrals; if he goes beyond seven days, he dies. And because *Manna* did

not

not fall on the seventh day, he who should have neglected it during the six days it fell down, would have found none upon the seventh, and so having no other food would have been liable to death. The following observation will afford us something like this.

A Mystery represented under the Character of the Day, wherein wounds are most painful.

THe third day hath produced the fulfilling of many mysteries; on the third day after warning given, God publish'd the Law in *Sinai*. On this occasion we fall to the consideration of another subject, expressed in *Hof.* 6. 2. *In the third day he will raise us up.* These words do carry a manifest allusion to a considerable circumstance in matter of wounds; it's known, that on the third day they are painfuller than on the first or on the second days, and the Scripture doth observe it in the History of the *Sichemites*, *Gen.* 34. 25. from thence is this Metaphor of the Prophet: The foregoing words are express for that, *He hath torn, but he will heal us; he hath smitten, but he will bind us up.* That which followeth doth import, that even then when our wounds shall be most painful, which hapneth naturally on the third day after the hurt, we shall be healed.

The sense of these words yet go much further. But that which is most mystical in the Oracles of God, is often cloathed with natural observations, as the Fruit is inclosed in the Shell, or the Diamond set in the thing of a lesser value, doth sparkle the more gloriously.

An instruction drawn from Levit. 25. *that the price of Lands was so much the less, by how much the nearer was the year of* Jubilee.

IN the year of Jubilee, all the lands that had been alienated returned to their former owners, and therefore the price of the sale, which properly was but a Lease, was according to the number of the years wanting to the next Jubilee. In these latter days, he that purchaseth Lands should not so much value them, as those who in former times were Purchasers;

chafers; then they purchafed for four or five thoufand years, but now the time of the duration of Lands is fo much the fhorter. A man doth purchafe for himfelf, and for his heirs for ever, that is to fay, to the end of the world. But the end of the world being much nearer, fo much the lefs time will our poffeffions continue, and fo much the lefs ought we to value them. To this the words of the Apoftle do relate, 1 *Cor.* 7. *Henceforth the time is fhort.*

A Doctrine drawn from a difproportion, touched on in Levit. 26. verf. 8.

THe words are, *Five of you fhall chafe an hundred, and an hundred of you fhall put ten thoufand to flight*; the proportion of five to an hundred is much different, from the proportion of an hundred to ten thoufand; the firft is of one to twenty, but the other is of one to an hundred.

The whole Law is full of myfteries, and the temporal favours propounded therein ought to put us in mind of more excellent things. In fpiritual graces, the
more

more they do abound, either in number or in greatness, the more do their proportion encrease. To this the Parable of the Pound, in *Luk.* 19. doth relate; the Pound taken from the bad servant was given to him that had ten Pounds already, and not to him that had but five: A complaint was made of the disproportion, but it was answered, That *unto every one that hath shall be given.*

Levit. 27. *Some inequalities in the Estimation of the Sex, and of the age of those that were to be ransomed.*

THey always paid more for a Male than for a Female, but not always in the same proportion. The Tax differed according to the difference of of age, but with much diversity.

From a month after the nativity, to the age of five years, the female paid three fifths of the sum paid for a male.

From five years to twenty, the female paid just half the estimation of a man.

From twenty years to sixty, three fifths again.

From sixty years to the end of her life, the two thirds of the sum. These

These inequalities of proportions have their reasons, although very hard to be found. The mariageable age of the female, and that wherein she ceaseth to bring forth; the age wherein a man is able to serve in the war, or to carry publick offices. All these circumstances, and others well weighed, could shew unto us the justness of such disproportions.

Three men who knew punctually, and from above, the place where they should die.

Aaron, *Moses*, and *Jesus Christ* had that fore-knowledge, no other ever had it. A man may guess of his fatal place, but cannot be sure of it, though he were already upon the Scaffold. How many accidents have interven'd betwixt the neck and the sword? Onely these three, the first Priest in *Israel*, the first Leader of that People, and the first-born amongst the dead, have been certain of the place where they should die; yet with this difference, *Aaron* and *Moses* knew not the place of their death but some few hours or few days before, but *Jesus Christ* knew afar off the place of his death:

Numb.

Numb. 20. 25. *Deut.* 32. 49. *Luk.* 13. 33. It is remarkable, that at the transfiguration of our Lord, *Moses* was one of the two that did speak of the place where he was to die, *Luk.* 9. 31. The *Israelites* who murmured at the report of the Spies, were condemned to die in the Wilderness, *Numb.* 14. 29. but the Wilderness was very large, and they wandred there a long time afterwards from place to place, so that none of them could know the particular place where he was to die.

Fifteen men have been warned from above, they were not to die before such a Time, or such an Event.

NOah knew that he was not to die before the Flood, and besides, that he was to out-live all those who were to perish under the waters. The *Israelites* being to enter into *Canaan*, God named twelve persons who were to divide the Land, *Numb.* 34. This came not to pass, but seven years after they were nominated; they were therefore sure to live all that time. *Hezekia* had a respite of fifteen years after his sickness. The good

Simeon

Simeon was forewarned, that he should not die before he had seen the Christ.

Our Saviour foretold that there were some which should not taste of death, till they had seen the Son of man coming in his Kingdom, *Matth.* 16. 28. but he named none in particular.

Here is one difference betwixt Christ, and all those of whom we have spoken; namely, that he alone hath known and fore-seen, not onely the years but the day, and the very hour, yea, and the very moment of his death.

God giveth to one man as many days as he taketh away from another, yea, from a whole Generation. The ordinary ages of the Israelites, *who were condemned to die within the forty years of their wandring in the* Wilderness, *was seventy years, the age of* **Joshua**

Joshua *was forty years above seventy.*

THe eldest of the *Israelites*, who died in the wilderness, went no further then seventy years, such as out-lived that time did not live but languish, *Psal.* 90. 10. That curse continued till it had devoured all that generation comprised in the sentence of death, which was throughly executed within the forty years of their dwelling in the Wilderness. *Joshua* out-lived them, and brought their children into the Land of *Canaan*.

Now in all he lived as long as the eldest amongst them, to wit, seventy years; and yet as many years more as they had wandred in the Wilderness, *viz.* forty years; for the days of his life were 1 10 years, which are seventy and forty. The forty years he had above the ordinary age of the others, were to him an addition of so much time, as God had taken from the others,

God

God doubleth the days of a man. After the Murmurers were condemned to die in the Wilderness, Joshua *lived yet as many years as he had lived till then.*

WHen God pronounced the sentence against those who had murmured, *Joshua* was fifty five years of age, and he lived after fifty five years more, for he died in his hundred and tenth year.

The proof of it is evident. The condemnation of the Murmurers was pronounced in the second year after the coming out of *Egypt*. From that time till *Joshua* entred into *Canaan*, there were thirty eight years, which being added to seventeen, which *Joshua* lived since, do make up fifty five years. Now, since *Joshua* was 110 years of age when he died, it must needs be he was five and fifty years old when the others were condemned to die in the Wilderness. That *Joshua* lived seventeen years after his entring into *Canaan* is out of dispute.

Thus the life of that excellent man was

was divided into two equal parts, distinguished by that memorable sentence which God pronounced. He was at that time fifty five years of age, and lived fifty five years longer; when God began to cut shorter the days of the other *Israelites*, he began to prolong those of *Joshua*, and continued to the doubling of them.

Four Miracles God wrought in the Conquest of Canaan; 1 *In the* Water. 2 *In the* Earth. 3 *In the* Aire. 4 *In the* Heaven.

1 IN the *Water*, when he made the River of *Jordan* to stand still, yea, to run back, at the onely presence of the Ark.

2 In the *Earth*, when he threw down the Walls of *Jericho*, onely at the sound of the Rams-horns.

3 In the *Aire*, when he slew his enemies with the Hail that fell upon them as stones, *Josh.* 10. 11.

4 In the *Heaven*, when he stopped the Sun and the Moon in their course.

Those wonders hapned successively, and

in their order, and generally in those parts that make up the whole world, tended to show unto the *Cananites* the universal power of the God of *Israel*. These people, as all the rest of the Heathen, acknowledged no Gods, but what were particular ones to one or to another Element, or to some part of the world; but those miracles shewed them, that the God of the Hebrews had an universal command over all in the Water, in the Earth, in the Aire, and in Heaven.

Three Memorable passages of the Israelites hapened by the diversion of the Waters; 1 Of the Sea; 2 Of Jordan; 3 Of Euphrates: A Gradation from the Greater to the Lesser in the Means imploy'd therein.

TO come out of *Egypt* they were to pass through the waters of the Sea, which divided to give them a free way. To enter into *Canaan* they were to pass through the Channel of *Jordan*, the

waters

~~waters~~ whereof gave place to them. And ~~to come~~ out of *Babylon* where they were Captive, the waters of *Euphrates* must be first turned another way, which was performed by *Cyrus*, who to take the City of *Babylon* diverted the course of that River. Now the taking of that City was a necessary preamble to the deliverance of the *Jews*, *Jer*. 50. 38. and 51. 32. Thus the coming out of *Egypt*, the entring into *Canaan*, and the departure from *Babylon*, came to pass by the division of waters.

But the two first passages, that of the Sea, and that of *Jordan*, were miraculously wrought, whereas the last was prepared by the hand of man; and even the second of the two first was in some manner less illustrious than the first, as a River is less than the Sea.

The wisdom of God, having sufficiently shewed his power by one or two acts, in one kind, taketh delight in lessening himself, that men might believe in him, as well for his least works as for the greatest.

A Gradation of four Means successively interven'd in the Conquest of the Cities of Canaan; The first was gain'd by Miracle, the second by Stratagem, the third by a voluntary Surrender, the fourth and the following by Force.

The most excellent means to attain to a Conquest, is the immediate and miraculous operation of God, which proceedeth immediately from him, even the evil it self, is always to be preferred to that which passeth through the hand of men.

The second means, inferior to the former, but nobler then the two following, is, when the victory is gotten by industry and prudence, which are the most commendable arms of a man.

The third means is, when the enemy wanting courage, doth submit without striking a blow.

The fourth means is, the force of the arm and of the sword.

All

All these four means in the same order, interven'd in the Conquest of *Canaan*: the first City Conquered, *viz. Jericho*, was gained by a miracle of God, who pulled down her walls to the ground. The second, *Ai*, was carried by a stratagem. The third, *Gibeon*, was surrendred by fear. All the other were taken by force.

The strange change of Persons in the succession of the Judges or Governors of Israel: after a valiant Man, a Woman; after a wise and pious Man, an unnatural Fool; after a Man of an Illustrious Birth, a Bastard; after an Old Man, a Child; and among the rest, a strong Man of Body, but weak of Understanding.

Debora succeeded the valiant *Ehud*, and *Shamgar*; the wicked *Abimelech*, to the good *Gideon*; *Jeptha*, the son of of a Harlot, succeeded to the noble *Jair*; and the young *Samuel*, to the old *Eli*. But what an inequality was there in *Samson* alone! a prodigious strength of body, seconded with a great weakness of judgment, which in the end caused his shame and his death.

Certainly God would have the *Israelites* to see, that their subsistence did not depend, either on the sex, or on experience, or on birth, or on force, or on wisdom, nor even on the goodness of those that ruled them.

But there is yet a more particular reason, as to the example following.

Wherefore God being willing to deliver the Israelites, *he gave them for a Deliverer, yea, for a perpetual Head and Governor, the son of an Harlot.*

A Bastard was incapable of any office, of any publick charge, the Law had debarred him from it, *Deut.* 23. and yet *Jephta*, whose birth was infamous, was chosen to command the people of God:

God: Was there not a man in all *Israel* worthy of that honor, but the son of a whore? the *Israelites* were given to Idolatry, which is a spiritual fornication; God raised them an Enemy. They crave pardon, and pray God to deliver them. God grants them their prayer, but will have them to have the shame to be delivered by the hand of a man begotten in fornication, and that for the time to come he should exercise authority over them. His end therein was to upbraid them for their Idolatry, and to let them know, that being infamous themselves by reason of their spiritual fornication, they were worthy to be commanded by the son of a harlot.

A marvellous and most exact disproportion betwixt Gideon's Troop, and the Army of the Midianites, Judg. 7. 16. and 8. 10.

Gideon had but 300 men, his Enemies were 135000, for there were slain of them 120000 men, and there remained 15000. Now what proportion was there from 300 to 135000? it was

just

just one *Israelite* against 450 *Midianites*. Moreover, if we do number the *Midianites* slain, who were 12000, it was precisely 400 *Midianites* for one *Israelite*: and those 400 against one, exceeded by one hundred the Troop of *Gideon*. Here is another wonderful inequality.

Lastly, the 15000 enemies that remained after the slaughter, were yet fifty against one *Israelite*; and yet were, defeated.

Thus the enemies were first 450 against one, afterwards 400, and lastly 50. The proportions of those numbers do shew, the excellent order the God of Hosts doth observe, even in the disproportion, and in the confusion of the Midianites.

Satan hath attempted to make men believe he did raise one from the dead, before ever God raised any.

SAtan causing an apparition to be seen, which represented *Samuel*, after his death, thought to brag he had wrought a miracle, which God himself had as yet never done: For from the death of *Saul*, to whom this pretended *Samuel* appeared,

G 3   there

there passed above 140 years before God did raise any from the dead. The first he raised was in the days of the Prophet *Elijah*, under the reign of *Jehosophat*. Satan then would have it believed, that he had prevented God, as to this kind of miracle. An abominable impudence.

The Evil Spirit which counterfeited Samuel, could not foretel to Saul on what day he should be kill'd.

TO *morrow*, saith he, *thou and thy sons shall be with me*; that is to say, To morrow you shall be dead. Now Interpreters do shew, and it appeareth by many circumstances, that neither *Saul* nor his sons died on the next day, but onely some days after.

That which I have to add is an Answer to a Reply that might be made, *To morrow*, that is to say, within few days, for that word is often so taken.

But we must know, that in a Prediction that term is never taken for an indefinite time; in Promises, or in Threatnings, or in Exhortations, it is so, but not when God doth foretel a time, for then he doth certainly

certainly mark it. But the Devil, who knew not well when *Saul* should die, used a word, which often doth not denote any prefixed time.

An interval of many months, within which, David composed no Psalm.

'TWas during the time of his impenitency, after the injury he did to *Uria*, till he had his first Child by *Bathsheba*, and was censured by *Nathan*; dureing those nine months he had no Prophetical Inspirations, and his Pen produced no other work, but the Letter written with the blood of *Uriah*. In all that time he did not write one Psalm, his hand was too guilty to be a Secretary to the Holy Ghost.

Why God, having pardon'd David, would never vouchsafe him the life of the Child he had by Bathsheba.

WE know with what fervency *David* prayed, and desired the life of that Child, but could never obtain it.

We ought here to observe an effect of God's wisdom. It might have been doubtful whether that child was *David's* or not, for the time of his birth shewed that he was then begotten, when *Urish*, the first husband of *Bathsheba*, was yet alive; had that child lived, being the first son of *David* and *Bathsheba*, he might have succeeded *David* in the Kingdom as well as *Solomon*, whom they had afterwards; but as his Birth might have been disputed, so his Title might have been called to question, and it would have caused a great trouble in the Royal Succession.

And although no doubt had been made of his coming from *David*, yet being conceived in Adultery, the Law made him incapable of the Crown; he might have had some Partizans, but he could not have wanted Competitors, armed with strong reasons, and that would have occasion'd casion'd Civil Wars, which by the death of that Child were prevented.

But there is yet a higher and more important reason, why God was not pleased that Child should live. Christ was to come from *David* and *Bathsheba*, not indeed by their eldest son, for our Lord is come from *Nathan*, who was but a younger brother; but it was necessary, for many weighty reasons, that Jesus Christ should be comprehended in the Genealogy of the eldest, because of the Legal succession which belonged to Jesus Christ, the line of the eldest failing; and from thence it comes, that St. *Matthew*, in his first Chapter, naming the Ancestors of Christ, makes him to come from *Solomon*. Now it was not fit that Christ should succeed, either Naturally or Legally, one of whom it might be doubted whether he came from from *David*, or was his lawful Successor. And upon this account was God pleased that that Child should die (though the first-born) and that on the seventh day of his nativity.

The

The seven days of the child of David, and the seven days of the Reign of Zimri, 1 King. 16. 15.

THese two have no relation, nor any thing answerable one to the other; yet the life of the first, and the reign of the last, have had one and the same measure of time; as short as it was, yet it hath been recorded in the Sacred History. And the distances between these examples may include many secrets unknown to us. Certainly, none of the Kings of *Juda* had so short a Reign as this King of *Israel*, who possessed the Throne but as many days as that child of *David* lived. Besides, the number of seven is here remarkable.

Solomon's Fleet spent three whole years in a Voyage, which might have been performed in less then one year; It is very likely, that for want of a Sea-Compass that
Voyage

[91]

Voyage was thus long: Why that Secret was not discover'd to Solomon.

His ships sailed along the *Mediterranean Sea*, and so came into the main Ocean about *Africa*. The going and coming back, at this day, would not take so much time. They were not so ignorant of the use of the Needle touched with the Load-stone. *Solomon* himself, so great a Naturalist as he was, did not know it, and God was not pleased he should, for many reasons.

First, God would not have his people should much apply themselves to Navigation, lest *Israel* should be corrupted by the Commerce with other Nations. And therefore of all the Tribes, onely three, *viz. Zabulon*, *Issacher*, and *Asser* had their habitations by the Sea-side.

He would not have them neither to go far from the Land of *Canaan*, for many weighty reasons.

Moreover, as to that natural Secret, God did reserve it to the latter times, for the discovery of the New World, which required a longer Navigation, and consequently a more particular and constant skill, than that of the Antiquity.

The

The Temple had stood thirty years after it was finished, when the Ten Tribes forsook it. When, Christ the true Temple, was thirty years of age, Jesus said to the Jews, Destroy this Temple, &c.

THese ten Tribes, who by the suggestion of *Jeroboam* forsook the Temple, did, as much as in them lay, annull the Holiness thereof, which was as much as if they had destroyed that Building. Their desertion hapned the thirtieth year after the Temple was finished; this is manifest to any, who will reckon the years of the Reign of *Solomon*, followed by the Revolt of the ten Tribes.

Now Jesus Christ was also in the thirtieth year of his age, when being in the Temple he said to the Jews, *Destroy this Temple, Joh.* 2. 19. The Chronology of the New Testament sheweth, it was a few months after Jesus Christ was entred into the thirtieth year of his age, *Luk.* 3. 23.

Thus he who was represented by the Temple, signifieth his own death under the

the name of the destruction of the Temple. But as the Temple was thirty years old, when the Apostate *Israelites* attempted to annihilate it; so Jesus Christ being thirty years of age, rejected by the *Jews*, and speaking in the Temple, remembred that circumstance.

The first Temple after finished, lasted fourteen times thirty years.

During the first thirty years, it had all the Tribes of Israel adhereing to that of Levi; the other thirteen thirties of years that followed, do answer the number of the thirteen Tribes, therein comprising that of Levi, whom the Apostate Israelites had degraded.

THe Temple was finished in the year 3000. During the space of thirty years, all *Israel* frequented it, as the onely lawful

lawful place where they were to worship. From the year 3030, when the ten Tribes forsook it, until it was destroyed by the *Babylonians* in the year 3420, we see that there passed 390 years, a term of time marked in *Ezek.* 4. 5.

Now these 390 years are as many thirties of years as there were Tribes, *viz.* 13, that of *Levi*, although supernumerary, because it had no possession, but was scattered among the other Tribes, yet it is added to the twelve, and considered in the number of the years of the Temple, because it was the Tribe to whom the service of the Temple belonged, and because the revolted *Israelites* had taken away their Rights from them, 2 *Chron.* 11. 14.

Thus after the thirty years all the Tribes adhered to the Temple, God measured as many thirty years as there were Tribes, till the destruction of the Temple.

A gradation in the extraordinary Means wherby Eliiah was fed, viz. 1 *By Beasts;* 2 *By an* Humane Creature; 3 *By an* Angel.

ALL these three means were employed therein successively: 1 The *Ravens* brought him food: 2 A Woman in *Sarepta* fed him: 3 An *Angel* gave him Bread and Water: 1 *King.* 17. and 19. Thus was he fed at several times; 1 By an unclean and ravenous Bird, yet faithfully administred him his provision. 2 By a poor Widow, that had not wherewith to subsist her self. 3 By a Spirit, far from all the refreshments of flesh and blood.

Sith the Resurrection of the Resurrection is to go before their bodily ascension into Heaven, how cometh it to pass, that the ascension of Enoc *hath preceded by many ny ages the Resurrection of all those who have been raised from the Dead.*

IN the persons of those who were raised from the dead, and of those who were bodily translated into Heaven, God hath shewed the Prologues of our Resurrection to come, and of the transportation of our bodies that are to be taken up into Heaven. But the Resurrection will be before that transportation. We may then demand, Why hath not God observed the same order in those wonders, that represented the wonders he is to work at the last times? For whereas we shall be raised from the dead, before we be taken up into Heaven, *Enoc* was transported into Heaven before any was raised from the dead. The first that was raised from the dead was the son of the widow of *Sarepta*, at the prayer of *Elija*, a long time after the transportation of *Enoc*.

This we may say, upon this with all likelihood, God in the first place hath been pleased to shew, that had it not been for sin, Man had been translated without seeing of death, as *Enoc* was by privilege, although he was mortal. Afterwards,

terwards, death having yet a long time reigned, God shewed, that the Resurrection of our bodies is a necessary forerunner of their ascension into heaven: whereof he shewed an example in two divers persons, raising one who was dead, by *Elija*, before *Elija* went up himself to heaven. He hath since continued at certain times the miracle of the Resurrection, till the Ascension of Christ, and a while since too. But so it is, that the Resurrection of the first that was raised from the dead was soon after followed by a miraculous Ascension, even of him by whom that dead was raised. And it cannot be objected, that those two wonders were not wrought upon one and the same person, for that was reserved till the days of Christ; before he raised himself, no man could ever be raised from the dead, to go up bodily into Heaven.

The Resurrection of one from the dead, was never the first Miracle of any Man, no, not of Christ himself. The Reason that can be given of it.

NOne ever raised any from the dead, without having first wrought miracles of another kind.

Before *Elija* raised the son of the widow of *Sarepta*, he had stopt the Rain and the Dew, hindering it from falling on the ground by the space of three years and six months; he had also multiplyed the Oyl and the Meal of the Widow.

Before *Elisha* raised the son of the Shunamite; he had divided the waters of *Jordan*, multipli'd the Loaves, &c.

Before St. *Peter* raised *Tabitha*, he had cured one that was lame from his birth, and one who was sick of the Palsey, *Act.* 3. 9.

Before St. *Paul* raised *Eutichus*, he had struck with blindness the Impostor *Elymas*, cured one who was born lame, and chased away the spirit of *Python*, *Act.* 13. and 14. and 16.

Before Jesus Christ himself raised any
from

from the dead, how many other Miracles had he wrought? He began them by feeding mens bodies, and afterwards proceeded to the cure of the living, before he came to the Resurrection of the dead.

For the most part, the greater Miracles have followed others of lesser moment. The Wisdom of God hath been pleased to act by degrees, to prepare by little and little the spirits of man.

Moreover, the particular Resurrection of some from the dead hath not onely been one of the greatest Miracles of God, but a Preludium of the general Resurrection which we expect. Now as the same shall not happen but in the time to come, the Types which prefigur'd it appeared not but after the curing of the sick, miraculous feeding, and other effects, the signification whereof is accomplished in this present life.

Of the Places where the dead have been raised. The first and the last Miracle of that kind. Both of them were wrought

wrought out of the Land of Israel.

The first was wrought in *Sarepta* of *Sidon* by the Prophet *Elijah*, who raised from the dead the son of the Widow: the last was wrought in *Troas*, a City of the lesser *Asia*, by St. *Paul*, who raised *Eutychus* from the dead. Both of them in the land of the Heathen.

God in the first place hath shewed, that his power over the dead was not limited within the land of *Israel*; moreover, that the Resurrection of the time to come was not onely for the *Jew*, or for any other *Israelite*, but for the *Gentiles* also; for the *Jews* believed it belonged onely to them, and to their Proselytes.

But chiefly God was pleased to shew that unto the *Gentiles*, which they believed to be impossible; the Resurrection of the dead seemed to them contrary to all reason, the Philosophers mock'd at St. *Paul*, who preach'd it, that Doctrine was ridiculous to all the *Gentiles*. Now that they might be convinced of the possibility of it, God was pleased they should see that miracle, even in their own land, yea, and it should both begin and end there.

King Hozias *usurping the Office of the Priests, to whom the judgment of Leprosie appertained, was himself also struck with Leprosie. And whereas the High-priest carried Holiness on his forehead,* Hozias *did carry Leprosie on his fore head.*

'Tis difficult to find the reason, why such and such a sin is found to be punished with such punishments rather then with another; yet for the most part the punishment is answerable to the offence, at least in some regard.

The rashness of that Prince caused him to take upon himself one of the noblest functions of the Priesthood; namely, to offer Incense in the holy place. But affecting the Office of the Priest, his pretensions aim'd at a Jurisdiction annexed to the Priesthood, upon leprous persons; for the Priests were to be the judges thereof, and gave the orders about their sequestration. Thus he who would be amongst those who judged of the Leprosie,

prosie, was put himself amongst the Lepers, to undergo the judgment of the Priests.

It was in his forehead the Leprosie appeared. The High-priest appearing before God, was to wear on his fore-head a plate of gold, wherein was written, *Holiness to the Lord*, *Exod.* 28. 36, &c. But *Hozias*, who would enter into the order of the Priests, bore on his fore-head a quite contrary mark to that the chief of that order wore. For there was nothing more inconsistent with the holiness of the Temple, and to the service performed there, than the uncleanness of a Leper.

Strange and wonderful concurrences of the proportions of Times, which went before, and followed, the going back of the Sun, in the days of Hezekia.

15 *Jubilees.*   15 *Kings.*
15 *Weeks of Years.*   15 *times* 40 *Years.*
15 *Years.*

THe year wherein the *Israelites* divided the land of *Canaan*, after they ended

ended the Conquest, is a Date of great importance, necessary to measure the times of the abode of *Israel* in the Land of Promise. This year was the 2566 after the Creation; from that year to the going back of the Sun, at a time when the Kingdom of *Juda* was in great danger, *viz.* 3295. we see there passed 735 years; now 735 years do make up fifteen Jubilees, every Jubilee consisting of forty nine years, which are seven times seven years.

From thence to the *Babylonian* Captivity, which began in the year 3400, there were 105 years, which make fifteen times seven years, or fifteen weeks of years. These fifteen weeks of years began by the fifteen years miraculously added to *Hezekia*'s life.

Hezekia was the fifteenth King, begining at *Saul*, who ruled the people of God: As therefore there had then been fifteen Kings in the order of succession, so God added fifteen years to the life and reign of the fifteenth King. As for the reasons of that Analogy, I have produced them in my *Observations on the Decalogue*, and shall onely repeat this, That the life of *Hezekia*, prolonged by fifteen years, was an earnest of the subsistance of that Throne, which fifteen Kings had already sate upon.

That Throne subsisted yet after the recovery of *Hezekia*, seven times fifteen years to the time of the Captivity; those who reigned after the begining of the said Captivity, *Jechonias* and *Zedekia*, were but Vassalls to the Babylonian King.

Thus those fifteen years of *Hezekia* were the seventh part of the time that passed to the Captivity; and that time that ran to the time of the Captivity, was one seventh in comparison of the time which had passed from the conquest of *Canaan* to the beginning of these fifteen years of *Hezekia*. To conclude, from the Conquest to the going back of the Sun, where the fifteen years added to the life of *Hezekia* began, there were fifteen Jubilees, which were followed with fifteen weeks of years, ending at the beginning of the Captivity, and including the fifteen years of *Hezekia*.

To all this we may add, that from the begining of the Captivity, to the last ruine of *Jerusalem*, and the final destruction of the State of the *Jews*, (forty years after the death of Christ) there was fifteen times forty years; for from the year 3400, whereat the Captivity began, to the year 4000, in which *Jerusalem* was destroyed by the *Romans*, there passed 600 years, which are fifteen times forty. Such have been the measures and proportions of times, since the *Israelites* were

put

put into the possession of the land of *Canaan*, till they utterly lost it. The Intervals have had their particular measures proportioned the one unto the other, and to a total sum of years.

If the Sun had leaped ten Degrees forward, according to the offer was made, the Question is, By how much his swiftness would have then surpassed the swiftness of his ordinary motion.

HEzekia did not accept of that offer, but required, that the Sun might go back, as it did; many hold, that that going back was done in a moment, but that is not without dispute. It is more certain, that if the Sun had leap'd forwards by so many degrees as God offered to his choice, it would have been in a lesser time then that Luminary doth ordinarily employ in going so long a way: For what wonder had it been if the Sun going forward, and following his ordinary course from East to West, had not gone swiftlier than he used to do? Now

Now to understand how great this swiftness would have been, we must first see what were the measures of the ten degrees mentioned in that Story; if they were so many hours, as the *Jews* think, they would have been 150 Degrees in the *Æquinoctial* line, fifteen degrees for one hour; a very long way, and which required about five of the six parts of that time the Sun employeth in one natural day.

If they were onely half hours, as most of our Interpreters do hold, yet was the Sun to run swifter than ordinary during five hours.

But a modern Writer doth much shorten it, conceiving the ten degrees to be those, which in the *Æquinoctial* line we do account for two thirds of an hour: And so, according to his opinion, the Sun should not have gone back but onely by two thirds of an hour. And when God offered the alternative, to cause the Sun to hasten ten degrees forward, it should not have been any more than by two thirds of an hour.

Now although we should take it in this sense, which is the most diminitive that can be given to that Story, yet we should still find therein a prodigious wonder.

But we must see also, how much less than the two thirds of an hour the Sun should have spent in compassing that way.

It

[107]

It is the most common opinion, that the Sun should have leaped in a moment of time, which is as much as to say, That in a moment he had made as much riddance of his way, as he is used to do in two thirds of an hour. And certainly the miracle, which God offered, did consist in this, that the Sun should dispatch his way in as short a time as possibly he could.

Thereupon the Philosophers will deny, that a local motion can be made in a moment. Let it be granted, but the swiftness of the longest motion may be augmented, God impelling a body to such a degree, that the motion shall be perfected in a time almost imperceivable by its shortness. It serves of that, that;

Instead of a moment let us put the case, that the Sun leaping forward had spent therein a minute, and that his way had been but the two thirds of an hour; in that one minute he had dispatched as much way as he had done naturally in forty minutes, which are the two thirds of an hour; and thus his swiftness had been forty times greater then that of his ordinary motion. Nay let us suppose, that he had employed ten minutes to leap forward, his motion had been four times swifter than it is ordinarily.

Now is known by demonstration, that in one minute he ordinarily doth
move

move 2500 *Germane* Leagues, and more, a wonderful swiftness and rapidity, such as our imagination can hardly follow. One would never believe any thing could be added to so great swiftness, and nevertheless God had augmented it four times, yea, forty times, nay, it may be a hundred times as much, if *Hezekia* had desired it; a prodigious wonder.

Why God did not offer to He-zekia *to cause the Sun to stand still, as he did by* Joshua, *but to make it run extraordinarily.*

GOD hath often wrought miracles in several creatures of the same kind; As for example, He hath raised many from the dead, cured many of the Leprosie, &c. but as to the motion of the celestial bodies, he was never pleased to shew but two miracles, one by stopping, and another time by changing their motion; doubtless, that the general order of the world, which dependeth on that of the heavens, should not be often interrupted.

Now

Now in this rarity, there being but these two miracles, God hath been pleased to shew the abundance of his power by the diversity of it; therefore he hath not reiterated the first miracle, but was pleased that the second should totally differ, yea should be contrary to the former.

Nebuchadnezzar by three Wonders learned to know God; the last being more effectual than the two former, his folly the chiefest means whereby he became wise.

THe miraculous discovery of the dream which he had, was the first argument that did convince him, *Dan.* 2. The deliverance of the three young men preserved in the fornace, was the second motive which made him open his mouth in the praise of the God of *Israel*; but he never was so wise as after a madness of seven years.

A strange means which God used to rectifie that man's understanding, permitting him to fall into a long and extreme tremo madness to make him wise. This would prove the subject of many rare Questions, both Natural, Moral, and Theological.

The last Miracle *of the Old Testament, the preservation of* Daniel *in the Den of Lions. The Inspirations of the spirit of Prophesie continued in Israel 130 years after the cessation of Miracles there.*

After that deliverance of *Daniel*, we do not read of any other Miracle wrought under the Old Testament. That of the Pool of *Bethesda*, where the Angel came down by Intervals for the curing of the diseased, hath no certain date; and it is very probable, that it did not begin but towards the beginning of the New Testament, *Joh. 5.*

Now that deliverance of *Daniel*, which is the closing of all the Miracles of the Old Testament, came to pass immediately after the *Persians* became Masters of *Babylon*, *Dan.* 6. their Empire continued 130 years. Within that time the
Jews

Jews had many Prophets, as *Haggai*, *Zecharia*, *Malachi*, and other holy Writers, as *Esdras* and *Nehemia*: but they had no more Miracles, till the time of the New Testament drawing near.

In all Ages of the Church, the Prophesie hath always lasted a longer time then the Miracles. Between the Creation and the Flood, for the space of 1656 years, amongst the many divine Inspirations the first Patriarchs had, there was never but one Miracle, namely, the translation of *Enoc*, 987 years after the Creation of the world. But the Prophesie (as being more necessary than the Miracles) hath been more frequent, and of a longer continuance.

Why the Church, being under the dominion of the Babylonians, Persians, *and* Romans, *hath had both Prophets and Miracles, but had neither of them under the dominion of the* Grecians.

During the Captivity of *Babylon*, the *Jews* had the Prophets *Ezekiel* and *Daniel*,

Daniel, and for Miracles, the deliverance of the three young men in the Fornace, and the prodigious change of *Nebuchadnezzar*. Under the *Persians*, *Daniel* continued to Prophesie unto the Church, *Dan.* 9. 1. and 10. 1. he himself became a miracle to them, being delivered from the jaws of the Lions. He was followed by many more, who prophesied even almost to the end of the Empire of the *Persians*. But under that of the *Grecians*, which continued 300 years, the Church had neither Prophets nor Miracles. That Empire having destroyed the Empire of the *Persians*, began by *Alexander* in the year 3600, and ended in *Cleopatra* in the year 3900. All that long while there was a cessation both of Miracles and Prophesies, even to the time of the New Testament; this hapned to that end, that the Church seeing those Lights extinguished, should breathe the more after the brightness of the Sun of Righteousness, who was to rise presently after the destruction of the *Grecian* Empire: For not many years after, *Judea* being already under the *Roman* Monarchy, and Christ at the very gates, God began again to work miracles, and lighted the Prophetical Lights, which continued to the closing of the New Testament.

The dangerous Assertions of many famous Interpreters, who think, that the 74 Psalm was composed on the subject of the Persecution of Antiochus.

THe fore-going observation doth lead us to this. All the pieces of the Old Testament, as well as those of the New, came from divine Inspiration; such Inspiration is not found to have been in any since *Malachy* and *Nehemia*, till the New Testament; the Writings composed in that interval can pass but for the works of men. And this is one of our Arguments against the *Apocripha*. Now the persecution of *Antiochus* was not till one hundred years and more after *Malachy* and *Nehemia* had put the last hand to the Writings of the Old Testament; How then can a Writing of such a date have place in the Canonical Scripture? This Psalm is far more antient than *Antiochus*, notwithstanding all the probabilities that can be alledged to the contrary.

The admirable dispensation of God in the distribution of the Empires represented unto Daniel, *and successively divided amongst the off-spring of the three sons of* Noah.

The first of those Empires, *viz.* that of *Babylon*, was given to the generation of *Cham*, *Nimrod*, coming from *Cham*, was the founder of it, *Gen.* 10. 6, 8, 10.

The second Empire, *viz.* that of the *Medes* and *Persians*, was held joyntly by the posterity of *Japhet* and *Sem*; for *Helam*, from whom the *Persians* came, was the son of *Sem*; and *Madai* was the son of *Japhet*, *Gen.* 10. 2, 22.

The Empire of the *Grecians*, and that of the *Romans*, were wholly possessed by the Race of *Japhet*, whose Genealogy is to be seen *Gen.* 10. Let him that readeth understand it.

It is to be observed, that in the distribution of those Empires, God hath kept an order quite contrary to that of the birth of the three sons of *Noah*; for the

the posterity of the youngest, who was *Cham*, and were noted with infamy, had the honor of the first Empire; the race of *Japhet*, who was the eldest, did but attain onely to the second Empire, leaving it presently to one descended from *Sem*, namely, to *Cyrus*, who was a *Persian*. But the last Empires that were near to the coming of Christ, were reserved for the race of *Japhet*, that they might propagate their *Grecian* tongue, which was afterwards the Language of the New Testament, far and wide amongst the Nations, and that finally they might themselves be perswaded to dwell in the Tents of *Sem*, to fulfill the Oracle, *Gen.* 9. 27.

A miraculous observation in the Prediction of Esay, *touching* Cyrus, Esa. 45. 3, 4.

GOd caused it to be spoken to *Cyrus*, a long time before he was born, *I have called thee by thy name*; now besides the Emphasis these words do carry, this ought to be observed.

The Histories do relate of that Prince, that having an Army of many thousands of soldiers, there was not a soldier in all his

his Army whom he could not call by his name; as soon as ever he saw them, he could call them by their own name, without being prompted by any one.

That effect of his memory hath a relation to what God had said to him, *I have called thee by thy Name*; as *Cyrus* knew the names of every one of his soldiers, so God knew the name of *Cyrus*, who was his soldier, and call'd him by it.

Yea, it may be, that God giving him that prodigious memory, and intending he should make use of it to remember the names of every one of his soldiers, aimed at the remembrance of the proper terms of the Prophesie, the fulfilling whereof was found in a man who could call by his name every man in his Army, as God had called him himself by his name.

As many Provinces as the Empire of Persia *did possess, so many years it did continue after the Prediction of its ruine.*

THis Empire which began by *Cyrus*, and continued in his Successors, was

was of 130 years. Now in the third year of *Cyrus, Dan.* 10. 1. which was also the third year of the Empire, its ruine was foretold, which came to pass by the Victories of *Alexander, Dan.* 10. 20. his last victory, which was the destruction of the Empire of the *Persians*, hapned then 127 years after that Prediction. Now that Empire was composed of 127 Provinces, *Hest.* 1. 1. Thus God having denounced the suppression of the Dominion of the *Persians*, he respited it as many years as it possessed Provinces, 127 years for 127 Provinces.

As those things did not meet casually, so the Sacred History doth present unto us several other wonderful correspondencies upon like subjects, among which, this is to be observed.

From the time the Temple was purged of the abominations of Antiochus, *till the same Temple was destroyed by the* Romans, *there were 245 years, which are 35 weeks of years, or the half of seventy weeks.*

I 3   The

The *Purification* of the *Temple* was made three years, and a part of the fourth, after the prophanation of it; and the destruction of the same Temple hapned after a War of three years, and part of the fourth.

THe profanation and the purification of the Temple had been foretold in *Dan.* 7. 25. now that profanation continued three years and ten days, viz. to the year 3755. 1 *Mac.* 4. 52. From that year 3755, wherein the service of the Temple was re-established, untill it was destroyed by the *Romans* in the year 4000, there were 245 years, which are the half of the 70 weeks of years. A most remarkable period.

Now this hath been strange therein, that two so contrary events, as the purification of the Temple, and the destruction thereof, should have the like time of calamity to go before them; for before the *Romans* destroyed the Temple, they plundered all *Judea* for the space of three years, and a part of the fourth; whereas,

after

after the Temple was profan'd under *Antiochus* for the space of three years, and part of the fourth, the service of God was again there re-established.

But the *Jews* themselves had already profan'd the Temple several ways, when God destroy'd it; besides, the holiness of the building was annull'd, after the Vail was rent at the death of Christ. Therefore whereas after the calamity of three years, God formerly re-established the service of the Temple; on the contrary, at that time, after the calamity of three years, he ruin'd the Temple it self.

The Empire of the Grecians *began by a great Warrior, and ended in a Woman.*

THat Monarchy having been founded by *Alexander*, surnamed the Great, and after his death having been divided into four Kingdoms, by degrees they came to nothing, one after the other. The last that subsisted was that of *Egypt*, which continued until, being possessed by a Woman, *viz. Cleopatra*, it was suppress'd by *Augustus Cesar*. Many observations might be made on this subject.

Divers

Diverse measures and proportions of Times given to the Empires of Babylon, Persia, *and* Greece.

A Certain space of time was given to each of them, *Dan.* 7. 12. but the measures were different, and with diverse proportions.

The Empire of *Babylon* continued 70 years, which was also the term of the Captivity. That number of 70 years was marked-out to fulfil the Sabbaths of the Land, 2 *Chron.* 36. 21. The Empire of the *Persians* continued 130 years, which was 60 years more then that of *Babylon* lasted. It was necessary, that that Empire under which the Temple was to be builded, and which was to produce other effects, requiring a long time, and that concerned the Church of God, should be of a longer continuance than the former. It did surpass it therefore by 60 years.

But for several other weighty reasons the *Grecian* Empire lasted five times 60 years, which expired before the death of Christ. For from the time *Alexander* the Great subdued the *Persians*, until *Egypt*, the last piece of the *Grecian* Empire, was incor-

incorporated into that of the *Romans*, there were exactly 300 years, or five times 60; and from that time to the death of Christ, 60 years more. It may be obferv'd, that *Alexander* the Founder of that Empire, reigned but fix years.

The years which paſſed from the beginning of the Captivity of Babylon, to the deſtruction of the ſecond Temple, meaſured by whole Hundreds.

THat interval was of 600 years, which were divided as followeth.

Two hundred years from the beginning of the Captivity, to the end of the Empire of the *Perſians*. There endeth the Hiſtory of the Old Teſtament, and the tenth Prophetical year, as we have ſeen already.

Three hundred years from the end of the Empire of the *Perſians*, to the end of the Empire of the *Grecians*.

One hundred years from the end of the Empire of the *Grecians*, to the deſtruction of the ſecond Temple, and of the State of the *Jews*.

From

From the closing of the History of the Old Testament, to the destruction of the second Temple, which was the suppression of the service thereof, there passed the tenth part of the age of the world, after the tenth Prophetical year.

WE have seen, that the History of the Old Testament ended when the Kingdom of the *Persians* was hastning to its period; this came to pass in the year 3600, which was also the end of the tenth Prophetical year. Now from that time to the destruction of the second Temple, in the 4000 year of the world, there passed 400 years, the tenth of the age the world had then contim'd from the Creation. And forasmuch as that destruction hapned forty years after the death of Christ, we see these forty years were the tenth of the 400 which had run after the History of the Old Testament was finished, as these 400 were the tenth of the 4000 which were fulfilled at the ruine of the second Temple.

An

An Addition of many Historical Observations, included in these foregoing, and set down according to the order of the Times.

A Conjecture why the Scripture nameth not the time, viz. the year or the day, when Sin began.

IN vain do men undertake to know how much time passed from the Creation of the Angels, to the revolt of many of them; or how long *Adam* was in the state of Innocency. 'Tis not mention'd on what day, nor at what hour of the day, nor yet in what year, sin entred the world: 'Tis very likely, and that upon very strong reasons, that *Adam*

continued

continued but very few days in his primitive integrity. Yet the History doth not name neither the day nor the year of his fall, nor in what age it was.

And as the Scripture never expresseth the total sum of the years of the life of a wicked man, as many have observed, so it would not mark the time sin was born: Many sins committed since are there circumstanced, by the expression of the time when they hapned; but the first sin that produced all the others is there mentioned, without the least designation of the term of its birth.

All the conjecture which we can give thereof is this: The Scripture relating the Creation of the works of God, hath distinguished them from those that are not of his making, and yet nevertheless hapned soon after the Creation. Now this is one of the marks of that distinction, that of all the works of God, it is said on what day they began to be; but the day sin was born, is not marked in the Kalendar of the holy Ghost.

Yea, long after the Creation, the Scripture forbore to express the year wherein *Cain* killed his brother. That silence hath many causes, but we see but very few of them.

A vulgar prejudice of those, who think that the Angels appeared with Wings whensoever they were seen of men.

Thus were they represented on the Propitiatory, and thus they may have appeared to the eyes of *Adam*, when they were set upon the Avenues of the Garden to hinder him from coming in again: but certainly, when they appeared to *Abraham* and *Lot* in *Sodom*, who gave them food, they did not appear in the figures of men with wings, for then they would not have been taken for true men, whereas the said Patriarchs nevertheless thought them to be such. Those Histories and many others are commonly falsifi'd in Pictures, and the vulgar imagination already prepossess'd, is thereby confirmed in that ignorance.

Since the Judgment given against Cain, *God hath never immediately pronounced to any sinner the sentence of his condemnation, but onely to one.*

TO the three first Offenders that ever were, the *Serpent, Eve,* and *Adam,* God himself pronounced the Sentence; and yet to the next offender after them, namely, *Cain*: but since, although he hath condemned many transgressors, and drew the sentence, yet he never pronounced it to them with his own mouth, but to one onely, mentioned 1 *King.* 13. 20, &c. to all others he ordinarily caused it to be pronounced by some Prophet, as messengers of his justice, whereof there be many examples.

Doubtless it is to shew us, that he is much more inclinable to mercy, than to rigour, even when he exerciseth justice: It is as if he would have judgment to be pronounced, as it were, in his absence, he withdrawing out of pity.

Of

Of the three several times of the Ascension of Enoc, of Elija, and of Christ.

AT each of these three times there reigned some notable impiety, which choaked the belief of the life to come. In the days of *Enoc*, Atheism was almost general throughout the whole world. In the time of *Elija*, the *Baalism* domineer'd in *Israel*. And when Christ was on earth, *Sadducism*, denying the Immortality of the Soul, and the Resurrection of the Body, was in fashion amongst the *Jews*.

To convince those impieties, and to confirm the belief of the life to come, at every one of these three times, God gave a visible example thereof.

The Generation of Cham, *although the holy Ghost hath noted it with infamy, had the*

the honor of the first Empire erected upon Earth.

Nimrod, descended from *Cham*, was the first King, before ever any of the race of *Sem* or *Japhet* had any Kingship, *Gen.* 10. 8; &c. So *Esau*, debarred from the blessing, had great Lords among his posterity, whilst the posterity of *Jacob* was in great bondage in *Egypt*.

That dispensation containeth many secrets, which have yielded much matter to Interpreters.

The History of the Times whereof the Angels have appeared.

WE insert it here, because the first time the Angels spake to men was in *Abraham*'s time, which now doth offer it self; but this is the order of their apparitions.

1 After the Cherubins, who were plac'd at the entrance of the Garden of *Eden*, for above two hundred years the Angels appeared not unto men: In the days of *Abraham* they began again to appear.

2 From that time they appeared from time

time to time for the space of 204 years, until the going down of *Jacob* into *Egypt*.

3 After that, for 215 years, they were not seen till the vision of the burning Bush, where the Angel appeared to *Moses*.

4 Afterwards their Apparitions were very frequent, and continued till the writing of the Old Testament was almost finished; the last under the Old Testament to whom the Angels appeared unto was the Prophet *Zacharia*.

5 Since that time there was a cessation of their Apparitions for above 400 years, till the beginning of the New Testament; then an Angel appeared to *Zachary*, *John Baptist's* father.

From that time the Angels continued their Apparitions, and were seen of many, and at several times; as, of the *Virgin*, of *Joseph*, and of the *Apostles*, until the New Testament was completed.

But since the Scripture was totally perfected, the Angels appeared no more. The last Angel that appeared is he who dictated the the *Revelation* to *S. John*.

The oldest Trade that we read of hath been that of buying and selling Men.

IN *Gen.* 17. 12. it is spoken of servants bought with the price of silver; of all sorts of Commerce, this is the first mentioned in the Scripture: If it hath not been before all others, at least it is very antient, and us'd a little after *Canaan* was condemn'd to slavery.

Wherefore God hath often employed one Angel alone to do great Matters, and hath often sent many Angels together onely to deliver a Message.

ONe Angel alone hath been able to open the Iron-gates, and to cause the chains of the prisoners to fall off, and to set those at liberty, such as were there most strictly kept, *Act.* 5. 19. and 12. 4. &c. One Angel alone was able in one night

night to flay 185000 men. One Angel alone was able in three days to cause 70000 men to die of the Pestilence. One Angel could exterminate all the first-born of *Egypt*, in the space of one hour. Why did God employ one Angel onely on each of these great exploits, when as many were sent together onely to speak a word? Must there be a company of three Angels to go and tell *Abraham*, he shall have a son by *Sarah*? Were two Angels necessary to denounce that Christ was risen? Was not an Angel sufficient, without joyning to him another, to tell the Apostles that Christ shall come down again from heaven, where they had seen him go up? *Luk* 24. 34. *Act.* 1. 10.

But we ought to consider, that in these occurrences the Angels were sent, not onely as Messengers, but as Witnesses of the Word they were sent to deliver; they were to attest that it came from the mouth of God. Although his truths need not the testimony of the creatures, yet the weakness of men hath need of it; especially, when the things in question are beyond humane belief; as was the birth of *Isaac*, the Resurrection of Christ, and his second coming. Thus, to help the incredulity of men, and for a greater confirmation of the truth, God hath been pleased his Word should be sometimes in the

mouth

mouth of two or three Angels, as of so many witnesses; as amongst men they do give belief unto two or three Witnesses that are unreproachable, and conformable in their depositions.

Why the Fire that fell down upon Sodom, was sent by good Angels, and that which fell upon the servants of Job was sent by Satan; A general Consideration thereupon. When God is willing to make use of Spirits to afflict men, he employeth bad Angels to chastise good men, and on the contrary, good Angels to punish bad men. Onely one Exception of this Maxim.

A Most remarkable proceeding of God! If he be pleased to destroy *Sodom*, to exterminate the firstborn of *Egypt*, to destroy the Army of *Senacherib*, or cause *Herod* to die, he gives

gives the commission thereof to good Angels; but if he will afflict *Job*, either in his own person, or in the persons of his; if he will have St. *Paul* to be buffeted, Satan is he who hath order for it. Hardly an example shall be found of any good Angel employed by God for the chastisement of his children; that Angel onely excepted, who in the days of *David* caused so many *Israelites* to die of the Pestilence, concerning whom we cannot be certain, whether all, or any of them, were the children of God.

But the good Angels are properly ordained to guard those who are to receive the Inheritance of Salvation, and not to cause unto them any calamities. And if thus it might seem, that contrary to what we may judge at first, it would not be so good a sign to be beaten by the hand of a good Angel, as by the hand of Satan: yet we must always say, *Deliver us from evil.*

Why Abraham, *who prayed for the life of* Ishmael, *yea, and for the lives of the Inabitants of* Sodom, *did not pray at all*

all for the life of Isaac, *when he was commanded to sacrifice him.*

O That Ishmael *might live before thee,* said that Patriarch; we know also how many Petitions he did put up for those abominable Monsters, who were to be burnt the next morning: But having received an order to slay *Isaac* his onely son, the son of the Promise, he spake not a word tending to the saving of his life, but prepared himself to put him to death; no doubt but he had a wonderful conflict within himself arising from divers causes; but there are some reasons for the silence of the Scriptures in this occasion: Yet it were more credible, that indeed *Abraham* opened not his mouth at all to save *Isaac*'s life, which may seem very strange, considering the tenderness he had of him, and several other great motives.

Now it seemeth, that the principal cause that might oblige him to make requests for *Isaac*, was the same that dissuaded him from it; he knew *Isaac* was to be the father of many Nations, and doubted not of the truth of the Promise made unto him, nor of the future accomplishment

plishment of it; from whence he inferr'd, that the death of *Isaac* should not at all hinder *Isaac* to become a Father. But as this is naturally impossible, he knew also, that God could do an extraordinary work in the person of *Isaac*. He reasoned with himself, *that God was able to raise him from the dead*, Heb. 11. 19. and what then, said he, if God will work that wonder? shall I require him to deprive himself of that glory? It is remarkable, that as yet God had not raised any from the dead, that kind of miracle had never been seen yet. It was therefore less expedient yet to demand of God to forbear a miracle, which as yet he had never wrought, and was to begin it in the person of *Isaac*.

The Birth of Christ procured, both without and against the intention of the Patriarchs his Ancestors.

Jacob loved *Rachel*, and had not had *Leah* had he not been deceived; yet Chrrist was to come of *Leah*, *Jacob* did not as yet know it, but he knew it lying on his death-bed: *The Scepter*, said he, shall not depart from *Juda*, &c. now *Juda*

Juda was the son of *Leah*; had he known that the Messiah was to come from her, he ought to have preferred her before *Rachel*. But God would shew, that the birth of Christ proceded not either from the choice, or the fore-sight of men, even of those men from whom he came. Would not *Isaac* have given unto *Esau* that great blessing, which belonged to him onely who was to be one of the Fathers of the *Messiah*.

One of the Ancestors of Christ endeavoured to kill him many Ages before he was Born.

Gen. 37. *Juda*, one of the Patriarchs, and from whom Christ is descended, would have burnt *Thamar*, big with child as she was; but she bore him in her womb from whom Christ was to come, *viz. Phares*; to choak him before he was born, was it not as much as to annihilate Christ himself, yea, a long time before he had any existence in the flesh? We ought here to take notice of what we have said in the fore-going observation.

Why the Scripture doth recite the ridiculous Contract betwixt Rachel *and* Leah, Gen. 30. 14.

When *Leah* made that bargain, she had already four sons, the last of whom was *Judah*, from whom Christ was to come: Had she known that she had already a son, who, according to the flesh, was to be the father of the Saviour, would she have envied *Rachel*? The Scripture relateth this (which would otherwise have been frivilous) to shew, as aforesaid, that salvation cometh not from the wisdom or the foresight of the Ancestors of Christ: Which maketh expresly against the *Jews*, who believe they shall be saved by the merits of the Patriarchs.

The blood of a Kid, for the blood of Joseph, *Gen.* 37. 31, &c.

The flesh of Man is different from that of Beasts, and that of Beasts on earth

earth from that of Fishes, or of the Fowl, 1 *Cor.* 15. So likewise the blood of Man is different from that of brute Beasts; the difference (although at first it appeareth not to the eye) might yet be discerned, if not by looking near, at least by some means a cunning Naturalist could invent. But *Jacob* discern'd not the blood of a Kid from the blood of a Man; this artifice whereby he was deceived was not so obvious, as that he himself used to his father *Isaac*, whom he deceived with the skins of a Kid he made use of to counterfeit *Esau*. In those weaknesses of the Patriarchs, one might observe many marks of the wisdom of God.

Why in the midst of all the Plagues of Egypt, *even in the death of the First-born, God preserved the life of* Pharaoh.

IF *Pharaoh* had died then before the children of *Israel* departed out of *Egypt*, 'twould have been thought, that their departure had been facilitated, by this disorder, the intermission of affairs,

the

the fears, the emulations, and other accidents, which often happen upon the death of a King, and either change the designes, or stop the execution of them. In such a case the deliverance of the *Israelites* would not have been so illustrious, and it would have been attributed rather to the weakness of *Egypt*, than to the power of God.

Moreover, God would have the greatness of the danger to shew the greatness of the deliverance, and that therefore *Pharaoh* with a mighty Army should pursue the *Israelites*, and bring them to such a pass, as to expect no succour but from heaven. Thereunto *Pharao* was reserved, and therefore God would not have him to die sooner, *Exod.* 9. 15, 16.

Why God being willing to punish with death those that were guilty of the Idolatry of the golden Calf, he destroyed them not by any miraculous punishment (either by Fire, as Nadab *and* Abihu; *or by opening the Earth to swallow*

low them up, as Corah; *or by some other extraordinary means*) *but commanded* Moses *and others to slay them with the sword.*

Such sins as men think not they are to punish, God doth himself punish, and, for the most part, immediately. But to shew that men ought to punish Idolatry, he would have their hands to be the Executioners of those who had made the golden Calf. In the same manner he commanded that those should be put to death, who adher'd to the Idol of *Baal-peor*: He might himself have exterminated them, without committing it to any other; but to make a Penal Law of it he ordained, that men should inflict the punishment thereof.

Why God hath been pleased that the knowledge of the signification of the Names, representing the matter or stuffs belonging

belonging to the Ceremonial Law, should be lost.

Most of the *Hebrew* names expressing them are unto us as so many Riddles, yea, even unto the *Jews* themselves. We do not know what kind of Cedar was the Timber of the Tabernacle, nor what was that colour of purple (the invention whereof is now lost) in the Curtains of the Tabernacle; nor all those precious Stones set in the Breast-plate of the High-priest: We know not the forms of the Instruments of Musick, on which they sang their sacred hymns; nor whether their Philacteries were Fringes, or Bands, or Borders; nor of what colour was the twist or string, whether Purple, or Seagreen, or Sky-colour; nor the Ingredients of the Confection the Priests were annointed withal; and many other things, the nomenclature whereof is very obscure, and the Interpretations as uncertain; whereas all those words were very easie to be understood, when God caus'd them to be written and pronounced.

But his intention was to abolish the *Mosaical* Ceremonies at the end of a certain time; and becanse they being suppressed, none might re-establish the practise of them, he caused the signification
of

of most of the words, wherein the Ceremonial Law was set down, to be forgotten. Hence it is, that though the *Jews* should have full liberty to build again their Temple, and to put in use again all their antient Ceremonies, 'twould be impossible for them to do it.

The Tables of the Law were shut up in the Ark, and none had power to see them: What was then the use of them?

IF they had been exposed to the view of men, they would have amused themselves in looking upon the work, instead of searching after the sense thereof. The Law is spiritual, and ought to be regarded with spiritual eyes. But as *Moses* did put on a veil over his face, that the children of *Israel* might not look on that which was the end of the Law, 2 *Cor.* 3. 13. so it seems that for the same cause the Tables were hidden from them: What use then did they make of them? They were an earnest of the presence of God unto them. How did they know that those Tables, shut up in the Ark, were the work of God? Because God miraculously

and

and suddenly punished those that were so bold, as to prie thereinto, witness the *Bethshemites*, 1 *Sam.* 5. or onely but to touch it, as *Uzza*, 2 *Sam.* 6.

The Miracle that continued the longest.

'TWas the preservation of *Manna*, reserved and kept in a pot of gold, *Exod.* 16. 32., and *Heb.* 9. 4. *Manna* (that onely excepted which was gathered for the Sabbath-day) did corrupt the next day, and bred worms: But the portion of that food, which God commanded to be kept, that posterity might consider it, did continue many ages without the least corruption. We cannot precisely say how long it lasted; but though it should have been laid up but about the latter end of the last year of the abode of the *Israelites* in the Wilderness, and should have continued but as long as the Tabernacle served, *viz.* until the first Temple was finished, there would have been 447 years. Never any other Miracle lasted so long.

in Israel, *none was ever condemned to the Penalty of Banishment. The Errors of many Interpreters upon certain terms of the Law.*

OF some kinds of sins, the Law saith, That the person found guilty *shall be cut off from his People*, (as he that neglected Circumcision) or *cut off from the Assembly of Israel*, (as he who, during the time of the Passover, should have eaten any leven'd thing) and the like, touching many other breaches or omissions of the Ceremonial Ordinances. But the terms of that penal Law are diversly interpreted. Many Expositors do believe, that these words do signifie a banishment: But, 1 A man might be cut off from the Assembly, although he still abode in the Land of *Israel*; so the *Bastard*, the *Moabite*, the *Ammonite*, could dwell in the Land of *Israel*, and yet they were excluded from the Assembly. 2 In all the History of the Old Testament, there is not one Example found of any *Israelite*, who was judicially banished from his Country for any offence whatsoever;

there

There were other penalties, either more rigorous, or gentler, but not that of banishment. 3 Although he who had accidentally killed a man, was commanded to leave his house, and the City of his habitation, and to retire himself into a place of refuge; yet he continued in the Land of *Israel*, and even in some City of the *Levites*, and went not into any strange Country. 4 Although the Law-giver imposed temporal punishments on Delinquents, yet he had a care of their souls, and would not expose them to the danger of becoming Idolaters. Now in what danger, as to that, would that man have been, who should have been obliged to live amongst Idolaters, far from the publick Exercises, and of the sacred Instructions which were enjoyed but in the Land of *Israel*.

Sometimes God commanded his children to go and dwell, for a time, in the land of the Infidels, as to the *Shunamite* and her son, 2 *King*. 8. and afterwards to *Joseph*, and to the *Virgin*. But, 1 The difference is great between a place of Exile, and a place of Refuge; in the one, a man is subject to a constraint; in the other, he enjoyeth his liberty. 2. Such as God sent into Foreign Countries, he preserved them from the contagion of the Idolaters by his special assistances, as

L *Joseph*

Joseph in *Egypt*, and *David* amongst the *Philistines*.

And even when God hath transported the whole Nation, and caused them to sojourn amongst Infidels (as *Israel* in *Egypt*, the ten Tribes in *Assyria*, and the *Jews* in *Babylon*) and many of them hath been corrupted with Idolatry; it was an act of his justice to punish their former Idolatries, in confining them to the Land of Idols, there to fill the measure of their abominations; but he hath not committed that jurisdiction into the hands of men. As for the faithful, who have been overwhelmed in the general calamity, he hath provided them of Antidotes against the infections of Paganism, as *Daniel* and his Companions. And this is an effect of his grace, which men cannot give, so he gave them no authority to expose their souls to so manifest a danger as might have been occasion'd by the banishment.

Never was any Pestilence in Israel but one, and that onely for three days.

'TIs that pestilence which hapned after *David* had nombred the people,
2 *Sam.*

2 *Sam.* 24. the Scripture mentioneth not any other among the *Israelites.* Amongst the publick scourges, this is the least frequent, unless it be in such places where the constitution of the aire, the multitude, and other accidents, do cause a mortality: sometimes, as this which God sent upon *Israel,* it proceedeth immediately from God; but the evils or calamities that come immediately from him, are never so frequent, nor so general, nor of so long continuance, as those where the hand of men doth intervene, as the War is; on which many excellent considerations might be brought.

The Pestilence which was in Israel touched no Woman, nor any Male under twenty years of age.

IT carried away 70000 men, as the History expresseth; we must understand, that in the enumerations of persons, which are in many places of the Old Testament, the name of *Man* is the name both of the Sex, and of the Age; of the Sex, to distinguish him from Women; and of the Age, to distinguish him from those

L 2   whom

whom the holy Tongue calleth *little ones*, for so it calleth all those that are not yet of age to bear arms; and that age was prescrib'd, for in their Musters none were listed for the War unless he was twenty years of age, 2 *Chron.* 27. 23.

Now its easie to understand, why the Pestilence neither took away, nor touch'd, any woman, nor any male under twenty years of age. The numbring of the people, which *David* caused to be made, was to make him know how many fighting men he had, and consequently what were the forces of his Kingdom. Women therefore were not then numbred, nor those who were under twenty years of age. But as the action of *David* was unlawful, so it had a punishment answerable to the offence; *David* thought to glorifie himself by the number of his fighting-men, and God lessen'd the number of his fighting men, sending a mortality amongst them. It reached not to any one whom either sex or age rendred uncapable of the War, and whom *David* had not numbred; but to those onely who had been the subject of his pride, 2 *Sam.* 24. 9.

We see sometimes some kinds of Epidemical diseases, that assault onely those of a middle age, when they are at the highest of their vigour; and on the contrary do do spare Infants, and the weakness of decrepit and sickly old men: The Physicians give natural reasons for it, but doubtless there are higher causes, although not always known.

The proportion of the number of those who died of the Pestilence, and of those whom David had caused to be numbered.

THe list of these is greater in the first Book of the *Chronicles*, chap. 21. 5. than in the second of *Samuel*. chap. 24. 9. this difference, a reason whereof is given by Interpreters, includeth no contradiction at all. But let us see what hath been the proportion of those who died of the plague, to those who were numbred by the commandement of *David*; the least number of these amounted to 1300000, and there dyed 70000, who were not above the eighteenth part of those that were numbred.

If you take the greatest Catalogue, which containeth 1570000, it appeareth, that the 70000 thousand swept away by the Pestilence were but the two and twentieth

tigth part of those that were numbred; God onely took away by death those 70000, who were above the round number of 1500000

In this dispensation of God, we may observe his indulgence, joyned with an inscrutable wisdom.

A necessary consideration on the words of the Psalm 36. 6.

I Washed my hands in innocency, and so have I compassed thine Altar. The Priests being to officiate, used to wash their hands and feet in the outward Court, which done, they approached the Altar; *David* therefore speaketh of what the Priests used to do. But *David* was of a Tribe whereof none ever assisted at the Altar, *Heb.* 7. 13, 14. How then doth he say, that he compassed the Altar? Certainly he could not speak it litterally of himself, its therefore onely an allusion to that act of the Priests; or it is a Psalm indited, as many others, to the Priests and Levites, to be pronounced in the behalf of *David*; and this indeed is the most probable: For by no means we must not believe, that ever *David* performed that Sacerdotal act. The consequences would

would be worse then at the first they seem to be.

A diminution of the Titles of Solomon *from one of his Books unto the other.*

IN his first Book, that of the *Proverbs*, he is styled the King of the *Israelites*, King of the whole Nation. In his second Book, that called *Ecclesiastes*, he is named but King of *Jerusalem*, King but of one City; nay, he is not called King *of Jerusalem*, but King *in Jerusalem*, a title yet more diminutive. But in the *Canticle of Canticles*, his last work, he hath neither Title nor Epithet, but onely his own name; In the two first Books he was a King, but in the last he is but *Solomon*,

This puts me in mind of a Monarch of the last Century, who in his last sickness would not be saluted by any Title of Honor, but commanded they should onely call him by his Christian name.

Why the Spouse in the Song of Solomon *doth speak before the Bridegroom.*

WHen *Eve* was presented to *Adam*, *Adam* spoke first; and according to all reason, it belongs to the Bridegroom to begin the discourse, and to express his affections: Much more doth it belong to Jesus Christ to speak first in the Dialogue, betwixt him and the Church his Spouse: Why then doth she prevent him in this Canticle? Certainly the Bridegroom had already spoken to the heart of his Spouse, before ever she opened her mouth, yea, and he dictated to her what she was to utter; the first words she pronounced, which are the first of this Canticle, are after to those the Bride-groom had spoken to her in her soul. She believed, therefore she spake. If this Canticle had but a carnal mariage for its subject, it would be against the order, nay, and against the good manners, for the Bride to make the Proposition, and to Court a Man to have him to her Husband.

The Angels having eaten the Bread of Men, returned them the like, causing them to eat the Bread of Angels, but far more substantial then that Bread they had received from the hands of men.

THe Angels had been entertain'd at *Abraham* and at *Lot*'s Table, and since, they brought bread to the Prophet *Elija*; and that food which was given him by an Angel had such a vertue, that it enabled him to walk forty days and forty nights without intermission, 1 *King.* 19. whether *Manna*, which, in the 78 *Psalm*, the Scripture calleth the Bread of Angels, was made or distributed by those celestial Spirits, is very disputable. But as concerning *Elijah* it is evident, that an Angel brought him both his food and his drink. Some might think, that the Angels were willing to requite that hospitality which men had shew'd unto them; but the food which they afforded unto men had a vertue, much above the food men could present unto the Angels.

The

The action of that Angel who brought meat to Elija was quite contrary to the first action that ever Angels did towards Men.

THeir first action towards man was to shut unto him the entrance into the Garden of *Eden*, to hinder him from eating the fruit thereof, and particularly that of the Tree of Life: They then took from man his ordinary food that was very excellent, that with pain he should purchase a meaner. But since in the person of *Elija*, they brought to man a more excellent food, and of greater vertue then all the meats of the world. An action quite contrary to the first which ever they did towards man.

Why God hath often punished Idolaters, who had plundred the Temple of the false gods, and hath given a reward to those who plundred and burned ed his own Temple; as namely, to Nebuchadnezzar.

THis first is witnessed by the Histories: amongst many Examples, we have that of *Antiochus*, 1 *Mach.* 6, and 2 *Mach.* 9.

As for the second, 'tis known how *Nebuchadnezzar* prospered, even after he had destroyed the Temple of God. This is very observable, that *Nebuchadnezzar* having taken the City of *Tyre*, God did further recompence his pains, by conferring on him the Kingdom of *Egypt*, *Ezek.* 29. 16, &c. But how cometh it, that God doth interest himself in the violation of the Temples of the Idolaters? what hath his Justice to do with the nullity of false gods, that he should take their cause into his hand? To this we may answer, 1 Whosoever doth lift up himself against that which he believes to be God, acteth against the dictate of his own conscience, which doth forbid him to attempt against the Deity. For although his blinded conscience makes him take imaginary Deities instead of his Creator, yet is it still a crime to make war against that, which the conscience commandeth to fear and honor as a Deity. 2 Those who plundred their false gods,

were

were not directly punished for such a sacrilege, but for other crimes, although sometimes that punishment came upon them in the very act, or in the place where they committed the sacrilege.

The other question, touching the prosperities of *Nebuchadnezzar*, doth seem more difficult to resolve; for the Scripture attesteth, that God gave them to him for a recompence: But must a publick Thief, the Scourge and Pest of Mankind, be rewarded with such a Salary?

We ought to observe, that the justice of God being willing to punish the *Jews*, and the Nations about them, caused the Arrest thereof to be signifi'd to them, and made *Nebuchadnezzar* the Executioner. The Predictions are frequent in *Jeremy* and *Ezekiel*, declaring to them, that *Nebuchadnezzar* should subdue them; but they believed them not. But God, who hath an interest in the honor of his Messengers, verifi'd their Prophesies, and particularly touching the destruction of the Temple; for he shewed according to his Predictions, that *Nebuchadnezzar* was employ'd by him, and fought under his Banner to destroy the State of the *Jews*, and the Temple it self. It is then no wonder if God gave victories to him, who executed the Decrees of Heaven, although for his own advantages, as a mercenary servant.

Why

Why Daniel *having fore-seen the calamity of* Nebuchadnezzar, *advised him to repent; and having fore-seen the ruine of* Belshazzar, *said nothing to him of Repentance.*

THese two Histories are in the Fourth and the Fifth of *Daniel*; he interpreted to *Nebuchadnezzar* his dream, which denounced to him a madness of seven years, and that he should be driven out of his Kingdom: And to the end this Monarch might prevent this misfortune, *Daniel* exhorteth him to forsake his sins, and to do works of Justice.

A long time after, *Belshazzar*, the son and successor of *Nebuchadnezzar*, was also condemned to lose his Kingdom: *Daniel* read and interpreted the sentence to him, but gave him not the advice he had given to *Nebuchadnezzar*, for he spake not to him of amending his life to avoid his ruine.

We must know, that God hath prefixed a time for the repentance of sinners, as we have already seen; to some he
giveth

giveth a longer time, to some a shorter, within which they are to repent: If they suffer the time to expire which God hath prefixed to them, their repentance cometh too late to prevent their calamity; and it happeneth to them as it did to *Esau*, who came not soon enough to obtain the blessing.

But the Prophetical spirit which was in *Daniel* shewed him, that the Repentance of *Nebuchadnezzar* might yet come seasonably enough to remove the storm that threatned him. But it was not so in *Belshazzar*'s case, the time wherein he was to repent was already gone. And therefore the Prophet being divinely instructed, doth not speak to him of the means of preventing ruine that was unavoidable.

Chronological

Chronological Tables of several Matters contained in this *Harmony of the Times*,

Together with diverse Illustrations, necessary Repetitions, and additions of new Points.

GENERAL TABLES.

The Years of Years.

Each of them is of 365 Solary years, which are as many years as there are days in a year.

THe first year of years doth end then in the 365 year of the World, of the Sun, and of *Adam.*

The second year of years endeth at the year

year of the world 730, was juſt 200 years before the death of *Adam*, for he died in the year 930. Thus the firſt man went two Ages beyond the ſecond year of years.

The third, fourth, and fifth year of years ended, within the life, of *Noah*: That Patriarch ſaw the end of three years of years; two before the Flood, and one after.

The ſixth year of years ended at the year 2190, which was ſeven years after the death of *Abraham*.

The ſeventh year of years ended at the year 2555, then did the Sun ſtand ſtill; as he was ending his ſeventh year of years, he obſerved a Sabbath for the ſpace of a whole day.

The eighth and ninth year of years ended in the year 3285; and the year following, which was in the year 3286, began the tenth year of years. Now in the tenth year of this tenth year of years, in the year 3295, the Sun went back by ten degrees. Thus his going back of ten degrees came to paſs the tenth year of his tenth year of years. The Sun then in ſome ſort paid, as it were, a Tenth or Tithe to his Creator.

The

The Prophetical years, each of them is of 360 Solary years.

THe first and second Prophetical year ended in the year of the world 720, when *Enoc*, the seventh man after *Adam*, (and who prophesied) was 14 weeks of years old, and when his son *Methuselah*, who lived the longest of all men, was 33 years of age, the number of the years of Christ upon earth.

The third, fourth, fifth, and sixth Prophetical year expired in the year 2160; it was 77 years after the Promise.

The seventh Prophetical year ended at the year 2520, it was seven years after the coming out of *Egypt*.

The eighth, ninth, and tenth Prophetical year ended in the year 3600, and then also ended the writing of the Old Testament; and from thence to the death of Christ, in the year 3960, there passed just another Prophetical year, which was the eleventh.

The three and thirty Periods of 120 years, expired in the 33th and the last year of the abode of Christ upon earth.

The most remarkable are the three following.

The five and twentieth, which ended the same year wherein the building of the first Temple was finished, viz. in the year 3000: for there had been 25 times 120 years since the Creation.

The thirtieth, which ended with the tenth Prophetical year, in the year 3600. But as the number of those periods answereth the number of the years of Christ, we are here to mark a notable difference; at the end of this thirtieth period of 120 years, the History of the Old Testament stopped, the Prophetical Inspirations ceased, and the holy Ghost forbore to come down any more in an extraordinary manner. But at the beginning of the thirtieth year of Christ, the holy Ghost came down upon him with Majesty, and the voice of God, which was not heard before in so long a time, caused it self to be most distinctly understood.

The three and thirtieth Period of 120 years was accomplished in the 33th. year of Christ. The

The Septenaries of Years since the creation of the first Adam, to the conception of the Second.

THis Catalogue begins with the first seven years of the world, afterwards there are seven times seventy years. this cometh into the year 497. Afterwards there are seven times seventy weeks of years, this cometh into the year 497. Afterwards there are seven times seventy weeks of years, or otherwise seven seventies of weeks of years, which follow the year of the world 497.

Of these seven seventies, here are the most remarkable in their clasure.

The first endeth at the translation of *Enoc*, the seventh man after *Adam*, in the year 987.

The sixth endeth at the Captivity of *Babylon*, in the year 3437. After which year, for the fulfilling of the seventy years of the Captivity, there passed yet thirty three years, as many years as Christ afterward abode upon earth.

The seventh and last seventieth ended at the year of the Conception of Christ, in the year 3927, after the Promise concerning the Seed of the Woman. Now 3927 years are seven years, seven times seventy years, and seven seventies of weeks of years.

Seven times seventy weeks of years, followed by forty years more, ended the Captivity of Babylon: *And seventy weeks of years, followed by forty years, ended the State of the Jews, in the destruction of the second Temple.*

THe seven times seventy weeks from the Creation of the World, ended in the year 3430, which was the thirtieth year of the Captivity. From thence to the end of the Captivity, which was in the year 3470, there were forty years.

From the end of the Captivity to the death of Christ, there passed seventy weeks of years, which were one seventh
in

in comparison of the years which had run to the thirtieth year of the Captivity. The death of Christ made the year 3960 remarkable.

And from the death of Christ to the destruction of the second Temple, there were forty years.

Thus, between the seven seventies of weeks, fulfilled since the Creation, and the seventy weeks that ran to the death of Christ, there was an interval of forty years. And again, between the end of the seventy weeks, and the destruction of the second Temple, an interval of forty years.

The tenth and last part of all the time which ran from the Creation to the burning of the second Temple; that Tenth subdivided into another Tenth, and the illustrious marks which have distinguished them from the other times.

THe second Temple was destroyed in the year 4000, the last 400 of that sum

sum were the tenth part of it. These last 400 years did begin when the year 3600 ended; now the year 3600 ended the History of the Old Testament, and the tenth Prophetical year. Thus these last 400 years began at the close of the History of the old Testament, and ended by the suppression of the Ceremonies of the Old Testament in the destruction of the second Temple; and these last 400 years were the tenth of the age of the world when the Temple was destroyed.

Again, these last 400 years were decimated; for their tenth and last part, which was of forty years, began at the death of Christ, and ended in the destruction of the Temple.

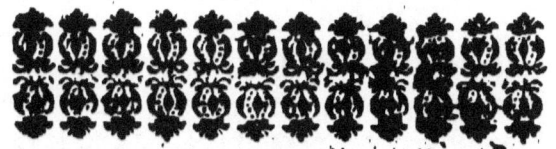

THE PARTICULAR TABLES OF The Years of the World.

The Seventh year.

THIS year is not remarkable by by any particular mark, yet it is illustrious; it is the first of all the Sabbatical years. The Septenary of years hath been since made famous in many great affairs, I will not touch upon Examples, which other Writers have observed; but I will produce some, the observation whereof is particular to our selves, as, the seven last years of *Methuselah*, the seventh year after the death of *Abraham*, the seventh year after the coming out of *Egypt*; the seventh of the Palsey of that Man, who was cured by the Son of God, *Joh.* 5. 5. and others, which we shall mention in their proper places.

Now from this seventh year of the world, to the Conception of Christ, when the Son of God was made of a Woman, in the year 3927, there have been seventy weeks of years, and seven seventies of weeks of years.

The year 120

Endeth the first of the 33 Periods of time, which were from the fall of *Adam* to the 33*th*. and last year of Christ's sojourning here.

The year 235

The nativity of *Enoc* followed, with the distinction made between the children of God, and the children of men. From *Enoc* to the Flood there were eight generations. Which is remarkable for the causes we shall see on the year 1656.

The year 365

Endeth the first Prophetical year, and from thence to the death of Christ, when he sealed the Vision and the Prophesie, in the year 3960, there passed ten Prophetical years.

The year 365

Endeth the first year of years, the Sun having run his course as many years, as he doth days in a year.

The year 497.

From thence to the Conception of Christ seven seventies of weeks of years.

The year 720.

Endeth the second Prophetical year, as also the fourteenth week of years of the Prophet *Enoc*, and the thirty third year of his son *Methusela*.

The year 730

Endeth the second year of years. Just two hundred years before the death of *Adam*.

The year 930

Adam dieth; the years of his life were thirty years, and thirty times thirty years. At the age of thirty years Christ began his Ministery. From the time the Ten Tribes forsook the Temple, that represented

sented Christ, until the Veil of the Temple was rent at the death of Christ, there passed the number of the years of *Adam*, 930. From the fall of *Adam*, to the falling away of the Ten Tribes 3030 years. From the death of *Adam* to the death of Christ 3030 years.

The year 987.

This is altogether mysterious. It endeth the first seventy of the weeks of years, that ran from the year 497, to the Conception of Christ.

It was the same year of the translation of *Enoc*, which began the second Septenary of the 77 Generations, in the Genealogy of our Lord.

Christ is the seventieth Man after *Enoc*, as *Enoc* is the seventh man after *Adam*.

Enoc was the third went out of this world. Christ the third of those went up bodily into heaven, being preceded by *Enoc* and *Elias*.

The departure of *Enoc* was preceded by that of *Abel*, who died a violent death, and by that of *Adam*, who died a death natural. Those two ways; the violent death, and the natural, have been opened until, and represented now, in *Abel* and in *Adam*, the two first men that departed out of this world. There
remaineth

remaineth a third way, *viz.* the transmutation and translation of those that shall be found living at the last day, 1 *Cor.* 15. 51. this third way was represented in the Person of the third Man who departed out of this world.

That translation of *Enoc* was the first Miracle that God wrought after the Creation of the world; and the last Miracle he will work, before he destroyeth the world, will be the translation of those that shall ascend to heaven.

The year 1636.

God prefixed to the world the term of 120 years, the eighth part of the age of men at that time, *Gen.* 6. 3. A long time after, since the *Israelites* had divided the land of *Canaan*, 2560, they possessed it seven times 120 years, to the Captivity of *Babylon*, which began in the year 3401. God gave them then seven times as much time as he had given to the old world, when he did threaten them with the Flood.

The year 1650

Doth begin the last seven years of *Methuselah*, those seven years he had above the age of any other man that ever lived:
the

[172]

the last of these seven years of *Methuselah* was also the last year of the old world, when it perished by the Flood in the year 1656. The same year of the destruction, a little before it came to pass, God caused him to be seen of men, who had lived a longer time then any other man. The example of so great a blessing so near unto the Flood was a warning to them, that God would have greatly prolonged their days, had not their impenitency abridged them.

The year 1651.

'Tis the second of the seven years of *Methuselah*, in that same year his son *Lamech* died, five years before his father, which were also five years before the Deluge. *Lamech* is the first that we read of who died a natural death before his father; he is the seventh man that died after *Adam*; he is all made of Septenaries, which are expressed in our Harmony of the Times.

The year 1656.

The Flood. *Noah*, then the chief of Mankind, was the eighth Generation after *Enoc* inclusively, in whose days men began to call on the name of the Lord,

Gen.

Gen. 4. 26. Thus in this eighth Generation, after the term of the eighth part of the ordinary age of man at that time, eight persons were saved in the Ark.

In the Deluge, God did some works, which were contrary to those of the second, and the third day of the Creation, he mingled the waters that are above with those that are below; he caused also the earth to be covered with waters, to teach men, that the earth was covered with them when God created it, 1 *Pet.* 3: 5, 6. In the last six months of the year of the Flood, there was neither born, nor did there die, any humane creature, nor Beast, nor Bird; God for that time having suspended both the birth and the death of all living creatures of the earth and of the aire. Not one creature either died or was born in the Ark, during the whole year of the Flood.

From the Flood, to the Promise made to *Abraham* in the year 2083, there were 427 years. *Abraham* was the tenth Generation after *Noah*, as *Noah* was the tenth after *Adam*. A long time after *Abraham*, from the foundation of the first Temple, in the year 2993, to the first ruine thereof, in the year 3420, there were also 427 years. Also from the interruption of the foundation of the second Temple, in the year 3473, until the
final

final ruine of the *Grecian* Empire, in the year 3900, there were likewise 427 years, which are 61 weeks of years.

The year 1658.

The Nativity of *Arphaxad*. Of all the Ancestors of Christ, *Arphaxad* was the first that was born after the Flood.

He was the twelfth Generation after *Adam* inclusively; and the twelve Patriarchs, the sons of *Jacob*, were the twelfth Generation after *Arphaxad* inclusively. And *Nathan* the son of *David*, from whom Christ came, was the twelfth Generation after *Juda* (one of the Patriarchs) inclusively.

The year 1723.

The nativity of *Heber*, which begins the third Septenary of the seventy seven Generations in the Genealogy of our Lord.

Heber living, and at the same time when *Phaleg* was born unto him, hapned the confusion of the Tongues. *Heber* was the fourteenth Generation after *Adam* inclusively. Christ, who conferred the gift of Tongues, was the fourteenth Generation after the Captivity of *Babel*, where the Tongues were confounded, or rather

rather where one Tongue was confounded into many, *Matth.* 1.

The year 1757.

The nativity of *Phaleg* followed by the division of Tongues; from hence to the death of *Heber*, the father of the *Hebrews*, in the year 2187, there were 430 years; and so much time was from the Promise, in the year 3082, to the Law, in the year 3513; and as much from the Law to the annointing of *David* in *Bethlehem*, in the year 2943.

The division of Tongues was followed by the erection of the first and most antient Monarchy, in the person of *Nimrod*, who was come from *Chasma*. That accurs'd race had the honor of the first Empire.

The year 2008.

The nativity of *Abraham*, two years after the death of *Noah*: He lived 175 years, half of the 350 which were the years of *Noah* after the Flood.

The year 2094.

The second time the Angels shewed themselves unto men, *Gen.* 16. 7, &c.

The

The nativity of *Isaac*, which begins the fourth Septenary of the 77 Generations in the Genealogy of the Son of God. *Isaac* is the first whose conception was miraculous.

The year 2113.

From thence to the going out of *Egypt*, in the year 2513, there were ten times forty years, *Gen.* 15. 13. the last of these ten times forty doth end with the second fortieth of the age of *Moses*: These ten times forties were followed by another forty years spent in the Wilderness, and ending with the last fortieth of the years of *Moses*.

The year 2168.

The nativity of *Jacob*, the 22 Patriarch after *Adam*. After him the Church became to be the body of a Nation, ruled by 22 Judges successively, from *Moses* unto *Samuel*: 22 Priests, until the destruction of the first Temple; 22 Kings, 22 Generations from the Captivity to Christ.

The

The year 2245.

Jacob goeth to *Laban*, he was then seventy seven years of age; he serveth seven years, or one week of years, to have a wife; he maried being eighty four years of age: after which, he had as many sons, as he had lived weeks of years before he was maried. His family consisted of seventy souls when he went down into *Egypt*, *Gen.* 46. 27. He preferred *Rachel* before *Leah*, for he was ignorant that Christ should come from *Leah*.

The year 2276.

Joseph being sold, continueth thirteen years in slavery, according to the number of the thirteen Luminaries that had done homage to him in his Dream: His eleven brothers, represented by so many stars, went to submit themselves unto him, before *Jacob*, who was represented by the Sun: Although the Sun and the Moon were in his Dream expressed to be the first, according to the order of dignity, yet in the order of time, *Jacob* was the last who personally did homage unto *Joseph*.

Again, as the Sun and the Moon are sufficiently distinguished from the eleven Stars, so the two last years of the servitude of *Joseph* were distinguish'd from the eleven Stars going before; for two years before his

his deliverance and preferment, he had interpreted the Dream of the two Officers of *Pharaoh*, which interpretations, at the end of two years, were the occasion of his liberty and greatness, *Gen.* 41. 1, 9. &c.

The year 2298.

Jacob and his sons, who had been represented by the Sun and the Stars, do homage unto *Joseph*; since that, *viz.* 257 years after, in the year 2555, the Sun in effect did homage to one descended from *Joseph*, *viz.* to *Joshua*; and from the time the race of *Joseph* forsook the Temple and the Service of God, in the year 3030, until they were transported into *Assyria*, in the year 3287, there were 257 years. The glory and the ignominy of a Family have often the like measures of time, until their final extinction.

The year 2460.

The nativity of *Joshua*. A hundred years after, in the seventh year of his Government, he divided the Land of *Canaan* amongst the Tribes of *Israel*.

The year 2513.

The Angel appeared to *Moses* in the burning

burning bush. There passed 215 years (all the time of the sojourning of the children of *Israel* in *Egypt*) without any Angel appearing or speaking unto men.

The miracle *Moses* wrought, by order of the Angel, changing a Rod into a Serpent, is the first Miracle that ever was wrought by man. Seven men under the Old Testament had the gift of Miracles; 1 *Moses*. 2 *Aaron* his brother. 3 *Joshua*. 4 *Samuel*. 5 The Prophet sent to *Jeroboam*. 6 *Elijah*. 7 *Elisha*.

That year is that of the *Israelites* coming out of *Egypt*; *Moses* was then eighty years old, as many years as *Joseph* had govern'd *Egypt*.

The Tribe of *Judah* had, at that time, *Naason* for their Head, who begins the fifth Septenry of the seventy seven Generations in the Genealogy of the Son of God.

From the coming out of *Egypt*, to the foundation of the first Temple, in the year 2993, there were twelve times forty years, 1 *King*. 1.6. The first of these 12 times 40 years were spent in the Wilderness. From the time of the foundation of the first Temple, to the interruption of the second, in the year 3473, there were also 12 times 40 years. From that interruption, to the end of the last but one of the weeks of *Daniel*, and of the years of the abode of Christ on earth, in the year 3953, there were also twelve times forty years. From the time of the finishing of the second Temple, in the beginning of the year 3520, to the destruction of it, in the year 4000, there were also twelve times forty years. This twelfth fortieth begins at the death of Christ.

At that same year 2513, expired the ten times forty years, foretold unto the Patriarch *Abraham*.

The year 2515.

The Murmurers condemned to die in the forty years of their sojournings in the Wilderness. See the year 2570.

Israel beaten by *Amalek*. Why the people of God have so often been beaten in war by their enemies. See my *Observations on the Creed*.

The year 2520.

Endeth the seventh Prophetical year.

'Tis the seventh year after the coming out of *Egypt*, the seventh year of the sojourning of *Israel* in the Wilderness. The thirty three years which followed, and expired when the *Israelites* entred into *Canaan*, do answer the thirty three years of the sojourning of Christ on earth, and
which

which expired in the Redemption. And as the entring of *Israel* into *Canaan*, under the conduct of *Joshua*, hapned at the time of the Feast of the Passover, *Josh.* 5. 10. so the Redemption accomplish'd by *JESUS* hapned at the time of the same Festival.

The year 2553.

Moses dieth, having lived three times forty years, the last whereof he passed in the Wilderness.

Israel entreth into *Canaan*, having *Joshua* for their Leader. None of the *Israelites* who entred into *Canaan* had then attained the age of threescore years, *Caleb* and *Joshua* excepted; whom God had reserved for two antient eye-witnesses of the wonders he had wrought in *Egypt*. See my *Observations on the Decalogue*.

The government of *Joshua* continued seventeen years, which was the age of *Joseph*, *Joshua*'s predecessor, when his brethren sold him. And there passed seventeen years from the entring of *Jacob* into *Egypt*, until the time of his death. And seventeen years *Rehoboam* reigned over *Juda*.

The year 2555.

The miraculous Solstice, for the space of one whole day, a day of Sabbath for the Sun, as he was finishing his 365 weeks of years, seven times as many years, as he numbreth days in the year. It endeth the seventh year of years.

The Sun and the Moon do homage to one descended from *Joseph*. See the year 2298.

The year 2560.

It is the seventh of the Government of *Joshua*, and of the entry of *Israel* into *Canaan*; it is the year wherein they divided the Land of Promise: They possessed it to the Captivity of *Babylon* for the space of 840 years, which are twelve times seventy years, as many years as there were portions, according to the number of the twelve Tribes.

And from the time they were transported into *Babylon*, unto the return from thence into the Land of *Canaan*, there passed seventy years, to fulfil the Sabbaths of the Land, 2 *Chron.* 36. 21. This was the time of the Captivity.

And from the end of the Captivity, which ended in the year 3470, to the death

death of Christ, in the year 3960, there were seven times seventy years.

Thus, they had twelve times seventy years of possession, seventy years of Captivity, and seven times seventy years from the Captivity to the Redemption: In all, twenty seventies of years.

From the same year 2560, which was the fifth after the Miraculous Solstice, to the going back of the Sun, in the year 3295, there were fifteen Jubilees, every one consisting of seven times seven years, which make in all 735 years. And from the retrogradation of the Sun, to the Captivity, which followed the years 3400, there were fifteen weeks of years, otherwise 105 years. Those fifteen weeks of years began by the fifteen years added to the life of the fifth King, *viz. Hezekia*.

From the same year 2560, to the death of Christ 1400 years, which are 200 weeks of years. Then Jesus purchased us that rest, which *Joshua* could not give, *Heb.* 4. 8.

From the same year 2560, when the Land of *Canaan* was divided into twelve portions, to the destruction of the second Temple, and of the State of the *Jews*, in the year 4000, there were three times twelve forties of years.

The year 2570.

Joshua dieth, having lived 110 years: His age was forty years above the seventy of the ordinary age of the *Israelites*, who were forty years in the Wilderness, *Psal.* 90. 10.

Since the sentence of death was pronounced against the Murmurers, in the year 2515. God doubled the age of *Joshua*, who was then fifty five years of age, and lived fifty five more, which amount in all to 110: His life was thus divided into two moities, distinguished by that memorable Sentence of the condemnation of the other *Israelites*.

The year 2949.

By the supposition of an apparition, representing *Saul*, Satan endeavoureth to prevent God in the Miracle of the Resurrection of the dead; for there was none raised from the dead till a long time after.

The year 2975.

About this time, *Nathan* the son of *David*, he began the ninth Septenary of the seventy seven Generations in the Genealogy of Christ. *The*

The year 2989.

Some do attribute to that year (which is the last but one of the Reign of David) the Pestilence which God sent; but this onely time, as far as we can find in the History, Israel was afflicted with the Pestilence. That heavy Visitation touch'd no woman, nor no male under the age of twenty years.

At that time hapned the War of Absolom, and that of Sheba the son of Bichri, against David. The end of his Reign and of his Life was extremely turbulent.

We reckon six Civil Wars in Israel, while the Tribes were united in the same Religion, before the sin of Jeroboam: 1 That of Benjamin against the other Tribes, for the Levite's wife. 2 That of the Ephramites against Jeptha. 3 That of Abimelech against the Sichemites. 4 That of the House of Saul against David. 5 That of Absolom against David. 6 That of Sheba against David.

The year 2990.

David dieth, being seventy years of age; not any other of all the Kings of Judea lived so long.

How

How came it to pass, that those Kings, whom God had established, had so short a life? That the people of God might aspire unto the Kingdom of the *Messias*, 'Twas necessary that the temporal Kingdom of *Judah* should be of a short continuance, and in the shortness thereof, God would have a great diversity, both of Kings and of Events, to be seen, and that for divers reasons. That diversity had not been so great, nor so abundant, if there had been but a small number of Kings; and there number had been very few, if every one of them had lived a long time; for three or four had filled all the time of the duration of that Kingdom. 'Twas therefore expedient, that one should soon give place unto another. And this is the reason why their lives were so short, in comparison of many other men who were their Contemporaries, as *Barzillai*, and *Jehoiadah*, 2 *Sam.* 19. 2 *Chron.* 24.

In that same year 2990, *Solomon* begins his Reign; he and his race possessed the Kingdom of *Juda* to the year 3420, which ended in *Zedekia*; this was 430 years, a number of the same length of time as that which passed from the Promise to the Law.

The

The year 3000

Endeth the twenty fifth Period of 120 years.

The Temple was finished. They had employed one week of years in the building of it; and from the finishing thereof, it continued sixty weeks of years, to the year 3420.

That same number of sixty weeks of years, is that of fourteen times thirty. The Temple, after it was finished, continued fourteen times thirty years; the first thirty years it was owned, and frequented by all the Tribes of *Israel*; but at the end of those thirty years, ten Tribes forsook the Temple, to worship in *Dan* & *Bethel*. The thirteen thirties which followed the first, answer the number of the thirteen Tribes, the Tribe of *Levi* being therein comprehended, whom the Apostate *Israelites* had degraded.

The year 3030.

The Temple had stood thirty years, when the ten Tribes forsook it. Christ, the true Temple was thirty years of age, when he said unto the *Jews*, *Destroy this Temple*, *Joh.* 2.

From the ten Tribes forsaking the Temple,

Temple, the figure of Christ, to the death of Christ, the second *Adam*, there passed as many years as *Adam* had lived. *See the year* 930.

In that same year 3030, God pronounced his sentence against a guilty man; it is the onely man, since *Cain*, against whom God immediately pronounced a sentence; to all others he caused it to be pronounced by some Prophet.

The year 3160, *&c.*

Joas King of *Israel*. In his time *Elisha* dieth, the seventh and the last who did work miracles under the Old Testament.

The year 3175, or thereabouts.

Jonas refuseth to take a journey of three days, which was the bigness of *Ninevey*, *Jon.* 3. 3. he is condemned to a prison of three days in the belly of the Whale. But from this restraint of three days, and his miraculous deliverance, God hath framed a mysterious Type, *Matth.* 12. 40.

The year 3252.

King *Hozias* attempting to usurp the Office

Office of the Priests, is struck with a disease, the judgment whereof belonged to the Priests, *viz.* a Leprosie; it seizeth him on the forehead; whereas the High-priest had Holiness written upon his forehead.

The year 3285

Endeth the ninth year of years.

The year 3295.

'Tis the tenth year of the tenth year of years, and the Sun went back ten degrees.
'Tis the end of the fifteen Jubilees, which are 735 years expired since the dividing of the land of *Canaan*: 'Tis the beginning of the fifty years which were added to the life of the fifteenth King, *viz. Hezekia*.

The year, 3302.

'Tis the seventh of the fifteenth last years of *Hezekia*; 'twas the 107*th.* Sabbatick year to the Land of *Canaan.* Reckon ye from the year 2560, which was the first year of the Rest of the Land, and so from seven years unto seven.

The

The year 3400

Endeth the twelve seventies of years expired since the dividing of the Land of *Canaan*; and the year following begins the Captivity of *Babylon*. From thence to the last destruction of *Jerusalem*, in the year 4000, there passed fifteen times forty years, the last whereof doth begin at the death of Christ, and endeth at the destruction of the Temple.

The Captivity of *Babylon* began fifteen weeks of years after the retrogradation of the Sun. Those fifteen weeks of years began at the fifteen years which were added to the life of *Hezekia*.

The year 3471.

The miraculous Writing, which contained the sentence against *Belshazzar*, fifty one years after his grand-father *Nebuchadnezzar* had caused the loss of the first other Writing, that was in the Tables of the Law. The first Writing was made presently after the *Israelites* came out of the bondage of *Egypt*; and the other was made on the point of their coming from the Captivity of *Babylon*.

Cyrus, who could call every one of his soldiers by their names, had been named by by God a long time before, *Eſa.* 45. 3, 4.

The preſervation of *Daniel* in the Den of the Lions, the laſt Miracle under the Old Teſtament; from that laſt Miracle to the cloſing up of the Old Teſtament, there were 130 years.

The return of the Captivity, under the conduct of *Zorobabel*, who was the forty ſecond Generation ſince the diviſion of the Tongues in *Babel. See the year* 1723.

The year 3473.

The interruption of the foundation of the ſecond Temple, twelve times forty years after the foundation of the firſt, which had been in the year 2993.

From thence to the end of the Empire of the *Grecians*, who had profaned the Temple, there were 427 years, as many years as the firſt Temple had continued ſince its foundation. The Empire of the *Grecians* ended in the year 3900.

In this year 3473, *Daniel* foretold the end of the Empire of the *Perſians*, which came to paſs 127 years after, *viz.* in the year 3600. This Empire was compoſed of 127 Provinces, and after that Prediction it continued 127 years, as many years as it had poſſeſſed Provinces, *Eſth.* 1. 1. *Dan.* 10. 1. 20. The laſt Angel

Angel that appeared to men under the Old Testament, is he who spake unto *Daniel*, and the last words the Angels brought unto men under the Old Testament were those which were read in the third Chapter of *Daniel*. In the fore-going year, which was the year, 3472, an Angel had also spoken to the Prophet *Zechary*, *Zech*. 1.1.9, &c.

The year 3600.

This year was the conclusion of many Periods, and memorable affairs. It ended the tenth Prophetical year, to give place to the eleventh, which ended at the death of Christ, in the year 3960.

It ended the time of the *Persian* Empire, that had continued 130 years, which were sixty years more then lasted the Empire of *Babylon*.

It ended the History, and the Prophetical Inspirations of the Old Testament. It was 130 years after the last Miracle of the Old Testament, hapned in the year 3471.

It ended the thirtieth Period of 120 years, by a contrary effect to that of the thirtieth year of Christ.

The year 3755.

The Temple was purged of the abhominations, which *Antiochus* had introduc'd duc'd therein. From thence, to the destruction of the Temple, in the year 4000, there were 245 years, which are thirty five weeks of years, the half of seventy weeks.

The year 3848.

Here beginneth the years of the life, or of the widowhood, of *Anne* the Prophetess, who was in the Temple, when Christ was there presented forty days after his Birth, *Luk.* 2. 36, &c.

The year 3900.

The end of the *Grecian* Empire, which had continued five times sixty years, five times as long as the Empire of the *Persians*, went in duration beyond the Empire of *Babylon*. And from the end of the *Grecian* Empire to the death of Christ, there passed also sixty years.

The year 3920.

This year began the Palsey of that man, whom Christ cured near unto the Pool of *Bethesda*, thirty eight years after, *Joh.* 5. the disease of this man was seven years before the conception of Christ. *See the seventh year.*

The year 3925.

The Angel appeared to *Zachary*, the father of *John Baptist*, and made the overture of the New Testament.

The year 3946.

The Nativity of the daughter of *Jairus*, who was raised from the dead twelve years after, viz. in the year 3958.

The year 3954

Beginneth the last week of the years of the sojourning of Christ upon earth; this week was divided into two halves, the second and the last containeth the three years and a half of the Ministry of Christ, and endeth at his Ascension, in the year 3960.

The year 3960.

Christ rose from the dead, gave his presence to his Disciples for the space of forty days. He gave the space of forty years to the *Jews* to repent in them, before he destroyed their Temple and State. These forty years were the tenth of the 400 which had passed since the closing up
of

of the Old Testament; and these 400 were the tenth of the 4000 which passed from the Creation to the destruction of the second Temple.

The year 4000.

Since the *Israelites* took possession of the Land of *Canaan*, in the year 2560, until they were driven out of it, in the year 4000, there passed 1440 years.

BUT *now have I gone through all the great Abysses of the Times; and founded so many unknown Depths, though not without great labour and vexation of spirit. In this vast extent, how often hath sleep gone back from mine eyes? how often had I rolled from one gulph to another, had not God given me wings to flie over so many Precipices? To Him, who is the King of Ages, be the Honor of it.*

Reader.

READER,

This Work would be less defectuous, if I had therein inserted some Points contained in some of my former Treatises; but I haue forebore it, to avoid Repetitions: Yet take these few Heads of them.

In my Observations on the Creed.

HOW often the general Order of the world hath been interrupted, since the Creation.

Notable Examples of the Providence of God, in the Fatalities of the Times, and Places, and other Circumstances.

From whence it comes, that among the publick scourges, those that pass through the hand of men, are frequenter, more general, and of a longer continuance, then those which come immediately from the hand of God.

Of the wonderful Providence of God, permitting that the righteous men should

should die by the hand of the wicked.

Why in the War, the People of God have oftentimes been beaten by their enemies, and why the Good Cause hath miscarried.

Why God hath never sent but one Angel, or two at the most, when he would destroy men, and often hath employed many, when he hath been pleased to preserve but one man.

If man had continued in his original innocency, there had been never any miracle but of one kind.

The first and the next cause of the abode of *Jonas* for three days in the belly of the Whale.

An Observation on the four general Judgments, mentioned in the Scriptures.

An admirable mystery seen in the several departing of the three first Men, whom God had taken out of the world.

A Catalogue of the actions which have been celebrated with sprinkling of blood, in the time of the Law.

The number of the persons composing the body of the universal Church, is not onely prefixed or defin'd, but also ruled by measures and proportions.

Why the most notable Periods of the Church, and many signal Mysteries, have had their beginnings in a Wilderness.

Some Examples of many great sinners,

re-established in their first estate.

Why *Abraham* is so highly praised, for believing that God was able to raise from the dead.

The first and the last of all Miracles.

Why *Adam* was not bodily translated into Heaven as well as *Enoch*.

In my Observations upon the Decalogue.

WHy 'tis never said that God hath repented himself of any thing, but of what onely concerned men.

A comparing of two miraculous Writings reported in the holy Scripture.

How long the Tables of the Law continued. A consideration on that subject.

Degrees among the Nations, as to the love or hatred which God bears unto them.

A consideration of the times wherein Atheism and Superstition generally raigned.

Why God, who often appeared in a visible form, would not shew himself in that manner when he published the Law.

The admirable proportions God doth hold in the dispensation of his judgments.

From

From whom the people are descended who go stark naked.

Wonderful Examples of divers subjects, on whom God caused his mercy and his justice to be seen.

Why heretofore God took such a particular care of the Patriarchs and their children; nay, even of those who were wicked, and now he is not pleased to give such directions as he did then.

Why God employed but six days in creating the world, and employed seven to overthrow the Walls of Jericho.

The reason of the number of fifteen years, added to the life of Hezekiah.

The age of the Israelites, when they passed from the Wilderness to the Land of Promise.

The measures and proportions whereby the life of man was shortned from time to time, since the first Ages.

None of the Kings of Juda exceeded the age of seventy years.

A moral consideration on Samson's losing both his strength and his sight, and recovering the one and not the other.

One man onely, to whom God divinely shewed the way how to make himself rich.

A Conjecture on the opinion of the Jews, touching the just price of sales.

Why Moses, who had wrought so great, and

and such various Miracles, yet never raised any from the dead.

Before I proceed to the Matters of the New Testament, I thought it necessary to remove certain prejudicating Arguments which the Jews make use of, to nullifie the authority of the Apostolical Writings. This I reserved to the ensuing Treatise.

THE EXAMINATION

Of Seventeen

JEWISH PRINCIPLES,

TOGETHER

With a Preparatory Advertisement for the Confutation of certain Calumniators, Enemies to the *Harmony*.

By JOHN ESPAGNE, *Minister of the Holy Gospel.*

LONDON,

Printed by *William Godbid* for *Hen. Herringman*, at the *Blew-Anchor* in the Lower Walk of the *New-Exchange.* M. DC. LXII.

AN
EXAMINATION
OF THE
JEWISH ORACLES,
TOGETHER
With a Preparatory Advertisement,

&c. Executor to the Harmony.

By JOHN EPAGNE, Minister of the Gospel.

LONDON,

Printed by *William Godbid* for *Hen. Herringman* at the *Blew Anchor* in the Lower Walk of the New Exchange, M DC. LXII.

READER,

THE Jews *have many Principles, which at the first sight seem to be indifferent, but indeed they do make void the Authority of the New Testament; and he that lets them pass without contradiction, doth insensibly renounce Christianity:* They are the Inventions *of their* Rabbins, *whose Traditions pass for Oracles amongst them: You shall but in vain alleage unto them either* Moses *or the* Prophets, *as long as the* Jew *gives them the* Rabbins *to be Collateral unto them, with an equal right of suffrage. Those men are greatly deceived, who in disputing with such Adversaries, do believe,*

lieve, that they must at first come directly to the *Question* concerning the Messias. On the contrary, we ought to begin by the overthrowing of their Principles, viz. Their Traditions: Now they are destroyed if we let them see, that they consist of evident Blasphemies, gross Absurdities, fabulous Tales, formal Contradictions, and other Monsters, repugnant even to common sense. I have shewed some scantlings of it in a short verbal Conference I had lately with one of the most famous Rabbins of this Age, and had he accepted of the continuation thereof, either by word of mouth, or by *Writing*, as was offered him by me, I am certain he should have had yet a thousand times worse success. The

The First MAXIM of the *Jews*.

ONE *Angel is never employ'd in two Embassies, or in carrying of two Messages.* Bereshith-Rabba, *quoted by* Rabbi Moses *the Egyptian; otherwise* Bar-Majemon.

The Examination.

IF that be granted them, we must renounce all the New Testament, which they undertake to cut down by the root. We read therein, that the Angel *Gabriel*, having delivered a Message to *Zachary*, the Father of *John Baptist*, six months after he carried another to the *Virgin*; which could not be, if this Maxim of the *Jews* be true. Moreover, the same Angel *Gabriel* had a long time before performed the office of a Messenger,

Messenger, being sent to *Daniel*. From whence it will follow, that after that time he never carried any Message, and by consequence, never spoke either to *Zachary* or the *Virgin*.

But these blind *Jews* have not observed that one and the same Angel *Gabriel* under the Old Testament, carried two several Messages at several times, and to the same person, viz. to *Daniel*, chap. 8 and 9. the first in the third year of *Belshazzar*, and the other in the first year of *Darius*; one of them touching the four Empires, and the other touching the stated period of the desolation of the second Temple, and the profusion of the seventy weeks.

Moreover, What inconvenience would there arise, if one Angel be employed in two Messages? On the contrary, it was convenient, that the same Angel, who had already spoken unto men, should be sent again to them for a greater confirmation. Thus, when *Daniel* was sorrowful, God sent him a message by the same Angel, who had spoken to him heretofore, *Dan.* 9. 21. And as for *Zachary* and the *Virgin*, God sent them word by the same Angel who had marked the seventy weeks; from whence they might collect, that the time of the Redemption was drawing near. Was not the same Angel, who had

fore-told

fore-told the meaſures of that time, the fitteſt to declare the fulfilling of his Prediction, when the term thereof was ready to expire. To the contrary, it was expedient, and it hath conduced to the ſtrengthning of the faith of thoſe who were waiting for the Redemption; that the ſame Meſſenger, who had foretold the time, ſhould come again towards the end of that time, to put them in mind of his Prediction, and to advertiſe them, that the accompliſhment thereof was at hand. And in this eſpecially we may ſee an effect of the wiſdom of God.

Moreover, We might alleage to the *Jews*, that Angel who appeared twice to the wife of *Manoah*, *Judg.* 13. 13, &c. for theſe were two ſeveral Voyages, and two ſeveral Meſſages, although both tended to the ſame thing, and repreſented the ſame ſubject.

To be ſhort, This Maxim of the *Jews* doth even contradict the Old Teſtament.

The

The Second MAXIM of the *Jews*.

TWo Angels are never employ'd in carrying of one Message. This is in the place above-said, *viz.* in *Bereshith-Rabba.*

The Examination.

THis assertion of the *Jews* is different from the former, but tendeth to the same end, which is, to give the lie to the New Testament in two fundamental Articles, *viz.* the Resurrection and the Ascension of our Lord. For we do read, that his Resurrection was joyntly declared by two Angels; and likewise as he ascended into heaven, two Angels together, in the same time and place, did speak to the Apostles, *Luk.* 24. 4, &c. *Joh.* 20. 12, &c. *Act.* 1. 10, &c. Now those Histories would be false, if it were true, that two Angels were never sent together about one message.

But here again we may observe the blindness of the *Jews* in the midst of the
greatest

greatest Lights: Can they deny that two, nay, three Angels, were sent together to speak to *Abraham*? and though one of them was the chiefest, yet, did they not all speak unto him? *Gen.* 18.9. And though but one of them should have delivered the errand, did they not all three come upon the same Message touching the birth of *Isaac*? What then shall become of this Maxim of the *Jews*, which contradicteth so illustrious an Example of the Old Testament?

They ought also to have considered that which is very remarkable in this Question. When God hath employed two or many Angels, to deliver one and the same Message, his end was, that they should not onely be Messengers, but also Witnesses of the truth of his Words. For as amongst men, they do relie upon the Depositions of two or three Witnesses, so the testimony of two or three Angels hath confirmed the faith of those to whom they have spoken. This we have already observed in the *Harmony of the Times*.

P   The

The Third MAXIM of the *Jews*.

NO *Man can become a Prophet unless he be born an Hebrew.* Rabbi Manasseh Ben-Israel, Conciliat. in Pentateuch.

The Examination.

A Long time since their Ancestors have spoken in the same manner, saying, that the *holy Ghost*, i. e. *his extraordinary gifts, do never come down upon a Gentile*; but this prejudice of theirs hath been found to be false: For with amazement they have seen, that the *Gentiles* have received the miraculous gifts of the holy Ghost, even that of Tongues, which never any Prophet had under the Old Testament, *Act.* 16. 44, *&c.* And God himself had forewarned, that he would pour down his spirit upon *all flesh*, *Joel* 2. 28. so far was he from promising for ever to confine his Spirit to their Nation, or make it hereditary to them onely, and to debar from it all other Nations.

Their

Their Rabbins themſelves are not all of the ſame opinion about this point, for one of the moſt famous amongſt them, *Rabbi David Kimchi*, doth hold, that the Prophet *Obadia* was not of the Stock of *Iſrael*, but a Proſelyte of *Idumea*: However, he doth confeſs, that a man that was not born an *Iſraelite* could yet be a Prophet. If the *Jews* reply, that the *Idumeans* were *Hebrews*, deſcended from *Abraham*, it will then follow, that the ſpirit of Propheſie was not peculiar to *Iſrael*, but communicable to other Nations. But by the word *Hebrews* they underſtand onely the *Iſraelites*, that they might appropriate to themſelves, though in vain, the faculty of becoming Prophets.

They ought rather to have conſidered, that *Judaiſm* had never any Prophets; for had ever any of them the ſpirit of Propheſie ſince they rejected Chriſt? On the contrary, *Chriſtianiſm*, and the beginnings of it, have been animated by that ſpirit which hath authorized it, not onely by the gift of Propheſie, but alſo by that of healing, of working wonders, great works, the diſcerning of ſpirits, the diverſity of Tongues, and the interpretation thereof, 1 *Cor*. 12. 9, 10. How comes it to paſs, that the ſpirit of Propheſie hath not aſſiſted *Judaiſm* againſt the *Chriſtians*; but hath ſupplyed the

Christians against *Judaism?* Or if they deny, that the spirit of Prophesie hath been on the first *Christians*, how comes it to pass, that that spirit never came down upon any *Jew* to oppose *Christianity*, as *Moses* opposed *Pharaoh*'s Magicians, *Elija* the false Prophets of *Ahab*; *Micaija*, *Zedekia*, and *Jeremia* many Impostors, who bragg'd much of Revelations contrary to his own? If ever the *Jews* had need of the spirit of Prophesie, it was then when *Christianity* began to appear, and the destruction of the second Temple was drawing near; but that spirit was gone from them, and they never had it afterwards.

The Fourth MAXIM of the *Jews*.

DAvid *is not reckoned amongst the Prophets, although the holy Ghost hath spoken by him. As for what is mentioned*, 2 Sam. 23. 3. The God of Israel said, the Rock of Israel spake to me; *the sense of it is, That God hath*

hath caufed it to be fpoken to him by the mouth of fome Prophet. Daniel alfo is not accounted amongft the Prophets, although he had feen an Angel, and had heard his Words; for after he knew the bufinefs in queftion, he called that a Dream. Rab. Mofes the Egyptian, in Doctrin. Perplexorum.

The Examination.

Diverfe reafons have induced us to give a Note on this Maxim of the Rabbins. 1 The *Jews* on the fame, do build others, which will follow in order. 2 They would give a lie to the New Teftament, where *David* and *Daniel* are exprefly called Prophets, *Act.* 2. 30, 31. *Matth.* 24. 15. 3 Their boldnefs is remarkable, to take away the quality of a Prophet from thofe, whom they confefs to have fpoken by an extraordinary gift of the holy Ghoft, and to have received inftructions structions from the mouth of Angels, and by Dreams and divine Visions. 4 They do speak in terms contradictory. 5 They shew how weak their reasoning is.

For first, as for *David*, What makes them say, that God never spake immediately to him? *David* telleth us the contrary in the same Text, 2 *Sam.* 23..2. *The Spirit of the Lord spake by me.* 2 As for *Daniel*, is he not a Prophet to whom *God hath made himself known in vision, or to whom he hath spoken in a dream? Numb.* 12.6. doth not this description of a Prophet belong to *Daniel*? 3 This grand Rabbi and his followers fall into a contradiction; for in the same place he acknowledgeth him for a Prophet, who in a Dream seeth a Parable, and in the same Dream receiveth the Interpretation of it, as it hapned to *Zachary*; but the same hapned to *Daniel*, *chap.* 2..19. and all the seventh chapter along.

But they say, *That yet, after the Dream, and the Interpretation of it, he doth still give it the name of a Dream*, *Dan.* 2. 19. *and* 7. 1, 2, 15. *and* 8. 27. What of that? Because *Daniel* relates that he hath had Dreams, wherein God gave him marvellous revelations, even making him to know the very thoughts of *Nebuchadnezzar*, and the successions and forms of divers Empires; are not these Revelations

lations therefore Prophetical? Because, say they, he repeateth, that they happned to him in a Dream. What a wild Argument is this to degrade a Prophet! is there any spark of judgment in this discourse?

Some will demand, Do they not acknowledge, that the *Psalms* and the Book of *Daniel* have proceeded from the holy Ghost, and to be Canonical and true pieces of the Old Testament? They do indeed confess it, and give them the Title of *Hagiographes*, Why then not that of *Prophetical?* It is a *Jewish* Logomachy, or a frivolous distinction. But it was necessary for us to mark it, because the *Jews* would make use of it against the Arguments we oppose to some other of their Maxims, as we shall see in its due place.

The Fifth MAXIM of the *Jews*.

PRophesie *withdraws from a Man that's a Captive, or in Slavery, or in Banishment, and is not Master of himself.* Proverb. Siræ. and Rabbi Moses

Moses in Doctrina Perplexorum.

The Examination.

IF we should grant to them, that all the Apocalypse, which shutteth up the New Testament, and indeed all Prophesies, would be declared null: For it is said, that St. *John* received it being in exile, confined to a very small Island, where he was not Master of himself, but had his abode there as a Prisoner.

But who told them, that the Spirit of Prophesie is never found in a Captive, or in one who hath not the disposal of his own person? do they fear that the spirit it self should be prisoner if it were a prisoner? Was it not in a prison *Joseph* foretold that which should come to pass to the two Officers of *Pharaoh*, even to the naming of the very day? If that Prediction was not Prophetical, how shall we then call it? Nay, it was in the prison where the Spirit of Prophesie began to come down on *Joseph*, who never had it before.

When *Daniel* knew how to repeat and interpret the Dream of *Nebuchadnezzar*, it could not be but by the spirit of Prophesie, although the *Jews*, by a distinction full of vanity, which we have now observed, dare say the contrary. But in what condition was *Daniel* then? In that of a prisoner, and such a one that was in danger of death, *Dan.* 2. 13, &c.

Lastly, here is an Example not to be replyed against; *Jeremy*, to whom the *Jews* dispute not the quality of a Prophet; had he not Prophesies in the Prison, yea more then once? Let them but read that which is written, *Jer.* 32. *verf.* 2, 26, *&c. Jeremia was shut up in the Court of the Prison, &c. And the word of the Lord came to Jeremia, saying, &c.* Let them also see the 33*th.* Chapter, *The word of the Lord came to Jeremia the second time, while he was yet shut up in the Court of the prison, &c.* This word was a Prophesie of the re-establishment which was to come, contrary to all likelihood, after the ruine of the State of the *Jews*, and the transportation of the people into *Babylon*: And their Masters the *Rabbins* do confess it to be a Prophesie. What a spirit then of madness is this, which makes them say, That a Prophesie never came unto a Prisoner?

As for banishment, was not *Ezekiel* an Exile when he was in the Captivity of *Babylon*? and when he had such high Revelations,

velations, and in so great a number, which the *Jews* confess to have been Prophetical, was he not in Captivity?

We see then, that neither Banishment nor Captivity could hinder, that the Spirit of Prophesie should indite the *Apocalypse*, nor that the Angels should speak to the Apostles in the Prison, and deliver them out of it, *Act.* 5. 18. and 12. 7. nor yet that *Paul* and *Silas* should cause an Earth-quake, and make the foundation of the Prison to shake, and loose all the Prisoners, *Act.* 16. 25.

The Sixth MAXIM of the *Jews*.

I*N time of Persecution Prophesie ceaseth; andespecially then, when we are under the yoke of Profane Nations.* Rabbi Moses.

The Examination.

This Maxim is included in the foregoing, and is confuted by the same Reasons;

Reasons; but we will add thereunto that which followeth.

The intention of the *Jews* is to prevent the Objection we make to them, *viz.* That so long since they had no Prophets; whereas in their bondage in *Egypt*, and in the Captivity of *Babylon*, God did never leave them without Prophets, but for a little while. To which they answer, That a man who is persecuted, or a subject to other Nations, is incapable of the Spirit of Prophesie. And that being all of them in this dispersion, and persecuted, none of them can have the Spirit of Prophesie. That even if there were any Prophets among them, the Prophesie would withdraw from them, so soon as they should begin to be persecuted.

Upon this account, 'tis in the power of Persecutors to hinder the Spirit of God, to stop his influences, and to keep him from assisting, by his Revelations, those that are persecuted for his sake, even when they stand more in need of his presence.

But that impiety is refuted by it self, and is condemned by the Examples we have already brought, specially by that of *Jeremia*, who was persecuted even to an Imprisonment, and yet still received new Prophesies. Whereunto we do add this, When did *Elija* hear the voice of God in
Horeb,

Horeb, and received of him the Prophesie concerning *Hazael*, *Elisha*, and *Jehu*? 'Twas when *Elija* was flying from *Jezabel*, who was looking after him to put him to death, 1 *King*. 19. When did *Micajah* foretel the unhappy success of *Ahab's Battel*? 'Twas when *Micajah*, having been smitten on the cheek, was condemned to a prison, and there to be hardly used, 1 *King*. 22. 27. When did *Amos* foretel to *Amazia* the Priest, that his wife should be an harlot in the City, that his sons and his daughters should fall by the sword, that his land should be be divided by line, that he should die in a polluted land, and that *Israel* should surely go into captivity out of his land? All these were revealed to the Prophet *Amos* when he was impeached of high-treason, and was to be banished out of the Land of *Israel*, *Amos* 7. 10, &c. 'Tis therefore not true, that Persecution can put a stop to Prophesie. The true cause, and the time of the cessation of Prophesies and Visions, are set down in *Daniel*, *chap*. 9. 24. If the *Jew* doth read it, let him consider it.

The

The Seventh Maxim of the Jews.

The holy Ghost doth not rest upon a Man that's sad, but on him that's merry and chearful. (In Pirke Aboth. and Prov Ben Siræ. and R. Moses in Doct. Perplex.)

The Examination.

THat Maxim is very jolly, but confuted by the Sacred History. If by the holy Ghost they onely understand the gift of Prophesie, yet is it not so, that 'twas never conferr'd on any but such as were in mirth. What then? if a man be afflicted for his sins, he is incapable of the spirit of Prophesie, whilst he remains in so lawful a sorrow, so necessary and so pleasing to the Spirit of God? From thence a fine imagination would follow, That there was one day every year, *viz.* that of the *Expiations*, whereon as the Prophetical Spirit never came down upon men; for it was a day of mourning, when all the *Israelites* were

were bound to afflict their souls, *Levit.* 16. 23, 31.

But the Prophetical Spirit is so far from flying from a man, because of his sorrows, that on the contrary, that same Spirit hath often made sad those upon whom it came down, and remained with them in the height of their sorrow; witness *Jeremia*, witness *Ezekiel*, chap. 3. vers. 14. *The Spirit lifting me up, and taking me away, I went in bitterness in the heat of my spirit, but the hand of the Lord was strong upon me.*

Is it not true, that *Elija* was sorrowful even to the wishing of death, when God immediately spake to him, which is the highest degree of Prophesie, and gave them the Predictions we have observed upon the foregoing Maxim? 1 *King.* 19.

The *Jews* should rather consider, that the Son of God weeping out of sorrow, foretold them what hapned to them forty years after, that the enemies of *Jerusalem* should cast a trench about her, and that not one stone should remain upon another in that unhappy City? They themselves relate, that the *Romans* caused the Plough to pass over it, and that there remained no mark of a City. They should say to the contrary, that the most excellent Prophesies hapned, and were indited in sorrow: Which we could prove by many other Examples. The

The Eighth Maxim of the Jews.

OLd *folks are not capable of the Spirit of Prophesie. Almost all the Prophets were young, and onely* Moses *and* Aaron *Prophesied in their old age, which was miraculous.*

The Examination.

THis Maxim follows the former, and is read in the same places we have already quoted, and we bring it in to shew, how gross the ignorance or the inadvertency of the *Jews*, and that it is no wonder if they do so grosly mistake in other matters, less clear then this is.

Upon the Hypothesis we have already overthrown, they do build this assertion, that an old man, because of his peevishness caused by age, and other natural indispositions, cannot have the faculty of Prophesie, sith it requires a jovial and cheerful man.

But we could bring them *Daniel*, though they endeavour to blot out his name
from

from the Catalogue of the Prophets, who was not much less then ninety years old, when God gave him those admirable Revelations concerning the seventy weeks, the destruction of the second Temple, that of the Kingdom of the *Persians*, the end of the posterity of *Alexander*, the debates of the Kingdoms of *Syria* and *Egypt*, the vicissitudes of their Successes, their attempts and persecutions, &c.

That Chronology is out of dispute. *Daniel* was an Adolescent or young man, when he was carried Captive into *Babylon*: he passed there the whole seventy years of the Captivity, and three years after, that was also the third year of *Cyrus*, he received the Prophesie that we read in the 10, 11, and 12 Chapters; let every one judge whether he was not an old man. We might also mention *Isaias*, who prophesied above forty five years, and was not a child when he began to prophesie: *Hosea* and *Jeremia*, who prophesied almost as long; which may be gathered out of the number of years of several Kings under whom they prophesied.

But among all the Prophesies, that which *Jacob* had and pronounced upon his death-bed, is worthy admiration, *Gen* 49. It is known, that the Land of *Canaan* was divided by *Lot*, 245 years after *Jacob*'s death; how comes it that the Lot of each Tribe

Tribe doth meet with the prediction of that Patriarch? How comes it that the quarters, the manners, the conditions, and the particular qualities of each Tribe, specially the Kingship of *Juda*, are so visibly marked therein? How old then was *Jacob*, when he had that prophecy? he was 147 years old. Therefore the Prophetical Spirit was not inconsistent with the old age of a man.

We must here observe another Contradiction the *Jews* fall into: For that same *Rabbine*, whose words they do observe as so many *Oracles*, in that Book we have already so often alledged, doth write, that an old man, and he who is near unto death, are the fitter to conceive, or to apprehend the things of God, than he that is yet young. How then can they affirm, that young folks are fitter for Prophecy? He that is less fit for apprehending the things of God, can he be the most capable of prophecy?

Finally, Among the spiritual gifts God had promised, he saith; *Your old men shall dream dreams, and your young men shall see visions*, *Joel* 2. 28. It is because formerly the prophetical Revelations were often given, either in a Dream, or in a Vision, *Numb.* 12. 6. God then promised such Revelations to old men; But the *Rabbins* will not believe him.

Q   The

The Ninth Maxim of the Jews.

Moses *his Law seems to be defective in many things that are necessary.* (Rab. Manasseh Ben Israel Conciliat. in Pentateuch.)

The Examination.

This good *Rabbine* dares not openly say, that the Law is imperfect, but onely that it seems to be so. But if it falsly seems to him to be so, he ought to accuse his own imperfection, and not impute it to the Law of God. But his design (as well as of his Colleagues) is, to authorize the Opinions and the Traditions of the *Rabbins*, as necessary supplements to what is wanting (as they pretend) in the Law of *Moses*.

What are these wants? These are the chiefest they do alleage: When the Law speaks of the month of the year, it mentions not whether they be Solary or Lunary; a distinction necessary, that the true time for the celebration of the Feasts may be be known, *Exod.* 12. 2. It mentioneth not what are those parts of the Beast, whose fat is prohibited, *Levit.* 3. 17. It expresseth not the signes whereby they might discern the unclean Birds, *Levit.* 11. 13. It determines not the place where they should keep the Sabbath-day, whether in the House, or in the Court, or in the City, or in any other place of greater extent, *Exod.* 16. 29. It particularizes not the works which are lawful or unlawful on the Sabbath-day, *Exod.* 20. It mentioneth not whether the father may be the heir of his son, *Numb.* 27. It forbids not the mariage of a man with the wife of his father, or with the mother of his mother.

These are the most remarkable points wherein they say the Law is defective. Now most of these things are Ceremonial, and their time is expired; and though it it were necessary to know all these measures, we can shew, that there is not one of them which are not found in the compass of that Ceremonial Law.

But the two last points require two words of answer. On the first, This *Philo* the *Jew*, a famous Writer, and antienter then the *Talmud*, saith, that *Moses hath been silent of the succession of parents to their children, because such cases are unlucky, by the course of Nature children rather succeeding their parents:* Nevertheless

theless it hath preserved the right of parents; for indirectly it calls them to the same right it hath given to uncles. It giveth therefore the succession, 1 to the sons; 2 for want of them, to the daughters; 3 to brothers; 4 to uncles on the fathers side. Wherein it appears, that a father may have a better right to be the heir of his own children. So saith *Philo*, in the Treatise of the Laws. By which it appears, that the antient *Jews* do contradict the modern *Jews*, for they did not believe the Law to be defective in this case.

As for the other, is it not most evident, that the same prohibition which forbids the son to marry his own mother, forbids him also to marry his grandmother? and if it was needful the Law should expresly name the grandmother, would it not have been likewise necessary it should name the great-grandmother, and all the ancestors of a man to infinity? We had not then known, that the mariage of a man with his grandmother was unlawful, unless the *Rabbins* had told us so. They have taught us that which neither the Law of Nature, nor the Law of *Moses* did ever teach. Where is the shame of those men!

But because they use such pretences to cover their enormities, when they say, the Law is defective; 'tis requisite we should know, that they contradict one another. For

For their famous *Rabbine*, *Moses*, in the Book vve have alleaged, saith in express terms, That *the Law of Moses is perfect, and that there is nothing in it that's superfluous or defective*; and thereupon he brings the vvords of *Psal.* 19. 8. We see then, that the *Jews* do not agree, neither vvith God nor vvith themselves.

The tenth MAXIM of the *Jews*.

THere *are Angels that are corruptible, although there kinds be permanent.* (Rabbi-Moses in Doct. Perplex.

The Examination.

HEre is Paganism in the Doctrine of the *Jews*. The Heathens believe, that the Demons or Spirits having lived a long time, did at the last die one after another, and that yet their kind was preserved in other individuals succeeding the former, as amongst men and other living creatures. And this also is the conceit of that great *Rabbine*, who implyeth strange things

things unknown to all the Prophets: For first he tells us, that the Devils die; nevertheless he tells us not, whether their death proceeds from sickness, or from age; nor how long a time they do ordinarily live. And we may ask of him, whether that *Demon* who seduced *Eve*, be dead; for if there be any of them dead, 'tis a wonder that he should be still alive, seeing he is one of the antientest of them. 2 This fine Doctrine, which produceth new Demons in the place of those that die, teacheth us, that there are young Devils as well as old ones; which is an excellent distinction. 3 Who produces these young Demons, that do survive the others? who creates them? Is there every day a creation of new Angels? or if they be produced by generation, doth one Demon beget another? Ridiculous follies! which shew the wit of the *Rabbins*.

The eleventh MAXIM of the *Jews*.

OUr wisemen say, That the Expiation of the whole Church was made by Goats, because the whole Assembly of Israel,

rael, *when the Patriarchs sold Joseph, did dip his garment in the blood of a young Goat.* Rabbi Moses in Doctrin. Perplex.

The Examination.

THose pretended wise-men will not acknowledge him, who hath been *made sin for us, that we may be the righteousness of God in him.* Neither the blood of Goats, nor the blood of Bulls, hath ever expiated the least offence of man. But without entring into that matter, let us here observe the solidity of that Rabinical Imagination.

1. This Oblation of Goats is prescribed in the 16th of *Leviticus*; but there is not the least mention of the selling of *Joseph*, which hapned 237 years before the institution of that Ceremony.

2. That Offering was made for the sins of all the children of *Israel*, amongst whom was the race of *Joseph*, very numerous, and composed of two Tribes, *Ephraim* and *Manasseh*. But if this Offering tended to this, that the *Israelites* might expiate the crime which their fathers had committed

committed against *Joseph*, why should the children of *Joseph*, who had received the offence, undergo the expiation, as well as the children of those who had committed the offence? What answer will the *Rabbins* give to this? Surely none that's pertinent.

The twelfth MAXIM of the *Jews*.

IF any one of the *Karraims* desireth to be received into the number of the *Rabbanims*, he ought not to be received. Leo Mode.

The Examination.

THe *Jews* do not agree amongst themselves in the very principles of their Religion, but are divided into two companies: the first do hold onely to the Text of the Old Testament, the other add unto it the Traditions of the *Rabbins*; the latter are more numerous then the former, and call themselves *Rabbanims*, to distinguish themselves from the former, to whom they give the name of *Karraim*.

Now

Now the aversion is so great, that if one of these *Karraims* desires to be incorporated into the Sect of the *Rabbanims*, they will not admit him thereunto, but are altogether irreconcilable; if it be out of prudence, surely 'tis not according to piety or charity: We do observe this, That the genius of those *Rabbanims* may be yet further known, who are the same *Jews* we have in *Europe*. 1 Why do they admit a *Pagan* that will become a *Jew*, and reject a *Jew* who desireth most entirely to be one of their number? Is the distance greater between a *Jew* and a *Jew*, then between a *Jew* and a *Pagan*? Are not the *Karraims*, who acknowledge the Law of *Moses*, and all the Books of the Old Testament, and expect the coming of the same *Messias*, as the other *Jews* do, nearer to the *Rabbanims* then the *Pagans* and other Idolaters? Why then do they receive them into the number of the Proselytes, and reject those who are already *Jews*, both by Birth, and by Religion? 2 If salvation be onely amongst the *Rabbanims*, why do they exclude those who desire to be admitted among them? 3 If they believe that the *Karraims* (whatsoever promise they do make) will never prove good *Rabbanims*; Who made them Judges of the heart? But assuredly they are more jealous of their own Traditions,

then

then of the salvation of souls, or of the glory of God. 4. They shut the door on those, to whom God will have it opened: The Law excludeth from the Congregation of *Israel* but onely certain Persons and Nations, who are named in the 23*d*. of *Deuteronomy*; and yet that exclusion relates onely to publick Offices, as it may easily be proved; but the modern *Jews* do for ever exclude those from their Church, who are *Jews* as well as they, depriving them for ever from all the benefits of the Covenant; and this not for any faults expressed in the Law, but onely for having refused the Traditions of the *Rabbins*.

The 13th MAXIM of the *Jews*.

THe Resurrection of Man's Body shall be by the means of a certain incorruptible Bone which is in him.

The Examination.

THis Bone in their Language is called לוז, that is to say, a *Wall-nut*, or a *Hazle-nut*;

Hazle-nut; but I could never learn in what part of the body they place it, and I believe they themselves do not mark it; which neverthelefs they ought to do, that a due regard might be had of so confiderable a Bone.

Much might be spoken on this Fable, we shall content our selves to mark it with two dashes of our Pen: 1 What Scripture, what Anatomy, what Experience hath told those *Rabbins*, that there is a bone in mans Body, which can never suffer corruption, or lose its natural form? 2 Grant it should be so; Doth the Resurrection of the whole body depend on that bone? Suppose it be naturally incorruptible, can that natural quality produce the Resurrection of the whole body? Shall the Resurrection, which is so wonderful a work, be wrought by the vertue of a bone, as the production of a Plant is by the seminal vertue of the seed. 3 We must know, that many of the *Jews*, and the most learned of them, have a strange opinion about that subject; for they hold, that there shall be no Resurrection, but onely for pious men; yea, and that the soul of the wicked perisheth as the souls of beasts; so writeth their famous *Rabbi*, *David Kimchi*, upon the First *Psalm*. But their main design is to contradict the New Testament, which

teacheth,

teacheth, that the wicked shall also suffer after death. But if good men are to be raised by the vertue of a bone, which is in their body, have not the wicked such a bone also? why then shall they not also, by the vertue of it, be raised from the dead?

The 14th MAXIM of the *Jews*.

THe Nation of the Jews is wise and understanding; so saith the Lord, Deut. 4. 6. *The Nations shall say, This Nation is a wise and understanding People.* Rabbi Manass. Ben Israel, Vindiciæ Judæorum, Sect. 4.

The Examination.

CErtainly another *Rabbi* hath told me formerly, not without sorrow, that the *Jews* are the most stupid Nation in the world; that they love ignorance, and onely mind Letters of Exchange, and other affairs of this present world; and in that respect

respect they may boast to be wise and ingenuous. But the wisdome whereof that passage speaketh, which is mentioned by the *Rabbine* in his Writings, is far different from the other.

God saith unto them, That if they add nothing to his word, if they punctually observe it, *It shall be their wisdome, and other Nations shall praise them.* But have they fulfilled that condition? Have they not added to the Law of God? nay, have they not made it void by their Traditions? Do the other people of the earth praise them for their wisdom, as having the best Religion of all? On the contrary, Do not all other Nations mock at them? doth not God himself tax them as a foolish Nation, and more stupid then the Ox or Ass? *Esa.* 1. 3. Is not all the holy History full of reproaches and censures against their enormous follies? doth it not say, That, in this regard, they have gone beyond all other Nations? *Ier.* 2. 10, 11. It is to be observed, that that place of *Deuteronomy* alleaged by the *Rabbins*, is not directed onely to the *Iews*, who properly are those onely of the Tribe of *Iuda*, but to all the Tribes of *Israel*. Now when ten of the Tribes, who were the greatest part of *Israel*, forsook God, and worshipped the Calves of *Ieroboam*, were they wise? The Promise which imported, that they should

be

be held to be wife, was but conditional. But the *Rabbi* doth make an absolute prediction of it, which experience hath contradicted.

The 15th Maxim of the *Jews*.

CUrsed be those that do reckon the days of the Messias.

The Examination.

THey would say, that they ought not to compute the time to know when the *Messias* shall come: The meaning is, that having so long expected him, and measured all the ages, and almost all the moments, to find the day of his coming, and being so often deceived in their calculation, they are resolved to reckon no longer. And this is the sense of that *Maxim* which is so common among them: Now it cannot subsist but on a false Hypothesis, *viz*. That God hath not revealed the time when Christ shall come.

This deserves to be examined. We know that God hath revealed the times of diverse other occurrences that have hapned

hapned at the prefixed times: He foretold how many years should pass from the time he spake to *Noah*, to the Flood, *Gen.* 6. 3. How many years since *Ishmael*, the son of an *Egyptian* woman, persecuted *Isaac*, to the coming out of *Egypt, Gen.* 15. 13. How many years from the revolt of the ten Tribes, to the destruction of the first Temple, *Ezek.* 4. 5, 8. How many years the Captivity of *Babylon* should last, *Dan.* 9. 2. Did not the faithful under the Old Testament reckon those years unto the end of the term of terms? *Psal.* 102. 14. *Dan.* 9. 2. And now the Spirit of God which hath forewarned on what year such and such an event should happen, hath it not foretold what time Christ should come? Christ, who hath been the end and scope of the Prophecies, the hope of the Church, the joy of the Patriarchs; He to whom the Nations were to gather, and of whom they expected an everlasting Redemption; Should a prefixion of time, more necessary then all the former, have been omitted by the holy Ghost?

But the seventy weeks revealed to *Daniel*, and which he was enjoyned to be mindful of, do overthrow this Maxim of the *Jews*, what means soever they use to divert the sense of the Oracle.

Moreover, though the year of the death
of

of the *Messiah* should not have been foretold; do we not see, that all the events that were to go before it have appeared long ago? and those which not long after were to follow it, as the destruction of the second Temple, the overthrow of the State of the *Jews*, their dispersion, which hath already continued so many Ages, do they not all make it apparent, that the days of the *Messias* are already expired? In that regard indeed, they have some reason to reckon it no longer.

The 16th Maxim of the *Jews*.

Jesus *of* Nazareth *was put to death under the Reign of* Hasmanneens, *otherwise the* Maccabees.

The Examination.

This hath already been contradicted and confuted by the Learned; yet is it of concernment to put those in mind of it, who see not the consequences of this Maxim, which would seem indifferent to them: If we suffer it to pass, we must also renounce all the New Testament, which affirmeth,

affirmeth, that our Lord was put to death by *Pilate*, who was under the Empire of *Tiberius*, above seventy years after the suppression of the Reign of the *Maccabees*, to whom *Herod* the Great succeeded. Moreover, if our Lord died when the *Maccabees* had the Kingship, that date would make void the circumstances, which, by virtue of the Prophesies, were necessarily, either to go before, or accompany, the coming and the death of Christ, or presently after to follow it, as that which was to happen at the end of the seventy weeks of *Daniel*, after the Scepter and the Law-giver were taken away from *Juda*. For if Christ died at that time the *Jews* do mention, it will follow, that he is not the Christ, because then he would have come and suffer'd long before the time marked by the Prophets.

But the Heathen Historians (to whom this matter was indifferent) do in express terms attest, that *Jesus Christ* was put to death by *Pilate* the Procurator of *Judea* under the Emperor *Tiberius*. Those are the proper words of one of their most approved Historians, *Cornelius Tacitus*, who at no hand loved Christianity, but speaks of it as of a contagious disease. I have one reason more, which sheweth the falsity of that calculation of the *Jews*: It is certain, that Jesus Christ died by the punishment

R of

[242]

of the Cross, to which they used to nail the hands and feet of the condemned person. Now this kind of death was never practised by the *Jews*; for the Law, whereof they boasted to be great observers, ordained but four sorts of capital punishments, which they used according to the diversity of crimes, *viz*. 1 Beheading, 2 Strangling of the hanged person. 3 Stoning. 4 Burning. But Crucifying was not in use amongst them; and when practised, it was not by them, but by the *Greeks* and *Romans*, when they exercised Dominion over the *Jews*. How can it be then, that *Jesus Christ* was crucified under the Reign of the *Maccabees*, when that punishment was not practised at all in *Judea*, seeing the *Jews* had a free and entire jurisdiction, and the Law whereto they adhered, did not ordain the crucifying of any? And thus this *Jewish* invention doth vanish away.

The 17th MAXIM of the *Jews*.

THis year, which is reckon'd to be the 1657 from the Nativity of Christ, is the 5417 year

year of the Creation. Rabbi Manasse Ben Israel in the date of his Book, entituled, *Vindiciæ Judæorum.*

The Examination.

THE *Jews* being as bad Chronologers as they are fabulous Historians, do ecclipse 168 of those years which have passed since the Creation. The least age which knowing men give unto the world, at this present year, is 5585 years; and their calculations, which we need not to repeat, is easily verifi'd. But the *Rabbi* makes the world 168 years younger than it is indeed.

Whether it be through ignorance, or through malice, yet it always concerneth us to observe, that their computation doth break an infinite number of correspondencies between the New Testament and the Old, nay, gives the lie to both, and cuts the thread of the whole History, which we are able to prove in due time and place.

The particular Opinion of a Modern Author, touching the Salvation of the Jews.

RAbbi Manasse Ben Israel, in his Book, entituled, Vindiciæ Judæorum, in the second Section, doth alleage a Christian Author, whom, as yet, I have not seen, who speaks in these words, *We do yet look for a second coming of the Messias. And the Jews do believe, that this future coming will be the first, and not the second; and by that faith they shall be saved: For the difference lyeth onely in the circumstance of Time.*

The Examination.

ON this account, those who blaspheme against the Son of God, and die detesting him, shall be saved as well as those that die blessing of him; and maintains going to heaven by two contrary ways, even by that which leadeth to hell. 2 Do the *Jews* believe that the Messias, whom they look for, shall offer himself in sacrifice for their sins? and if they believe not that sacrifice, is there any pardon for them? 3 Do they believe that the Messias, whom they expect, shall be the same Person, and the same Man, who is already come once, and whose death they have procured? If they believe it, will they cause him to die again another time? If they believe him not (as indeed we know they do not) doth not the difference lie onely in a circumstance of time? Not onely they do not wait for the same Messias, the same Person, but are forging to themselves another quite contrary, who instead of dying for others, shall cause millions of men to die, and will fill the world with blood and slaughter. Do two Messias's so contrary differ onely in a circumstance? 5 There are some circumstances which are of the Essence of a

R 3 matter

matter of Faith. There have been some Hereticks who said, that the Resurrection of the dead was already past, and that consequently we are no more to expect it, 1 *Tim.* 2. 17. Could they be freed from blasphemy, in saying, that the difference was onely in a circumstance of time, the time past being put for the future? can common sense agree thereunto?

Let us in this place observe, that whereas the Prophets do sometimes express the time to come by that which is past, they never express the time past by the future. When they said, *Unto us a Child is born*, they spoke of what was yet to come, as if it had already come, to intimate, that the Prediction was as certain, as if the effect had already appeared. But when they spake of a thing already past, they never represented it as a thing yet to come; for, to what purpose should they do it? The future comes to pass, but the time past never comes to be future again. The time goes forward but never backward. And such Prophesies as do represent the future are turned into History when they are fulfilled, but History never turns into Prophesie.

FINIS.

AN ESSAY

OF

The Wonders of GOD,

IN

The Harmony of the Times that preceded CHRIST, and how they meet in Him.

His Genealogy, and other Mysteries preparatory to His First Coming.

Written in *French* by JOHN D'ESPAGNE, *Minister of the Holy Gospel.*

And now published in *English* by his Executor.

LONDON,
Printed by *William Godbid* for *Henry Herringman*, at the Sign of the *Anchor* in the *Lower Walk* of the *New-Exchange.* M. DC. LXII.

HE worth of the Author is so universally known, and so apparently visible in his Works, that it may well serve for an Apology of my silence on this subject, and to justifie the pains I have now taken to publish this last Peece of his, which is the Second Part of his Harmony of the Times.

Death, who snatch'd him away, and hindred the finishing thereof, hath nevertheless caused a certain perfection to be seen, that may give admiration to some in this Age, and frustrate the hopes of others, of being able to come near the painting of such a Venus after such an Apelles.

His intention was to continue this Harmony to the close of the New Testament, but death seized on him when he came to that of Christ's, and hath left us the regret of losing with him the rest of that incomparable Peece, which I could no ways

ways conceal the publishing, because so
many Persons of quality, both here and
beyond sea, and also of both our Universities, have so earnestly desired what fragments soever I had of that most excellent
man. Besides this, I thought my self
obliged thereunto, by the honor he did me, in
making me the sole Executor of his last
Will and Testament.

None can be ignorant, that during
these late times of horror and confusion,
both in our Church and State, how precious the Word of God was, and that
in stead thereof, and the pure Administration of the Sacraments, we had nothing but extemporary prayers, with their
Sermons stuff'd with Blasphemy, Heresie, and Sedition, where none could joyn
with them without betraying his conscience toward God, and his fidelity to
his Prince; which obliged, or rather constrained me, first, to frequent
the French Church, then assembled at
Durham-house, to be a partaker of those
excellent Sermons and Doctrines of our
Author, who then was followed by many
of the Nobility, and the best of the
Gentry, who rendred both to God and Cæsar their due.

The respect I had from them of that
Assembly, engaged me to abide with
them

*them, ever since, and to take no part
with them in the trouble of providing
them a place to assemble in, after the
demolishing of* Durham-house. *Which
makes me remember the prophetical
words of our Author, for asking him
then, What we should do now for a
place to assemble in, made me the same
answer* Abraham *made to* Isaac, *when
he said to his father,* Behold the fire Gen. 22.
and the wood, but where is the Lamb 7, 8.
for the burnt-offering? *who replyed,*
Deus providebit; *which presently after
fell out to be true: For it pleased God
to touch the hearts of many of the Nobility to procure us an Order of the
House of Peers, to exercise our Devotions at* Somerset-house Chappel; *which
was the cause not onely of driving away
the* Anabaptists, Quakers, *and other Sects
that had got in there, but also hindred
the pulling down of* Somerset-house,
*there having been twice Order from
the late usurped Powers for selling the
said House; but we prevailed so, that
still we got order to exempt the Chappel
from being sold, which broke the design of those that had bought the said
House, who thought, for their improvement, to have made a Street from
the Garden, through the ground the
Chappel now stands on, and so up the*

r 3   *back-*

back-yard to the great street of the Strand, by pulling down the said Chappel; but it pleased God to provide so, that still there was order to preserve this Chappel, which consequently also preserved Somerset-house.

These things being considered, none, I hope, will blame me to relate, what I have said of a man, who hath merited so much of the publick, and of me in particular, and to revive the memory of him in his works: And when hereafter the rest shall be all printed together, I shall not fail (God-willing) to contribute thereunto all the Reliques I have by me of this excellent Author.

And to conclude, seeing it hath pleased God, after so many confusions and dis-orders, which happened as well in the Church as in the State, to re-establish again on the antient foundations both the one and the other, and to cause that the Church, as the floating Ark did, at last find a Mountain to rest on; or as the Disciples of Christ, who were the true Church, being on the Sea, and tossed by the tempest, but when Christ their beloved Master came in to them, then all was made calm again: So it hath pleased God, that not onely the Church in general hath had the effects of his goodness, but also in particular this French Church of West-minster, *minister*, *having always maintained the purity of its Doctrine amidst such horrible confusions, and at last by his mercy, and the especial favour of his Majesty, hath found a place of rest, and a nursing Father to have care of it; obliging all the Members thereof in general continually to pour out their prayers for the preservation of his Person, the encrease of his Greatness, and the felicity of his Reign; which in particular are the real and continual humble requests of His Majesty's*

Most humble, most obedient, and most faithful Servant and Subject,

HENRY BROWNE.

Of the Times that preceded the Days of *Christ*, and how they meet in Him. His Genealogy, and other Mysteries, Preparatory to His *First Coming.*

Six days for the Creation finish'd in Adam. *Six periods, each of them of 660 years, from the creation of the first* Adam, *to the death of the Second. The correspondency of the six Periods with the six days of the Creation.*

FROM the Creation to the Death of Christ we do reckon 3960 years, which are six times 660. And as the first *Adam*, the last work of the Creation, was framed on the sixth

sixth day, so the Second *Adam* was produc'd about the latter end of the sixth Period of 660 years. Such are the measures and divisions of the Time which ran from the Creation to the accomplishment of our Redemption.

That which now presents it self is worthy to be attentively considered. Whensoever God made any general and miraculous change, contrary to the order of any work of the Creation, every one of such changes hapned within some of the six Periods, answering to that of one of the six days, whereunto that change is opposite. The Examples will clear this.

Four great changes have hapned in the world, one in Earth, two in Heaven, and one in the production of Man. On Earth, when it was wholly covered by the Flood. In Heaven, when the Sun staid, and since when it went back. In the production of Man, when a Virgin brought forth a Child. For although Christ alone hath had such a birth, yet ought he to be considered, not as a particular man, but as being the second *Adam*, opposite to the former, in several respects.

All other changes hapned in Nature, (as the division of the waters in the *Red-sea*, the going back of *Jordan*, the speaking of *Balaam's* Ass, and other wonders) were but particular ones. Likewise, we
do

do not here reckon the other Miracles, as the rising of the dead; for death is not of the Creation, which alone we consider here.

Therefore as to the changes we here speak of, here are the times when they hapned, answering the days of the Creation, whereunto they are opposite.

I. On the third day of the Creation, God caused the waters that covered the whole earth to withdraw, and made the dry land appear. To the contrary, within the third Period of the years of the world, God covered the whole earth with waters by the Flood.

II. On the fourth day of the Creation, God having made the Sun and the Moon, he ordained they should uncessantly run; but in the fourth Period he caused them to stop in their course.

III. On the fifth day of the Creation, the Sun began to be seen; he had already lighted the whole preceding day, vvhich was the fourth; but there vvas then no eye, as yet, to see his light. The light is onely for such creatures as are endued vvith sight, *viz.* Animals having life and sense; but there vvere none such until the fifth day of the Creation. In the fifth Period of the years of the vvorld, about the latter end, God caused that great Luminary to go back. But vvhereas upon the fifth day

day

day of the Creation, the eyes of the living creatures began to see the Sun going from the East to the West, in the fifth Period they savv him going to the contrary, from the West to the East.

IV. On the sixth and last day of the Creation, the first *Adam* vvas made, earthly, and a living soul. In the sixth Period, tovvards the latter end, the Second *Adam* vvas made, heavenly, and a quickning Spirit.

Let us reckon each of these Periods of 660 years, and vve shall see, that all these changes are included vvithin the times to vvhich vve have assign'd them.

The first Period endeth at the year of the vvorld 660.

The second Period begins presently after, and endeth at the year of the vvorld 1320. Within these tvvo first Periods God hath produced no general change in the vvorld.

The third Period hath been from the year 1320 to the year 1980. Within that intervvall falls the year of the Creation 1566, vvhere hapned the Flood.

The fourth Period hath been from the year 1980 to the year 2640. Within that Interval falls the year of the Creation 2555, vvhere hapned the miraculous Solstice in the time of *Joshua*.

The fifth Period vvas from the year 2640,

2640, to the year 3300. Five years before the end of this Period the Sun went back in the days of *Hezekia*.

The fixth and laſt Period was from the year 3300, to the year 3960. About the latter end of that Period, *viz.* in the year 3928, the Virgin brought forth a Child; and in the laſt year of that Period, the ſecond *Adam* expiated the ſin of the firſt *Adam*, in the year of the Creation 3960.

If the world was created in the Spring-time, as its very likely, this term of 3960 years falls to be expired in the ſame ſeaſon. And theſe ſix Periods, as the ſix days of the Creation, were followed by Chriſt's eternal Reſt, whoſe Sabbath is not limited by the Evening and the Morning, as is that of the Creation.

Of ENOS *his name, wrong ſpell'd in ſeveral Verſions,* both Latine *and* French.

THe *Hebrew* name of that grand-child of *Adam*, and one of Chriſt's Anceſtors, is *ENOSH*. The *Greek* Tongue, which is the Original of the New Teſtament, wanting an aſpiration for the end of that word, ſaith onely *ENOS*; but the Tranſlators

Translators instead of *Enos*, write *Henos*, are without excuse. The word *Enos*, or rather *Enosh*, in *Hebrew*, signifies a sad or mournful man. Why that name was given to that Patriarch, is a question by it self. But however, the Aspiration set by diverse at the beginning of that word, takes away the signification, and leaves it none at all. Whereas all the names of those antient Patriarchs are significant, and point at some passage of the History of their time, which we ought not to annihilate.

A dangerous Note *in one of the* French Editions *of the New* Testament *upon* Luk. 3. 36.

THose Annotators speak thus: *Moses* onely mentions one *Cainan*; from whence it appears, that he hath not set all those that succeeded *Enos*.

They ought rather to have said, *Moses* mentions but one *Cainan*, or *Kenan*; therefore that second *Cainan*, thrust in by several in this place of St. *Luke*, is wrongfully supposed. Such is likewise the opinion of the best Interpreters.

For the justification of the inadvertency of the Copists, shall we say that *Moses* is defective?

defective? what scandal will it be to the *Jews*, yea, and to many Christians? I omit, that the addition of this *Cainan* produceth very great scruples in Chronology, as the learned have observed.

The first Millenary of the years of the world, expired seventy years after the death of the first Adam. *The fourth Millenary was accomplished seventy years, or a little more, after the Nativity of the second* Adam.

THe first man died in the year 930 of his age, which was likewise the age of the world, therefore the thousandth year of the world was the seventieth after the death of *Adam*. But many Chronologers reckon seventy years from the Nativity of Christ to the ruine of the second Temple, which we esteem to have hapned in the year 4000 of the world; from whence 'twould follow, that there have been seventy years between Christ's birth, and the end of the fourth Millenary; nevertheless

vertheless the Chronology which we follow, reckons seventy three. For some cause unknown to us, the birth of Christ hath fore-run by three years the beginning of the seventy years that were following to the ending of the fourth Millenary. But however, as the first thousand years ended not before the first *Adam* died, so the Fourth Millenary being near to its end, one might have guessed, yea, and be assured, according to the Prophetical Oracles, that it would not end before the coming of the second *Adam*.

The seven years of Jacob's *servitude with* Laban, *and the six years of an* Hebrew's *servitude.*

WHereas this Patriarch, out of his desire to marry *Rachel*, served seven years, the Law ordered onely six years for the *Hebrew* slave, unless he should voluntarily renounce to that privilege, *Exod.* 21. 2, &c. therefore he accomplisheth the sixth year of his service, and then he was set at liberty; the seventh year was the beginning of his Rest: As the seventh day was Sabbatical, so was the
seventh

seventh year, both as to the intermission of the tilling the ground, and the liberty of the *Hebrew* slaves. All these tended to the preservation of the memory of the day, wherein God rested himself from the works of the Creation. But it seems that neither *Laban* nor *Jacob* himself considered this; and that upon this occasion, the Law coming thereon, and being imposed on the posterity of *Jacob*, reduced the servitude to six years, appointing the seventh for the discharge and the Rest of Slaves.

There are some Nations among whom all Apprentices, of what Trade soever, are bound by the Laws to serve seven years before they be Free-men of their Profession; that turn of time is indifferent to the Christian Religion. But if the Law-givers, who have prescribed that number of years, have made choice of the Septenary number, as a memorial of the Creation, they should have appointed but six years for the Apprentice, that upon the seventh he might be free.

An admirable Propofition and Inclufion of the years of Chrift, *from his Birth to his Death, within the years that paffed from the birth of* David *to the death of* Chrift.

THe days of Chrift from his Birth to his death, were thirty two years and fix months, the years that ran from the birth of *David* to the death of Chrift were thirty two times thirty two years and fix months. The proof is eafie to any that knows never fo little of Arithmetick. We put the birth of Chrift about the Autumnal Equinox, of the year of the world 3928, and his death hapned about the Equinox of the Spring, in the year 3960; which makes thirty two years and a half: As to *David*, he was born in the year of the world 2920; from that year to that of the death of Chrift, there were 1040 years. The 1040 years make 32 times 32 years and fix months. I fay, 32 times 32 years, and 32 times fix months, a number multiplyed by it felf. The years of Chrift ending at his death, multiplyed by their own number, by going back, do therefore

therefore meet with that of the nativity of *David*. We know that the Prophets speaking of *Christ*, calls him often *David* in many respects; and it's observed, that the Reign of *David* in *Jerusalem* was of thirty two years and six months.

Of the fifteen years added to the life of Hezekia.

IN our Observations upon the Decalogue, we have touched a reason of that number of fifteen years; here is another consideration we bring thereupon.

That time of prolongation was granted to *Hezekia*, that he might see a son of his to be of age to reign; but then he had as yet no son: but in the interval of fifteen years he might not onely beget a Successor, but also see him of age to sway the Scepter; and that was the thing *Hezekia* desired to see afore his death.

Yet 'tis to be observed touching those fifteen years, that the two first passed before *Hezekia* had a son, he had him but at the third year: 'twas *Manasseh*, who was but twelve years old when his father *Hezekia* ended the last fifteen year of his life. To exercise the faith of *Hezekia*, God kept him in suspence till the third year;

year; as, after he had granted him his life, he appointed him the third day to go up to the House of the Lord.

Of the fifteen Stairs whereby men ascended, or went up to the Temple, answering the fifteen years added to the life of Hezekia.

THe Hypothese or Supposition we do here employ, is not indeed to be found in the Sacred History, *viz.* That for the coming into the Temple there were fifteen stairs about it, to go up into it; yet we ought not to reject all the Monuments that bear well framed Characters. The same Author who reckons those fifteen stairs, thereto applies those fifteen Psalms, called *Graduals;* namely, the 120th and the fourteen following, which were sung in going up to the Temple, one upon each stair.

Let this pass for a meer humane History, yet it is very likely: And supposing it to be true, there will be found a wonderful analogy. God doth promise fifteen years of life to *Hezekia*, and for an earnest

of

of his promise he tells him, *Upon the third day thou shalt go up to the Temple*, whereunto men went up by fifteen stairs. Therefore *Hezekia* had a promise to live as many years, as he should ascend steps to go into the Temple, fifteen years for fifteen steps.

The last fifteen years of Hezekia, *multiply'd by their own number, do reach to the year that follow'd the finishing of the second Temple.*

Hezekia began the fifteen years that were added to his life, in the year of the world 3295. The building of the second Temple was finished in the year 3519, and in the year following, which was 3520, the building ceased. The time that passed from the year 3295 to the year 3520, makes 225 years, which makes fifteen times fifteen years. Within that interval hapned the ruine of the first Temple. But at the end of the revolution of the fifteen times fifteen years, the second Temple was finished.

S 2 *Why*

Why among the Ancestors of Christ, who had Brethren, he descended from the youngest rather then from the eldest.

WHy came he from *Seth* rather then from *Abel*, who preceded *Seth*? from *Sem*, rather then from his eldest brother *Japhet*? from *Abraham*, rather then from his brother *Nahor*? from *Jacob*, rather then from *Esau*? from *Juda*, rather then from his three brethren born before him? from *David*, who was but the seventh son of *Jesse*? from *Nathan*, *Solomon*'s younger brother? from *Rhesa*, *Zorobabel*'s second son, rather then from *Abiud* the eldest? From that eldest son, *Joseph*, the Virgin *Mary's* Husband, descended; but the *Virgin*, of whom Christ was born, descended from *Rhesa*, who was but the youngest brother.

An example may be produced to the contrary. Of the Twins that *Juda* had by *Thamar*, *Pharez* was the first that came out of their mother's womb, and Christ came from him; but the holy History rehearseth, that that birth was monstrous,

the

the hand of *Zarah* appeared before the coming forth of his brother *Pharez*, which hapning contrary to nature, it could not naturally give him a primogeniture or eldership.

Now, why God, in bestowing that honor upon a family or kindred, to cause Christ to descend from them, hath chosen and preferred the youngest brethren, this one reason will suffice: It is known how much the Primogeniture hath ever been esteemed of, and what advantages and priviledges even the Law of *Israel* hath ever attributed thereunto. Yet sometimes, and by an order from Heaven, the rights that were ordinarily entailed upon the Primogeniture, have been transferred to the youngest; witness the example of *Esau* and *Jacob*, of whom it was said, that the eldest should serve the youngest. And as God intended to shew, that grace depends not on the age, so he hath thereby manifested, that the preheminency of Christ came not from any primogeniture of his Ancestors, seeing he descended from those that were but the youngest.

Of all such as Christ *descended from, according to the flesh, 'tis not reported, that any of them died a violent death.*

AMong the Ancestors of *Christ*, named by St. *Matthew*, chap. 1. there are many, from *Solomon*, inclusive, unto *Jechonias*, inclusive, that cannot be accounted among *Christ*'s Progenitors, but are comprehended in his Genealogy, for the reasons alledged by the Interpreters. But, as to these, who have been all Kings of *Juda*, many of them died a violent death; *Amazia*, *Joash*, *Ammon*, and *Josia* had such an end. But as to such as were *Christ*'s Progenitors, we do not read of any of them prevented by a violent death. Not any of those that were before *David*, who himself, although he many times had been in very bloody fights, yet he never received so much as a wound; nor his son *Nathan*, of whom *Christ* descended; nor any of those that came from *Nathan*; nor *Zerubbabel*, and so down to *Christ*, in his Genealogy, set down in the third chapter of St. *Luke*.

And it cannot be objected, that some of them may very well have died a violent death,

death, although the Scripture mentions it not. Is it likely, that if any of them had suffer'd Martyrdom, the Scripture would have suppressed the memory thereof, since they were the persons from whom came the grand Martyr *Jesus Christ*? Moreover, there are some deeds really hapned, wherein the silence of the Scripture is significant, and carries along with it some mysterie, which we ought not to annihilate. However, the Spirit of God, in the Catalogue of *Christ's* Progenitors, names divers of them, whom the holy Scripture relates to have died a natural death, but mentions none to have undergone a violent death.

It seems the same was reserved to him who closeth up the Sacred Genealogy, namely, *Christ* himself, to be alone he who should die a violent death, as otherwise he could not have died. *Isaac*, one of his Ancestors, was ready to have his throat cut upon an Altar, but the sword touched him not, and his death was natural, a long time after. The death of Christ, as that of *Abel*, the first man that died since the world began, ought to have been violent. But as the salvation of the world could proceed but from the violent death of *Christ*, and God from time to time shewed those who were to beget *Christ*, it was a thing of concernment, that none of them should die a violent death, that none of them might be taken to be the *Christ* himself.

Why some of the Children of Adam have lived longer then himself.

IT might seem, that the first man having been produced of a perfect Temperament, his fall would not have so soon shortned his life as to his children, who were mortal even from their very generation. Yet three of them had more days then he had himself; *Noah* had twenty years above him, *Jared* thirty two, and *Methusela* thirty nine.

Doubtless God hath been pleased to shew thereby unto men, that of *Adam* they hold death, and from the indulgence of God they hold life. *Adam* transmitted death to *Methusela*, and not a life of 969 years, for *Adam*'s life was but 930 years; and he could not give what himself never had.

Of the Times the nearest to the coming of Christ, *or which immediately preceded the same.*

Eighty four years before Christ's Nativity

Begin the years of the Widowhood of *Anna* the Prophetess, ~~whom~~ hereafter we shall see in the Temple, forty days after the Nativity of *Christ*.

Seven years before Christ's *Nativity.*

Began the Palsey of the Man, that was cured 38 years after, near the Pool of *Bethesda*, (*Joh.* 5.) A little before that same time, the lame man was born, who was healed at the Temples gate, above 40 years after, (*Act.* 4. 22.)

Consideration.

It pleased God that the power of *Christ* should appear in the healing of inveterate and incurable diseases. Here are two men whose corporal infirmities have by seven years preceded the birth of their Physician. Even afore *Jesus Christ* was born, God prepared him matter and subject on which to work such miracles, as hapned onely a long time after. And as to that lame man, whereas both he and his disease came into the world afore the coming of *Christ*, yet he was not healed but after *Jesus Christ* his leaving the world, even after his Ascension into Heaven.   A

A year and three months before Christ's Nativity.

Is the beginning of the History of the New Testament. It must be observed, that here we consider the order of the times, and not the order of the Books of the Scriptures. Now the deeds or historical matters hapned in the New Testament began at *Zacharias*, the father of *Christ's* Precursor, and are Registred in St. *Luke*, chap. 1. *vers.* 5, *&c.* Whereupon we bring in the following Considerations.

I. The History of the Old Testament ends at the Priestly Genealogy: and the History of the New Testament begins by a Priestly Genealogy, namely, that of *Zacharias*, *John the Baptist's* father. We must again here observe the order of the times. Now according to that order, the last History of the Old Testament is that, which cometh down to the beginning of the *Grecian* Empire under *Alexander*. At that time lived *Jaddua*, who was the High priest when *Alexander* came to *Jerusalem*. That *Jaddua* is mentioned by *Nehemia* in the Genealogy of the Priests, which we read in the 12 *chapter*, from *vers.* 10. to *vers.* 23. It appeareth then, that that place of *Nehemia* is the last piece

piece of the History of the Old Testament, and that it endeth at the Genealogy of the Priests: so that its ending is like unto the beginning of the History of the New Testament, which is also by a Priestly Genealogy.

II. A *Zacharias* was the last to whom the Angels appeared under the Old Testament, and a *Zacharias* was the first to whom the Angels appeared about the beginning of the New Testament: Of those two *Zacharia's*, the one was a Prophet, and the other a Priest.

III. The first word that came from Heaven about the beginning of the New Testament, was pronounced by an Angel; and that word of the New Testament was pronounced by an Angel; *Mal.* i. 1. and 22. 16.

IV. That first word, about the beginning of the New Testament, was pronounced in the Temple unto a Priest, about the hour of burning Incense. All these Circumstances, the Place, the Person, the Time, serving to the Ceremonial Law, served to the preparation of the entry of the New Testament, which is the end to which the Old Testament was relative. Upon the closing of the New Testament, then the Temple, the Priesthood, and all its Perfumes, soon vanished away.

V. This

V. This appearing of an Angel in the Temple, is the onely Apparition, that ever hapned there; never an Angel was seen in the Temple before, and never an Angel was seen there after. Before that Apparition the Angels were not seen then, but in figure, under the picture of the Cherubims. But as the coming of *Christ*, who is the true Temple, and the head of the Angels, drew near, God wrought a thing never hapned before, to cause an Angel personally to appear in the Temple.

VI. That Angel, who appeared in the Temple, is the same who had formerly foretold the ruine of the Temple, and the suppression of the Sacrifices, *viz. Gabriel*, *Dan.* 9. 26, 27. The term is known, which was by him prefixed for their duration. Their desolation was to happen soon after the death of *Christ*; and the *Christ* was to die at the end of the seventy weeks, which make 490 years, and began at that same time when the Angel gave that Prediction. Of these 490 years, 456 were expired when *Gabriel* spake to *Zacharias*: from whence it was easie to infer, that the ruine of the Temple was nigh; and so much the more, because that same Angel, who had foretold the same long before, was now come into the Temple, as the fore-runner of the destruction thereof. Such a circumstance was a warning to the

Jews,

Jews, that they should no longer look upon that Temple, but should prepare themselves to the receiving of Christ, whose coming was drawing near.

VII. The first Miracle mentioned in the History of the New Testament, offers it self at the same hour, and in the same place. A King *Uzziah*, who presumed to go into the Sanctuary, was smitten with Leprosie in the first Temple; and now a Priest being in the Sanctuary, is from God smitten in the second Temple. The first Miracle hapned about the entry of the New Testament, was wrought in the Temple; and the last Miracle hapned in the Temple was wrought about closing of the New Testament, when our Lord gave up the Ghost, as we shall say in its place.

The Conception of Christ *six months, after the Angel had spoken to* Zacharias. *From the Conception of* Christ *to his Resurrection, thirty three years and three months, therein including or adding thereto*

thereto the three days of his abode among the Dead.

With all the best Chronologers we observe, that the birth of Christ about the Autumnal Equinox, towards the Feast of the Tabernacles. *Christ* entring into his thirtieth year, began his Ministery, and exercised the same three years and a half, which ended at his death, in the solemnity of *Easter*. From whence it follows, that from his birth to his death there were thirty two years and a half: Whereunto if you add the time of the abode of *Christ* in the womb of his Mother, it will appear, that from his Conception to his Death, or, his Resurrection, which is the whole time of his Humiliation, there were thirty three years and three months. We cannot tell whether the three days of his abode among the dead ought to be included in that sum; if they ought to be added thereunto, there will be thirty three years, and three months, and three days.

Six months after the Birth of our Lord, a Writing was made between the Old Testament, which was finishing, and the New Testament, that was beginning.

SInce *Malachy*, there had not been any Writing inspir'd by God. The Oeconomy of the Old Testament was near its own end, to give room to that of the New Testament, which was to begin at the Ministery of *John the Baptist*. The time that ran from the Apparition of the Angel in the Temple, to the Baptism of *John*, was therefore as an interval betwixt both the Testaments, partaking of both, and reaching even to the death of Christ, which put an end to the Old Testament at the beginning of that interval, or soon after. Upon the eighth day of the nativity of *John Baptist*, his father *Zacharias* did write down his name; that Writing, which onely contained the name of a Man, was yet of a very great consequence, as having been indited by an Angel in the holy Place, and noting the fore-runner of the *Messiah*. That Writing

ing might be ftyled the laft of the Old Teftament, and the firft of the Nevv Teftament; or indeed, it hath hapned betvveen both, and it feemed to fignifie, that as the firft Teftament, had been given in writing, fo fhould alfo the second. The Pen of the Prophets having been ftaid for above 400 years, men might have imagin'd, that henceforth no more writings indited by the holy Ghoft, fhould be made. But that of *Zacharias* was as a Prelude of the Scripture of the New Teftament, which hapned fince.

GENERALITIES.

On the meafure of the time of the abode of Chrift *on earth.*

I. THe total fum of the years *Chrift* lived in this world, is never read in the Scripture, but is onely found therein in words. The whole number of the years of the Patriarchs, and other perfons, is found in the holy Hiftory; the 930 of *Adam*, the 365 of *Henoc*, &c. Why not alfo thofe of *Chrift*? Becaufe they have no end, and therefore cannot be numbred: We read indeed of part of

h's

his years, but who shall declare his duration? *Isa.* 53. 8. The years of his sojourning on earth ought to be numbred together with those of his Residence in Heaven. This is particular to Christ, death hath not interrupted his Eternity.

II. For other causes. The History of the New Testament never gives the whole sum of the years of any one. The daughter of *Jairus* hath her age marked then when she died, but she was raised from the dead, and 'tis not recorded how long she lived after. Further, there are some very antient persons mentioned, as *Zacharias*, *Elizabeth*, *Anne* the Prophetess; but how long they lived in all, the History expresseth not. The whole number of the years of the antient Fathers was observed, that it might serve to the Chronology that extended to the coming of Christ; the times included in that Chronology, were first reckoned by the Angels of the Fathers, and afterwards by the measures of other considerable Periods. But *Christ* being come, there was no necessity to learn how many years lived his Contemporaneous, or those that came after.

III. Although the Scriptures names not the whole sum of the time that ran from *Christ's* birth to his death, yet 'tis lawful to enquire into it; yea, the holy History invites us thereunto, sith it doth mark the

T particular

particular measures whereof the total of that sum consists; and very mysterious agreements are found therein, as we have seen in the enumeration of the years that ran from the birth of *David*, to the death of *Christ*. Here is another correspondence, which ought not to be neglected; from the revolting of the Ten Tribes under *Jeroboam*, to the destruction of *Jerusalem* and of the first Temple, 390 years passed. During that interval, the patience of God bore with the iniquities of *Israel* and *Juda*, the Prophet *Ezekiel* had order (*chap.* 4. *vers.* 4, 5, 6.) to represent that Patience by a Type of 390 days, during which, *Ezekiel* should bear the iniquity of *Israel*, and that of *Judah*: the number of the days answered that of the years. The number of the months that ran from Christs Nativity to his Death, is likewise the same; for thirty two years and a half that were between both make up 390 months. During all that while, *Christ* bore the iniquities of his people, and he expiated the same by his death; and bore, during those 390 months, not onely the iniquities of 390 years, but also the iniquities of 3900 years, and above, reckoning from the time of sin's entrance into the world. Yea, and he bore the iniquities that happened since, and that will yet happen.

The

The first Year of *Christ*.

Three several times when there was an universal Peace in the World.

1. Whilst they were building the Temple, in the days of *Solomon*. 2. When the Son of God came into the world. 3. When God gave rest unto the Christian Churches under *Constantine*, after so many and so long Persecutions.

The Tribe of Anne *the Prophetess.*

'TWas that of *Asser*, the youngest of the Patriarchs born of the Bondmaids, and in these two respects inferior to all his brethren. But since that Prophetess came of it, that Tribe was called the fourth, (*Rev.* 7. 5, 6.) *Judah*, who according to the order of his birth, was but the fourth, hath there the first rank among the twelve, as having had the honor to bring *the Christ*; and *Asser* having

ing brought that Prophetess, who gave glory to *Christ*, hath there the fourth rank, which before belonged to *Juda*.

The first and the last forty days of Christ upon Earth.

A Glorious Resurrection is like unto a new Nativity. And the Scripture speaking of the Resurrection of *Christ*, applies thereunto these words, *This day have I begotten thee*, *Act*. 13. 32, 33. Upon the fortieth day after the nativity of *Christ*, he made his first entrance into the Temple; and upon the fortieth after his Resurrection, he made his entrance into Heaven, whereof the Temple was the Figure.

Again, The first year of Christ, or, the second, according to some Expositors.
Christ gloriously Manifested, and presently after Persecuted.

ORdinarily, a Promise or a Prediction is presently backed by an event, that

that seems to annihilate and make void
the same. After the Posterity of *Cham*
was condemned to a servitude, presently
instead of serving, it got the Domination
in the person of *Nimrod*, who founded
the first Empire. After *Jacob* had obtained
the Blessing, that promised him the Dominion over *Esau*, *Esau* puts him to flight,
and also afterwards *Jacob* does him homage. After the two Dreams, that
noted the superiority *Joseph* was to have
over his brethren, his said brethren sell
him; and so many celestial Luminaries
as he had seen doing him homage, so many
years was he a slave. *Moses* having been
assured, that he should be the deliverer of
his People, is presently in great danger of
his person, flies away, and remains forty
years in exile, although he was armed with
a divine Commission, and the power of
Miracles; and being come to deliver the
Israelites, loe, their servitude grows heavier, and the task of Bricks is doubled to
them. But how many more Examples or
Divine Predictions have we, that seemed
to be eluded by contrary events that immediately followed them? So the Nativity of *Christ* having been foretold by an
Angel, published by a multitude of those
blessed Spirits, announced by a Star, acknowledg'd by the Wise-men of the
East: Loe, *Christ* is in danger of death,

T 3 and

and to avoid the reach of the Murtherers, he is necessitated to be carried away out of his own Country.

Why God, having sent warning to Joseph *and* Mary, *to carry his Son out of* Judea, *did not likewise warn the other Fathers and Mothers that were in* Bethlehem, *to carry away also their Children, to prevent their murther?*

Bethlehem was marked for the place of the Nativity of the *Messiah*, the time of that Nativity was come; if the rest of the children born then in *Bethlehem*, at the same time when *Jesus* was born there, had yet lived, some or other among them might perhaps have been deemed to be the *Christ*. Much less formal circumstances than these have often coloured the impostures of many that took upon them the Title of the *Messiah*, after the time of his coming was expired. To prevent such attempts, God's wisdom suffered not those children, born at the same

same time, and in the same place with Christ, should live. And that it might be known that they were all dead, he so ordered the matter, that their death happen'd by a notorious, publick, and signal means; and that it should be attended by a general mourning of the Inhabitants.

Why the *Angel did not carry* Jesus Christ *into* Egypt, *but gave that charge to* Joseph?

THe Devil tempting *Christ*, could alleage unto him, *The Angels in their hands shall bear thee up.* If ever it was needful they should do him that Office, it was upon that occasion. And yet, that Angel, in stead of carrying *Jesus*, is content to give that Commission unto *Joseph*, warning him of the danger wherein the Infant was. But its known, that where the ordinary means can serve, God is not wont to make use of extraordinary ways. He hath divided those Offices between that Angel and *Joseph*; *Joseph* could not dive into *Herod's* closet, to know the plotting of that Tyrant, therefore an Angel is sent to discover him that secret.

But *Joseph* could transport the Child, and therefore he leaves him the charge of it.

The Habitation of Christ in Galilee; and why a long time after he spake of the sign of Jona?

Since that time that *Jesus* was carried to *Nazareth*, a Town of *Galilee*, his ordinary abode was always in that Province, the reasons whereof are known; but the ignorants inferred from thence, that he was a *Galilean* by birth, and because of that they would not acknowledge him for a Prophet: For they had a prejudice among them, though false and abusive, that *no Prophet was to come out of Galilee*. But Christ declared to them, that they should be convinc'd by the sign of a *Galilean* Prophet, *viz. Jonah*; for that Prophet was native of *Gath-Hepher*, a Town of the Tribe of *Zebulon*, and *Zebulon* was in *Galilee*, (2 *King*. 14. 25. *Josh*. 19. 13. *Isa*. 9. 1.)

The

The twelfth year of Christ.

Of the eleventh year of the Reign of Solomon, and of the eleventh year expired since the Wise-men of the East published the Birth of the King of the Jews.

SEveral Interpreters, grounded upon ſtrong reaſons, affirm, that the coming of the Wiſe-men, who adored *Chriſt* at *Bethlehem*, was not ſo ſoon after his birth, but onely the ſecond year after, *viz.* either at the beginning, or about the middle of it: From whence it would follow, that the Diſpute which *Chriſt* had in the Temple with the Doctors, hapned in the eleventh year after the Wiſe-men declared him King.

The firſt Temple was finiſhed in the eleventh year after *Solomon* was declared King in *Jeruſalem*: And *Chriſt*, who is above *Solomon*, began to teach in the Temple in the eleventh year after he was declared King in *Jeruſalem* by the Wiſe-men.

The seventeen years of the age of Joseph *the Patriarch, when the Luminaries of Heaven did homage to him in a Dream; and the seventeen years of* Jesus Christ's *private life, at another* Joseph's *house, from the time of his dispute in the Temple, untill the Heaven was opened to him, and he was declared the Son of God, by the voice of the Father, and by the coming down of the holy Ghost.*

AT the age of twelve years he was in the Temple among the Doctors. From that time he lived as a private man, till the beginning of his thirtieth year, at which time he was Baptized, and proclaimed with the aforesaid Solemnities. That interval was of seventeen years, which was the number of the years of the Patriarch *Joseph*, when he was from heaven warned of his future promotion, *Gen.* 37. 2, &c.

The first words of Christ that are recorded to be pronounced in the Temple.

WE have seen the Message of the Angel to *Zacharias*, was the first word that God sent about the beginning of the New Testament, and it was in the Temple it self. The first word we read to have been uttered by *Jesus Christ*, was also pronounced in the Temple, though onely in one of the Courts; and in that word the Temple it self is mentioned, *Wist you that I must be about my Father's businefs?* God's wisdom hath been pleased to signifie, against the prejudice of the *Jews*, that the Temple served onely to the introduction of the New Testament, sith its preparatives began in the Temple.

The 15th year of *Christ*.

AT the beginning of that year, fifteen years before the Baptism of *Christ*, began the affliction of the woman which was bowed together, being bound by Sathan, *Luk.* 13. 12, 13. her misery lasted eighteen

eighteen years, *viz.* till the beginning of the three and thirtieth year of *Chriſt*, who delivered her.

So, before he wrought any miracles, God's providence prepared him several ſubjects for the ſame; as it's alſo ſeen in the following Example.

The 19th year of *Chriſt*.

About the latter end of that year, the daughter of *Jairus* was born, who twelve years after died, and was riſen again from the dead.

About the ſame time began the infirmity of the woman, whom our Lord healed of the bloody iſſue, as he was going to raiſe the daughter of *Jairus*, *Matth.* 9. 20.

The 29th year of *Chriſt*.

The beginning of John's *Baptiſm, and of the New Teſtament.*

From this time until *Chriſt's* death there were five Paſſovers, anſwering to the

the five days during which the Lamb was kept, before it should be killed, *Exod.* 12. 3, 4, 5, 6.

Upon the tenth day of the first month the Lamb was set apart, and upon the fourteenth it was killed. It was the term of five days. Now from that time that *John Baptist* made the beginning of the New Testament, to *Christ*'s death, there were *inclusivè*, five Passovers. Within the fifth and the last, the Lamb of God, whom *John Baptist* had shewed, was slain. Under the Old Testament, the five days that were accomplished on the day of the Passover, represented so many Passovers as should be accomplish'd at the death of *Christ*, after the publication of the New Testament.

Of these stones to raise up children to Abraham. Matth. 3.

These words carry a manifest reflection upon the words that are read in *Isaiah*, chap. 51. vers. 1, 2. *Look unto the Rock whence you are hewen*; out of these *John Baptist* frames that argument: If you your selves are proceeded from such a barren Rock, as *Abraham* was, when God drew of him *Isaac*; Will it be impossible to God to raise also stones out of that Rock?

The

The Ax is laid to the root of the Trees, Matth. 3.

Notwithstanding the saying of several Interpreters, that Ax signifies the Instrument of the revenge God was about to pour on the Jews; the *Romans* were that Instrument, who had already their foot at the root, ruling even in *Jerusalem*, and who afterwards did wholly cut off that State. Thus it is understood by the best Expositors.

But why the *Romans* are represented by the Ax, it remains to enquire. Let us at last hit upon our conjecture. The mark of the grand *Roman* Officers was an Ax that was carried before them; more or less were carried, according to the degrees of their Magistrature. Perhaps the Ax whereof *John the Baptist* speaks here, hath an allusion to that Ax of the *Roman* power, to say, that by it the State of the *Jews* should be destroyed.

The unquenchable fire, Matth. 12. 3.

That fire is not always that of Hell; the word often signifies a vengeance that tormenteth and consumeth to the end. such was that which God poured on the *Jews*; in the last ruine of *Jerusalem*, and which *John Baptist* here foretels. Yea,

Yea, it may be, that that unquenchable fire, whereof he speaks, ought to be understood literally. The Temple, whereupon the *Jews* put their chiefest confidence, was utterly burnt down. The *Roman* General was willing to preserve that Building; and his men having set it on fire, he endeavoured to have quenched it, but it was wholly impossible to hinder all that great Building from being totally consumed. In those flames also a great multitude of the *Jews* perished, that were fled into the Temple.

The 30th year of *Christ*, and the first of his Ministery.

NOt the thirtieth year complete, but but onely beginning, *Luk.* 3. 23.

From that time, till *Christ's* death, passed a week and a half of years, that makes three years and a half, the time of his Ministery, *Dan.* 9. 27.

That thirtieth year of *Christ* began by his Baptism and his Temptation in the Wilderness, with his Fast of forty days.

CONSIDERATIONS.

A comparison of the thirtieth year of Christ, *with the thirty years since the Promise made to* Abraham.

THat famous Promise, which bore, that *in Abraham all the families of the earth should be blessed*, cannot be understood but of the benefit of *Christ*, and that is out of controversie. But from that Promise till *Isaac* was declared the true son and heir of *Abraham*, there was the space of thirty years. Likewise from the Nativity of *Christ*, till he was solemnly by the voice from heaven declared the Son of God, which hapned at his Baptism; there passed thirty years.

There is yet another Parallel. The pretensions of *Ishmael*, who affected the succession of *Abraham*, were declared unjust and ill-grounded, and *Isaac* was declared the onely heir. Likewise, after the Baptism of *Christ*, it was said to them that were not the children of *Abraham*, but according to the flesh, no more then *Ishmael*, *Think not to say, We have Abra-*
ham

ham to our father. And soon after the true Son, in vvhom vve are made *Abraham's* children, vvas proclaimed from Heaven.

The Season of the forty days of Christ's abode in the Wilderness.

THe time of *Lent*, which is observed by many Christians, agrees not to the time of the miraculous Fast of *Christ*, whom they pretend to imitate; the forty days are immediately before *Easter*. But, from the fortieth day of *Christ*'s abode in the Wilderness, till the next following Passover, there passed a pretty long time, as it clearly appears by the deeds and circumstances related by the Evangelists. *Christ* having ended his Fast of forty days, returned to *John Baptist*, who then shewed him to his hearers, and told them, *Behold the Lamb of God*; and some of his Disciples followed Christ. From thence, *Christ* took the way of *Galilee*, *Joh.* 1. 15, &c. Three days after, happened the Miracle of *Cana*. Afterward, *Christ* went to *Capernaum*. All these hapned before that *Easter* that followed the forty days of *Christ*'s abode in the Wilderness, *Joh.* 2. 13.

13. Sith then they pretend to imitate that miraculous abstinence of *Christ*, why have they not chosen, in the revolution of the year, the same season wherein *Jesus Christ* fasted? If they say, that the season of that Fast is uncertain, yet 'tis still certain, that the Fast of *Christ* happened not at the season pick'd out by them to represent the same: Yea, 'tis certain, that many months passed since Christ came out of the Wilderness, to the following *Easter*. And according to the most exact Chronology, the forty days, in question, expired within the beginning of the month of *November*, a season, wherein Christ being pinched by hunger, after so long an abstinence, could find no fruit, nor no food in such a Wilderness: If there had been any fruits upon the Trees, the Devil would not have spoken of changing stones into bread.

All such as have miraculously fasted, have likewise miraculously fed others.

Moses caused *Manna* to come down from Heaven. *Elijah* multiplyed the Oyle and the Meal of the Widow.
And

And *Jesus Christ* multiply'd the Loaves, which fed many thousands of them. Every one of them three that thus fed others, hath been forty days and forty nights without feeding upon any creature. In the same Persons, Wonders of contrary nature have been seen.

Among many others, there is one difference observable. *Elijah* and *Moses* fed others before they fasted themselves, but Christ fasted before he fed others; yea, his miraculous Fast was before all his other Miracles.

Elisha did also multiply the Loaves, but he is not remarked by any miraculous Fast.

The days of Moses *his fast were not so hard as those of Elijah's fast, nor those of Elijah's fast so hard as those of* Christ's fast.

MOses conversed with God, who familiarly was speaking to him then. *Moses*, during his abstinence, was at rest both in his body and mind. To the contrary, *Elijah*, during his whole forty days,

was

was still travelling. But during *Chrift's* Fast, he was in a continual conflict of Spirit; He knew that his coming out of the Wilderneis was his coming into sorrows, and to greater sufferings then ever any man underwent.

Satan, *when he prefented himfelf to* Chrift, *did fay who he was*.

'Tis very likely, and 'tis the opinion of feveral Interpreters, that he feigned himfelf to be a good Angel; let us add, not onely a good Angel, but one of thofe Angels to whom God gives Commiffion of Rule over Kingdoms, *Dan.* 10. 13. 20. and 11. 1. In that quality, which Satan took upon himfelf, he offered to *Chrift* the Kingdoms of the world. Long before, all the Kingdoms of the Earth were promifed to the Son of God, *Pfal.* 2. 8. &c. Satan would perfwade him, it was he that fhould bring to pafs that promife, as having received the power over all Kingdoms, and authority, as he would make it to be believed, to difpofe of the fame. The Evangelifts, in few words, obferve the depths of that Adverfary.

Satan

Satan *took up* Christ *and set him on the* Pinacle *of the* Temple, *and on a high Mountain; but we read not, that ever any good* Angel *transported* Christ *from one place to another.*

THe Tempter alleaged to him the words of the Psalm, *The Angels in their hands shall bear thee up*; yet we read not that ever this happened, neither when it was needful to carry *Christ* from *Judea* into *Egypt*; nor when he was weary of walking, nor when he was upon the præcipices of the Mountain, nor in any other occasion, where it might seem, that the hand of the Angels would have come seasonably to his help: Other services they have administred to him, even presently after his Temptation in the Wilderness, doubtless to afford him some food, which otherwise he could not have come by, in a barren place, and not inhabited. Therefore, for want of ordinary means, the Angels administred unto him then: But they did not carry him out of the Wilderness, either because there were ways and passages whereby he might come out of it; or, which is of a higher confideration, and expressly in the History, because the same Divine Power that led him up into the Wildernefs, brought him likewife out of it, without any need of being carried by the Angels, who are but Servants, *Luk.* 4.

Never any man was carried by the Angels: What then do the words of the Pfalmift fignifie; They fhall bear thee up in their hands.

THe Angel that appeared to *Philip*, *Act.* 8. 26, 39, 40. and gave him order to go toward the Eunuch, who was pretty far from him, did not carry him thither; and after *Philip* had difcharged his Commiffion, he was fuddenly carried away to another place very far from thence; not by the Angel, but by the Spirit of the Lord. And we do not find that ever the Angels were employed to that kind of office towards men. The foul of the poor *Lazarus*, by them carried into *Abraham*'s bofome, contradicts not this
our

our saying. This is a service which the Angels never perform to men, but when he is passing from the Earth to Heaven, and not whilst he is yet walking on Earth.

That *Apocryphal* piece, which represents the Angel carrying the Prophet *Habakkuk* from *Judea* into *Babylon*, is neither preceded nor seconded by any Canonical Scripture.

As to the words of the 91 *Psalm*, it is known, they are but a general expression of the assistance or help of the Angels to the children of God, as if they should bear them up in their hands; not as if these words should particularly and literally signifie such an act.

Since the Angels performed that service to Christ, after his Temptation in the Wilderness, they never render'd him any visible service until the Eve of his Death.

IT was in his Agony in the Garden, that an Angel appeared unto him, strengthning him. When he went about to begin his Ministery, the Angels served him; and when

when he was about to finish it, they served him again: But in the interval, which was almost of three years and a half, the Angels forbore any service to him, though he might have commanded whole Legions of them to come down. Those miraculous works, which made part of his Miniftery, were not to be attributed to any concurrence of the Angels with him, as if they had been his Co-operators. Therefore, that it might appear they had no part in the glory of his Miracles, they kept themselves as remote from him. And even that Angel that was wonted to come down to the Pool of *Bethefda*, to heal there some difeafed perfon, was already withdrawn, when our Lord healed him that had the Palfey, hard by that Pool, *Joh.* 5.

Again, The 30th year of *Chrift*, and the firft of his Miniftery.

The firft Miracle of Chrift.

The Miracles of our Lord preferred

ferred before those of Moses, or any other.

THe opening of the *Red-sea*, the miraculous Solstice hapned at *Joshua*'s request, and several other wonders of the Old Testament, have indeed more shined, and have been full of more Majesty, then most of *Christ*'s Miracles. But *Christ*'s Miracles, who was come for men's salvation, have more redounded to mans profit. The bodies of men as the noblest of all visible creatures, for whom they were all made, have been the most frequent object of *Christ*'s Miracles: To give sight to a man born blind, was an act of greater beneficence, then to stop the Sun. Moreover, neither *Moses* nor *Joshua* ever raised any dead person; and the New Testament doth afford more examples of that wonder, then we can find in the Old Testament.

A gradation of Christ's Miracles to that of the bodies of of Men.

Before Christ raised any dead person, he healed many living; and afore he healed diseased persons, he afforded a nourishment to those that were whole, when he turned water into wine; he so begun his Miracles, that he went on by healing, and proceeded to the raising of the dead. That Gradation we have touch'd on in our Observations on the Symbole, but there is more in it: For, after he had acted on mens bodies, he finally displayed his riches farther, especially after his Resurrection, *viz.* on men's souls, by sheding into them the extraordinary gifts of the holy Ghost.

Of the Element on which the first Miracle of Christ was wrought.

Water, from which was made the first production of living creatures,
viz.

viz. Fishes and Birds, upon the fifth day of the Creation; the waters, I say, hath been the matter of several Miracles, which appeared the first on certain remarkable occurrences. The first plague of Egypt was the changing of the waters, turned into blood, wherein the fishes died. The first Miracle, after the *Israelites* had passed the *Red-Sea*, was the sweetning of the waters of *Marah*. The first Miracle of the Prophet *Elisha*, after he had divided the waters of *Jordan*, was to make wholesome the waters of *Jericho*, (2 *King.* 2.) and the first miracle of *Christ* was the turning of water into wine.

Why the first Miracle of Christ was not reiterated?

Most of the kind of Miracles wrought by *Christ* were wrought above once; diverse times he healed them of the Palsey; divers times he gave light to the blind, and divers times also he raised the dead: But this Miracle, which was the first of *Christ*'s Miracles, happened but once onely. Now why certain Miracles hapned but once, whereof we shall produce some examples in its proper place, there be many reasons. Although there be be no Miracle but what is very great, yet among the Miracles there be some degrees of necessity, according whereunto they hapned either oftner or seldomer. Wine not being so much necessary as Bread, *Christ* would not make use of his miraculous power to give Wine to men, but once onely; whereas twice he multiplied the Bread.

An Addition to what hath been said concerning the Preheminence of the Miracles of Christ, *above those of* Moses *and any other.*

NEither *Moses*, nor any other man whatsoever, did ever confer the gifts of the holy Ghost, that transcendent Miracle belonged onely to *Christ*; neither did any of them confer the gift of Miracles; neither of them did confer the gift of Tongues.

The Prophetical Spirit that came down on the seventy men, mentioned *Numb.* 11.25. was not transmitted to them by *Moses*, but immediately by the Lord. *Elisha* had not the power to communicate unto

unto *Gehazi* the vertue to raise a dead person., 2 *King*. 4. 29, &c. and the gift of Tongues hath been unknown under the Old Testament. The conferring of all those great wonders were peculiar, yea, singular to the Son of God.

Again, The 30th year of *Christ*.

The first Feast of the Passover falling within the time of his Ministery.

The place where Christ *began to foretel his Death and Resurrection*, Joh. 2. 19, 20, 21, 22.

WE have seen that the first words God sent out towards the beginning of the New Testament, and the first words we read were uttered by *Jesus Christ*, were pronounced in the Temple: And now the first words he ever uttered touching his Death and his Resurrection, were likewise uttered in the Temple. Both the Testaments have mutually interjoyned. The Temple, the place of the Sacrifices, hath been

been the first place where Christ spoke of his death, which was to put an end to the Sacrifices, and to the whole Oeconomy of the Temple. Another circumstance is here to be observed.

The time that ran since Christ *began to foretel his Death and his Resurrection, to the accomplishment thereof,* Joh. 2. 19, 20, 21, 22.

The Temple, whereof he was speaking, was his own Body; *In three days*, saith he, *I will raise it up*; those three days expired just and exactly three years after that Prediction; for it was pronounced on the first Feast of the Passover, that followed the Baptism of *Christ*; since which Passover, to the fourth, when Christ died and rose the third day, there were precisely three years complete. On the first Passover of *Christ*'s Ministery, He began to foretel his Death and Resurrection, and on the last Passover he accomplished that Prophesie.

The three years that passed from one to the other, seem even to be included within the proper sense of the three days,

that

that are marked for *Christ's* Resurrection.
It is known, that sometimes three days are
taken for three years, (*Amos 4.4.*) and
sometimes the number of certain years
answers the number of certain days. The
forty days, which the Spies spent in surveying the Land of *Canaan*, God ordered,
that the *Israelites* should be forty years in
the Wilderness, (*Numb. 14. 34.*) The
proper and natural signification of the
three days mentioned by *Christ*, hinders
not, but that they may have a respect to
the three years, which were immediately
to precede or determine those three days:
And so he hath not onely foretold how
many days he should be in the condition
of the dead, but also, though implicitely,
how long it should be precisely, from
the time of that Prophesie, to the accomplishment thereof, the exact measure of
three years.

The Question of Nicodemus,
*Can a man enter the second
time into his Mother's womb,
and be born again?*

THat man, though a Doctor in *Israel*,
had forgotten the words of *Job*,
Naked

Naked came I out of my mothers womb, and naked shall I return thither, (*Job* 1. 21.) The Earth is the mother of all men; all men come from earth, and return to the earth: But did ever any return thither, to come out of it the second time? *Nicodemus* had an express example of it in the Old Testament, in that dead man's corpse that was thrown into *Elisha*'s Sepulchre, and came out of it living, (2 *King.* 13. 21.) Other examples of that wonder appeared since: In *Lazarus*, who came out of the Grave, wherein he was interred some days before; in many bodies of Saints that rose from the dust, and came out of their monuments after the Resurrection of *Christ*. The Regeneration of which our Lord was here speaking to *Nicodemus*, is often represented as a Resurrection.

The 31 year of *Christ*, and the second of his Ministery.

ABout the beginning of *December*, the Dialogue betwixt *Christ* and the *Samaritan* woman; that it was in that season of the year, the Interpreters do infer it from that, that from that time there were four months to the Harvest, (*Joh.*

(*Joh.* 4. 35.) but the Harvest begun the next day after the Feast of the Passover, (*Levit.* 3. 10. *Deut.* 16. 9.)

In those four months that preceded the following Feast of the Passover, besides many other occurrences, we consider;
1 The first plot made against *Christ* (*Joh.* 4. 1.) during the time of his Ministery.
2 The first time it was attempted to put him to death, (*Luk.* 4. 29.) likewise during the time of his Ministery.
3 The first sick body he heal'd, being absent.
4 The first man possessed with a devil, that he delivered. 5 The first of the seven Sabbaths he hath solemnised by Miracles.
6 The first Leper he hath clensed. 7 The first sick of the Palsie he hath healed.

CONSIDERATIONS.

Sith the Tenor of the season is not always the same, whence comes it that it was ordained, that the Harvest should always begin the next day after the Feast of the Passover?

IT's known, that the seasons are sometimes later one year than another, though

though in the same Climate; how then to prefix one and the same annual day for all the Harvests? The same which prescribed it, included a promise of a constant tenor of the seasons, if the *Israelites* should not make themselves unworthy of it; which Promise we read in express terms, *Lev.* 26. 3, 4, 5, 6.

Five several degrees of Means whereby Christ *displayed his miraculous Power towards the Sick.*

THose means have been but signal, or demonstrations of this his Power: He hath then shewed it, either by the onely touching of his garment, as to that creature that was sick of a bloody Flux; or by touching of his hand, as to *Peter*'s mother in Law, and to the first Leper he cleansed, *Mat.* v. 40, &c. or by the applying of his spittle, as to the blind man, *Mar.* 8. 23. or again by his spittle mingled with clay, as to the man born blind; or by his meer word, as toward the son of that Court-Lord, mentioned *Joh.* 4. 46, &c. that son was sick in *Capernaum*, and *Jesus* was in *Cana*, the distance was almost a

days

days journey: But our Lord healed that sick person, though far from him, by his word onely, which at the same time, 'twas uttered by him in *Cana*, did work in *Capernaum*.

The first of the seven Sabbaths which Christ marked by his Miracles.

IN our observations on the Decalogue vve have seen, that the Evangelical History marks seven Sabbath days made famous by our Lord's Miracles; the Sabbath yve speak of here is the first of the seven: Upon that first Sabbath, *Christ* began to expel the evil spirits, delivers that possessed man, mentioned in *Mar.* 1. 21. and *Luk.* 4. 31, &c. Upon the same Sabbath he healed *Peter*'s mother in Lavv, and several other sick folks.

A digression against certain Persons, saying, they have the virtue of healing a sick body by the meer touching of their hand.

I Would not vouchsafe to mention that Imposture, much less to refute it, had it not found belief, then also, even among the vulgar spirits. A Lord of very high ranck, who had chosen me to have the direction of his conscience, being taken with a great and long sickness, forgot himself thus far, as to send, without my privity, for one of those wicked folks, called *Stroakers*. But that which hapned soon after was the death of that poor Lord, who yet had time enough to declare to me his fault, and ask God forgiveness thereof, as he did in my presence, shewing a great compunction for it.

Now, the bragging of these Impostors is grounded on that principle, whereunto many give faith; That the Seventh Son, whose birth is not preceded by the birth of any sister, hath that vertue to heal, by touching onely and stroaking with his hand. But who told them, that he that is but the seventh son hath that power, ra-
ther

ther then the eldeſt of the ſeven? Again, the ſeventh ſon of a *Turk*, or a *Pagan*, hath he alſo that faculty? *David*, who was the ſeventh ſon of *Jeſſe*, did he ever, in the diſeaſe of the firſt ſon he had of *Bathſheba*, tryed to heal him by the ſtroaking of his hands? If they ſay, that *David* had two eldeſt ſiſters; had he not occaſion to regret, that their birth had intercepted that rare privilege that was accruing to him? The holy Hiſtory ſpeaks of the ſeven ſons of one *Sceva*, a *Jewiſh* Prieſt, who medled with exorciſing, but not with healing any ſick perſons of natural diſeaſes; and at length the evil ſpirit did beat and wound them all, the ſeventh as well as the other, *Act.* 19. In a word, if birth could confer ſuch a vertue, every ſeventh ſon would have naturally as much power, as to healings, as the Apoſtles had ever from heaven: Yea, and the gift of healing, which the Apoſtles had, was not in them as a permanent habit. But ſhould any have it by his birth, 'twould be a perpetual faculty, reſiding in him as long as ſuch a man ſhould live. Away with ſuch ſuperſtitions.

The first sick of the Palsey our Lord cured, Mar. 2. 1. 15. *Why among so many diseased persons, the Son of God hath healed, he spake to none of their sins, but to the man sick of the Palsey.*

CHrist never mentioned any causes of the diseases, but for sin, because they could not be taken away but by him. And yet although all diseases come from sin, *Christ* never expressed that cause but in matter of Palsey: To that man that was the first cured of it, he said, *Thy sins be forgiven thee.* To another, whose History we shall hear by and by, *Sin no more, lest a worse thing come unto thee*; but he never spoke so to such as were afflicted with any other kind of diseases, as to them sick of the Fever, Dropsie, Hecticks, Leprous, Blind, or any way defective in their bodies, &c. Yea, and when he was asked concerning the man that was born blind, whether that affliction came upon him for some sin of his own, or for the sins of his father or mother; His answer was, That there was no such cause.

Now

Now why the sick of the Palsey, among so many Patients he healed, are the onely ones to whom he spake of his sins, the reason is very uncertain; yet let it be permitted to us to alleage this: Among the bodily infirmities that are of a long duration, the Palsey stops the course of many sins, as to the outward acts, which a man might commit, had he the sense and motion free. The Palsey that keeps him tyed, restrains many effects of the corruption of his soul; and if it happen that his body recovers its liberty, he ought voluntarily to avoid the sin, which he was compelled before to refrain from. But the Palsey, that was his Rod, is the disease, that stoppeth more sins, and that longer too, of any other bodily indisposition.

Again, The 31 year of *Christ.* The second Feast of the Passover falling within the time of his Ministery, and other Occurrences that followed it within the said Year.

CONSIDERATIONS.

*The Miracle of the Pool of Be-*thesda. *The first time the Angels were employed to the healing of the bodies of Men,* Joh. 5. 2, 3, 4.

THat miracle that consisted onely in the healing of the sick, was a Prelude of the ordinary miracles of *Christ*; but the Angels had never yet performed that office towards man, *viz.* to act in the healing of the sick. To the contrary, an Angel once caused formerly the Plague in *Israel*, in *David's* days. But the coming of *Christ* drawing near, those heavenly Messengers

sengers signified the same by such Miracles, as he himself was to work, and which indeed he wrought afterwards.

The thirty eight years of the sick of the Palsey, followed by other thirty eight years till the Water of the Rock dried up.

About the beginning of the Wars of the *Romans* against the *Jews*, all the waters that were about *Jerusalem* wholly failed, even those of the Pool of *Siloam*, and therefore those of the Pool of *Bethesda*. This is rehearsed by *Josephus*, the *Jewish* Historian. Now the War of the *Romans* began towards the 69th year of *Christ*: if we go up to his 31 year, wherein he healed that sick of the Palsey, we will find, that from that time the waters of the Pool of *Bethesda* were dried up, these past thirty eight years, as many years as the Palsey of that man had lasted, when he was healed hard by that Pool; which is admirable.

'Tis true, that some years after, *viz.* about the beginning of the Siege of *Jerusalem,*

salem, the waters began again to flow, and to fill the Pools; but they came again onely to vvater the *Roman* Army, and their Horses, till *Jerusalem* vvas ruined by them, and that City reduced into a Wilderness. In a vvord, thirty eight years after *Christ* had healed a sick of the Palsey of thirty eight years, hard by the Pool of *Bethesda*, God drying up the water of that Pool, would signifie, they were not to look any longer in that water for the Miracles that were wrought there before: that the Angel would not come down any more into it, yea, and that God had withdrawn himself from *Jerusalem*.

Another Consideration on the thirty eight years that followed the healing of the sick of the Palsey.

From the sentence of death pronounced by God against the *Israelites* that had murmured, after the return of the Spies, (*Numb.* 14.) to that their children prepared themselves to enter into the land of *Canaan*, thirty eight years passed: for that sentence was given about the end of the second year after their coming

ing out of *Egypt*: From that second year then, until about the latter end of the fortieth year of *Israel's* wandring in the Wildernefs, there were thirty eight years complete; which being expired, God commanded the *Israelites* to prepare themselves to pafs into *Canaan*. (*Josh.* 1. 1.)

But as two contrary events have often the prefixions of the like time, whereof we might give several examples; fo 'tis here; after the thirty eight years the *Israelites* accomplifhed in the Wildernefs, fince God condemned them to die therein, their children had warning to prepare themfelves to enter into *Canaan*. But to the contrary, after the thirty eight years that pafsed, fince the healing of the fick of the Palfey, till the beginning of the *Roman* War, God gave the *Jews* to underftand, and warned them, that they ought to prepare themfelves to go out of *Canaan*; as indeed they did, being foon after turned out of it, whereof the coming of the *Roman* Army was a token to them.

It might be demanded here; But what relation between the healing of the fick of the Palfey, and that calamity of the *Jews*? But we read, that the *Jews*, in ftead of acknowledging the Author of fo miraculous a cure, plotted alfo his death on that occafion, *Joh*. 5. 16. a more heinous crime then that of their fathers that murmured in the Wilderneis. And therefore our Lord denounced to the *Jews*, that that *Moses* who prayed for their fathers, would accuse the children, *Numb.* 14. 19. *Joh.* 5. 45.

The second Sabbath *which the Son of God solemnized with a Miracle.*

'Tis the same day of the healing of that sick of the Palsey, *Joh.* 5. 9, 10. And the first time the *Jews* imposed to *Christ*, that he was a breaker of the Sabbath; and it was on the occasion of what *Christ* either did or spake on that day.

Questions touching that sick of of the Palsey, and other deceased miraculously healed.

Since their being healed, how long did they continue in health? or did they never fall again to the same disease, or any other kind? The History decides it not; yet it appears, they were also subject to the same calamities, yea, and to greater ones.

ones. *Sin no more, lest a worse thing come unto thee.*

And it doth not avail to say, that *Christ* had not given them an imperfect health, but healed them wholly, as he himself said speaking of that sick of the Palsey, *Joh.* 7. 23. for, the health he gave them was perfect indeed, in that he left behind in them no relicks of disease; but that health might be altered, either by their fault, or by other causes: They remained sinners, and therefore capable of the infirmities sinners are subject unto; yea, it may be they were in greater danger then before, as we shall say by and by.

Such as were miraculously healed were in danger to be more sharply handled, then in their former diseases, in case they should make themselves unworthy of health.

'Tis not enough to give the reason of it in general, that after a notable deliverance, their ingratitude is more guilty, and deserves a more grievous correction. But there is here a more special cause, if we

[72]

we may so speak, or more particular: The benefits God immediately confers by his own hand, with the mediation of the natural causes, specially where they are impotent and unable to act for us; such benefits do lay on us a particular obligation towards God; but also with a greater guilt, in case of ingratitude: Guilt, which exposeth us to the danger of a more rigorous chastisement then the former. Therefore the sick of the Palsey was warned to beware of a relapse, which would be worse then all his former disease.

The third Sabbath solemnised by the Son of God with a Miracle.

'TWas when he healed the man that had his hand withered, *Matth.* 12. 10.

The raising from the dead the young man of Naim, *Luk.* 7: 11, &c.

Within the first year of Christ's Ministery, he never raised any dead;
yea,

yea, there passed above a year and a half from the beginning of his Ministery, before he began to work that kind of miracles. But towards the latter end of the second year, which is that wherein we now consider him, he raised two dead, the young man of *Naim*, and *Jairus* his daughter.

The number of the Wonders Christ wrought on the dead, answering to the number of the years of his Ministery.

Christ's Ministery was accomplish'd in three years and a half; he went therefore as far as the middle of the fourth year, and within that space of less then four years, he displayed four times his power on the dead, by raising of them, viz. 1 The young man of *Naim*. 2 *Jairus* his daughter. 3 *Lazarus* of *Bethania*. 4 The Saints that came out of their graves, after *Christ* raised himself.

An admirable dispensation of God, under the New Testament, in that after every example of Martyrdom, there is always an example of the Resurrection. A mysterious exception of that Rule.

IN the History of the New Testament, the examples of such as have been slain for the cause of God, wherein comprehended even the little Infants, from whom he hath drawn matter of glory, are thus ranked according to the order or the times. 1 The Infants murthered in *Bethlehem.* 2 *John Baptist* beheaded. 3 *JESUS CHRIST*, the grand Martyr, the faithful Witness, crucified. 4 St. *Stephen* stoned. 5 St. *James*, executed by the sword. 6 *Antipas* put to death for the testimony of *Jesus.* (*Rev.* 2. 13.)

Now, this is worthy of admiration, that every one of these Martyrs was followed by the raising of one or many dead; after a Martyrdom there hapned a Resurrection; and again, after a Martyrdom another Resurrection, and so always alternatively, though there hath been some interval of tim:, time, and other occurrences. So that since the Massacre of *Bethlehem*, a Martyrdom hath not followed the other, without first the intervening of the raising of some dead. See then the order of them in this Catalogue.

1. After the Martyrdom of the Infants of *Bethlehem*, hapned, though a long time after, yet within that time there were no other Martyrs, there hapned, I say, the raising of the young man of *Naim*, and of *Jairus* his daughter.

2. After the Martyrdom of *John Baptist*, hapned the Resurrection of *Lazarus* of *Bethania*.

3. After the Martyrdom of *Christ*, happened not onely his own Resurrection, which was ~~singular to himself~~ among all the Martyrs, but also the Resurrection of many Saints that were lying in the dust.

4. After the Martyrdom of St. *Stephen*, the Resurrection of *Tabitha*, (*Act.* 9.)

5. After the Martyrdom of St. *James*, the Resurrection of *Eutych*, (*Act.* 20.)

6. But loe, here is a great and remarkable exception; for the last of all the Martyrs mentioned in the New Testament, *viz. Antipas*, is not followed by any that hath been raised. That Martyr, the last of all, is different from all the former, in that after his death there is not any example found of Resurrection: Is it not to signifie,

Y that

[76]

that there remains yet a Resurrection, to accomplish the Parallel of the Martyr, and of those that have been raised from the dead? It is the last Resurrection, when *Antipas* himself, and all the other Martyrs not yet raised; yea, and all the Saints shall be rais'd in glory.

The two first persons whom the Son of God raised from the dead.

ONe of each Sex, *viz.* the young man of *Naim*, and the daughter of *Jairus*: That Maid was the first of her sex among the raised persons, for as yet there had been no example thereof. But under the New Testament, life was given to the dead, without exception of Male or Female, as being but one in *Jesus Christ*, (*Gal.* 3. 28.)

No little Infants raised from the dead under the New Testament.

ALL the dead to whom either *Christ* or his Apostles restored life, were come

come to their adolescence, as the two first aforesaid, or had passed it, as *Tabitha*; but none of the dead were raised in their Infancy, I say, under the New Testament. Under the Old Testament it had already happened; yea, the Miracle of the Resurrection began by Infants; the son of the Widow of *Sarepta*, and that of the *Shunamite*. Their Resurrection was followed by that of a man that revived in *Elisha*'s grave, and 'tis the onely person of age was raised under the Old Testament. But the Son of God did not reiterate that miracle, whereof there were already two examples, concerning Infants, but extended and amplifi'd it to persons gone out of their Infancy, whereof the Old Testament had afforded but one example. Whereupon we are to say what followeth.

Most of the Miracles of one kind have happened twice at least.

TWice the bitter waters were sweetned, in *Marah* by *Moses*, and in *Jericho* by *Elisha*. Twice God drew waters from the Rocks in the Wilderness. Twice God did write the Law in Tables of stone. Twice the course of the Sun was interrupted, when 'twas stopped by *Joshua*'s order,

order, and when it went back in the days of ~~Hezekiah~~. Twice *Elija* brought down fire from heaven upon the two Captains of fifty men. Twice was *Jordan* divided, by *Elija* when he was taken up into heaven, and by *Elisha* when he came from *Elija*. The same River had staid its courſe ~~long before~~, to afford a paſſage to the ~~Iſraelites~~ when they entred into *Canaan*. Twice did the Sea obey the Son of God, when he cauſed the ſtorm to ceaſe, and when he walked upon the waters. Twice he multiplyed the loaves. And above twice he wrought other miracles of the ſame kind. ~~Their reiteration tended to a more ample confirmation of the truth thereof, and to a stronger~~ conviction of the unbelievers. Likewiſe, the variety of the circumſtances tended to the ſame end; as by raiſing thoſe that were in their death-bed, and thoſe that were carried to be buried, and thoſe that were already in their graves, and thoſe that were turned into duſt. The diverſity of Sex is alſo noted in the miracle of the Reſurrection, whereof there are two examples, the daughter of *Jairus* and *Tabitha*.

The

The first and the last of those that have been raised from the dead under the New Testament.

Both were young men, that of *Naim*, and *Eutyches*. Why hath that kind of miracle, under the New Testament, begun and finished by persons of that age? Those particular Resurrections of some, although they have not given them perfection, nor an immortal life, yet have they been the preludes of the last Resurrection, wherein our bodies shall receive all the possible and convenient perfection. The Abortives, the little Infants, the Dwarf, the bowed old ones, will rise in a stature, vigour, and uprightness, answerable to that of the age that passed the imperfection of Infancy, and is not come to the corpulency of an unwieldy man, nor to the defects ordinarily attending old age.

And it availeth not to say, that among the Saints raised from the dust, immediately after *Christ*'s Resurrection, there might be some old men; for we could give several answers to that. But 'twill suffice to bring here a Maxim, which we shall justifie somewhere else, That in the

Y 3 Sacred

Sacred History, where question is of deeds of the same nature, the first and the last example are at the rule of others. But in the New Testament, the first and the last example of Resurrection have been two young men.

Why the Son of God raised certain dead, without being desired by any; and others after intreated it.

AS they were carrying the young man of *Naim* to bury him, none, no not his own mother, thought on imploring the mercy of *Jesus Christ*, that he might be pleased to raise that dead; and yet nevertheless, *Jesus Christ* brought him to life again: But the daughter of *Jairus* was raised at the intreaty of her father. It is to be observed, that before the young man of *Naim*, *Jesus Christ* had never raised any dead. He had made himself known by several Cures, and other Miracles, but not yet by any of that kind: His power had appeared on the living, but had not as yet extended it self to the dead. Therefore no addresses were made to him, for craving of him a miracle he had not as yet wrought. 'Twas then necessary, that the first time he wrought such a miracle, his goodness should prevent all petitioning. But having raised that dead, he was intreated to raise another, namely, the daughter of *Jairus*, (*Matth.* 9. 18.) after he had thereby encouraged the father. Also *Lazarus*, because he stanck, there was no hope of his Resurrection.

Four degrees of Means, whereby the Son of God manifested his Power to the Dead.

HE, to raise them, either taking them by the hand, as *Jairus* his daughter; or touching onely the Coffin, as the young man of *Naim*; or by his word alone, as *Lazarus*; or by the sole vertue of his Spirit, which he transmitted to the grave of those that were lying in the dust of the earth.

Chrift *is the firft, who in raifing the Dead commanded them.*

THE *Jewish* Doctors acknowledge, that the Miracles made by way of command were the marks of an excellency, peculiar to the Author thereof. The fenfe of this is, That among the proceedings or formalities the Servants of God ufed in working of their miracles, the higheft of them is this we now mention, *viz.* When they have commanded that the Miracle fhould happen. For the command, when followed by the effect, fhewed a fpecial authority given them from heaven, and put them in a more eminent degree, then when they onely acted by prayer, or by touching, or by any other fignes, or by fore-telling onely the Miracle that was to follow. *Chrift* hath rebuked Agues, Devils, and the Elements: *What manner of man is this, that even the Winds and the Sea obey him?* Let us fay more, *Who is this man, that even the dead obey him?* *Elijah*, and his Succeffor *Elisha*, being about to work Miracles of that nature, proceeded therein by way of requeft to God, and by long formalities reiterated in feveral intervals: but

but they spake not to those dead they intended to raise, much less did they command them to return to life. Christ is the first who hath spoken to the dead, in Imperative terms, *Young man, arise;* and, *Tabitha cumi;* and, *Lazarus, come forth.* After *Christ*, St. *Peter* used also the word of command towards one dead, *Act.* 9. 40. but that Apostle spoke then but as a Messenger, bringing the command which the Son of God was sending to that dead.

Six examples of Sleep followed by miraculous acts, three under the Old Testament, and three under the New.

1 THat of *Adam*, who being asleep, God framed *Evah* of him. 2 That of *Elijah*, who being awake, travelled forty days and forty nights without interruption. 3 That of *Jonah*, who after his sleep, remained living within the belly of the Whale, and came safe out of it. Under the New Testament, 1 That of *Christ*, who being avvake, caused the Tempest to cease: The presence of *Jonah* had occasion'd the danger of the Ship

wherein

wherein he was, but the presence of *Christ* saved the Boat which was in danger; and its the onely place we read of that *Christ* slept in. 2 That of *Peter* in the Prison, awaked and delivered by an Angel. 3 That of *Eutychus*, followed by his death and his resurrection. This last example is as a Type of the Resurrection, which will follow the sleep of death in all such as shall be found in that state at the last day.

The Gadarenes, who had prayed Jesus Christ to depart from them, were the first that were besieged during the Wars of the Romans *against the* Jews.

IN that War, the first place besieged was the Town of *Gadara*: They who had not accepted of the presence of *Jesus Christ*, were the first to whom the enemies presented themselves: They who came forth of their Town to beseech him to depart from them, were the first besieged and shut up within their Town, and afterwards compelled to go out of it, never to return thither any more.

A

A Particularity concerning the Daughter of Jairus.

AMong all the persons raised from the dead, she alone hath the number of her years recorded in the History; I mean, the number of years she had when she returned from the dead, which is not reported of any other. Now me-thinks this may be the reason of that singularity, the daughter of *Jairus* was the youngest of all the persons raised under the New Testament; all the rest, the young man of *Naim*, *Eutychus*, *Lazarus*, and yet more, were more stricken in years. We have seen, that neither *Christ* nor his *Apostles* have raised any little Infants. For the reasons given then by us for it, it may be added, That under the New Testament, God hath not been pleased to work that Miracle of Resurrection, but upon persons already of some discretion, who might have a permanent memory of their return from among the dead. Whereas Infancy cannot judge of the greatness of such a wonder, nor keep it in memory, the impression of it being but weak in that young age, and subject to be soon blotted out. But the daughter of *Jairus* was come out of her
Infancy,

Infancy, though but a little while before; and because she was the youngest of all those that were raised under the New Tement, the number of her years is marked therein, to let us know, that she was already able to consider the greatness of the Miracle wrought upon her, and to keep the memory of it, and therefore capable to bear witness of that wonder; which was the intention of *Jesus Christ*.

The *fourth* Sabbath *solemnized by* Christ *with a Miracle.*

'TWas in *Nazareth*, there he healed divers diseased persons; although the unbeliefe of his Country-men was a great obstruction to the working of his Miracles, *Mar.* 6. 1, &c.

An *example of the two Sparrows propounded by* Jesus Christ *to his Apostles*, Matth. 10. 29.

ONe of them doth not fall on the ground without the Father's will. But

But was it not enough to bring the example of one Sparrow, without speaking of two? Truly it seems to be an allusion relating to the two Sparrows imployed in the cleansing of a Leper, *Levit.* 14. 4, 5, 6, 7. for of those two Sparrows, the one was killed, and the other was let loose. But although it was a thing indifferent which of the two should be killed, and that it seemed to be a casual thing, yet God's providence had design'd which of them was to lose his life; and it was impossible any other should be killed.

The 32 year of *Christ*, the third of his Ministry.

CONSIDERATIONS.

THe first and the last of the Dead, since the publishing of the New Testament.

The Law and the Prophets were until *John Baptist*, the first who preached the New Testament, and who died for having maintain'd the truth. The last Dead mention'd in the Scriptures is also a Martyr, *Antipas*, *Revel.* 2. So doth the New Testament begin and end by Martyrs. Who knows

knows whether the world will not end by the violent death of some just person, as it began by the murther of a just man, *viz. Abel*?

The particular Reason why John Baptist was so soon taken out of the world.

'TWas indeed because he had accomplish'd the work of his Calling. But there is here a secret which is rectifi'd by the History. From *John Baptist*'s death, *Christ* remained the onely Prophet on earth. 'Twas necessary that the latter part of his Ministery, whereof remained about the space of a year and a half, should be accomplish'd, without the being of any other Prophet but himself. God's dispensation is here to be consider'd; at certain times there have been many Prophets in the world, at other times none, and then but one onely; such was *Noah*, a while after the Flood; such was *Moses*, at the coming out of *Egypt*; And this made a man so much the more illustrious, that he was the onely Prophet upon earth. It was therefore convenient, that the Prince of the Prophets should have a time, when

there

there should be no other Prophet besides himself. But a good part of the time of his Ministery was already gone, when *John Baptist*, though a prisoner, yet lived. It was then high time, that that Prophet, who was so great, should leave the world, that *Christ* might remain the onely Prophet, before he went up into heaven.

The greatest resemblance that ever was between two men, as to the Spirit.

'TIs of *Elijah* and *John Baptist*, we now speak of; there was never such an exact resemblance of spirit between men, as theirs was: For *John* came in the spirit and vertue of *Elijah*; yea, he was a second *Elijah*, although their issues were much different, the one having ascended bodily into Heaven, and the other put to death.

Why the Son of God going to his Disciples that were on the Sea, made not a way to himself through the waters, but walked upon them.

THe waters had given way to the *Israelites* in the *Red-sea*, and since when *Jordan* divided it self, to let them enter into *Canaan*, under the conduct of *Joshua*; and since to *Elijah*, when he went over that River to ascend into Heaven; and again to *Elisha*, when he returned from *Elija*. So that this kind of Miracle, of dividing the waters, had happened four times. But the Son of God was pleased to work an unknown Miracle on that Element, and unheard of till then, to be carried over the waters, and be born of them, either by rendring them solid, or any other way capable of bearing a man's body, or else being upheld onely by his own power: 'Twas a miracle altogether new, which he chose rather to work, then to reiterate a Miracle which already had happened several times, *viz.* the division of the waters. But this affords us the occasion of inserting here the following Observation.

Of

Of all the kinds of Miracles happened under the Old Testament, Christ being yet upon Earth, onely reiterated seven of them, and gave them a greater extent then they had had formerly.

THe seven kinds of Miracles which happened under the Old Testament were, 1 The shining face of *Moses*. 2 The Clowd that covered the Tabernacle, and which filled the Temple at its Dedication, under *Solomon*. 3 *Miriam* and *Naaman* healed of their Leprosie. 4 The effusion of the holy Ghost on the seventy men, *(Numb.* 11. 25.) 5 The healing of *Jeroboam*'s withered hand. 6 The dead raised by *Elijah* and *Elisha*. 7 Food multiplyed by those two Prophets.

We do not reckon here the miraculous Fast of forty days of *Moses*, *Elijah*, and *Christ*. For the Miracles of our Lord, since he entred into his Ministery, after his coming out of the Wilderness, began at *Cana*, where he wrought his first Miracle. Let us therefore see the seven kinds of Miracles

racles, or Wonders, which happened under the Old Testament, were reiterated by *Christ* within the time of his Ministry.

1. The face of *Moses* became shining, *Exod.* 34.

The face of *Christ* became shining as the Sun, and his clothes became as white as Snow: It happened at his Transfiguration.

2. The Clowd cover'd the Tabernacle, *Exod.* 40. and since, a Cloud filled the Temple, 1 *King.* 8. and from the midst of the Cloud, God spake several times, *Exod* 33. *Numb.* 11.

At the same Transfiguration, a Cloud compassed the Disciples, that were with *Christ* on the Mountain; and out of the Clowd came a voice from God, saying, *This is my beloved Son*, &c.

3. Two persons were cured of Leprosie, *viz. Moses* his Sister, and *Naaman* the *Syrian*.

Several Lepers were clensed by *Christ*, yea, 10 at one time.

4. The holy Ghost came down on the 70 men, and made them capable to prophesie that time onely. The same happened to *Saul*, 1 *Sam.* 10. 13.

The Disciples of *Christ* received the holy Ghost, that was permanent in them, to a large distribution of his gifts, conferred on them soon after, on the day of Pentecost, *Joh.* 20. 22.

5 *Jero-*

[93]

5 *Jeroboam*'s hand became withered, and soon after was cured, 1 *King.* 13.

Christ healed the withered hand of a man, who had been deprived of the use thereof longer then *Jeroboam*.

6 Three Dead were raised under the Old Testament, all the three were dead but a little before.

Christ raised not onely three dead, of whom one had been four days in the grave, but also many bodies of Saints that were lying in the dust.

7 *Elijah* multiplied the Widows Oyle and Meal, to feed her and her son therewith, 1 *King.* 17. *Elisha* maltiplyed the Oyle when children. was in the house of a poor woman. That same Prophet having but 20 loaves, filled therewith a great number of men.

Christ having but five loaves and two little fishes, fed therewith five thousand men, and abundance of women and children. Another time having but seven loaves, and a few small fishes, he fed therewith four thousand men, that had been three days without eating, and likewise a great number of women and children.

In most of these Parallels it may be seen, as to these seven kinds of Miracles, happened under the Old Testament, that *Christ* reiterated them with advantage in many respects.

Z 2 *Again*,

Again, The 32 year of *Christ*.

The third Feast of the Passover *which happened since his* Baptism, *and some Occurrences that followed it.*

CONSIDERATIONS.

Why Christ, *who raised several dead, healed but one deaf man? And why he used more formalities, and imployed more time in giving hearing to that deaf man, then in giving life to the dead.*

IF the greatest Miracles had been always the less frequent, some might have imagin'd, that it had been harder for God to work them, then the production of lesser Wonders; as if his power had been subject to the proportion he gives to his works. But to shew, that the greatest Wonders are equally easie to him, he gave more examples of them, in some kinds of Miracles then of others, that were much lesser. To raise a dead man is a

greater

greater Miracle, then to give hearing to many deaf men; and yet the Son of God, who raised many dead, during the time of his Ministery, gave hearing but to one deaf, *Mar.* 7. 32, &c. Let us yet add this: To raise a dead man is a greater Miracle, then to cure a sick man, though a dying. But of all the sick the Son of God healed, we find but one that was near death, *viz.* the Centurion's servant; but many that were dead indeed were raised by *Christ*.

That deaf man, whom the order of the times causes us to represent here, had besides an impediment in his tongue; yet that recovery of his hearing and speech, though the wonder of it was great, was less neverthelefs then the raising of a dead man. And yet for the healing of that man, the Son of God employed more formalities, much longer, and more various, then ever he did to any of all the dead he raised: He takes this Patient, he draws him aside, he puts his finger into his ears, he toucheth his tongue, applies his spittle to him; he looks up to heaven, he sighes, , he says to him, *Be opened:* He never used so many things to raise a dead person; one word onely, *Arise*, was presently followed by the effect. By this he was pleased to shew, that the signes or ceremonies used by him, were arbitrary, and that his power was not included therein, sith he used less in the working of his greatest Miracles, and more to the less.

The second wonder wherein *Christ* used much formality, was, when he gave sight to the blind mentioned in St. *Mark*, *chap.* 8. 22, &c. That Miracle followed the former.

Some kinds of Miracles Christ *reserved to himself, during the time of his Ministery.*

WHilst he was on the earth, no other ever gave sight to any blind, and no other raised the dead. He gave power to his Disciples, first to the twelve, and then to the seventy, to cast out Devils, and to heal all sorts of diseases and infirmities: but their commission reached not to the giving of sight to the blind, much less to give life to the dead. At least, we read not, that being yet in this world, his Disciples had ever done any Miracle of either of those two kinds. *Christ* reserved some, chiefly those two, that are of the greatest, that there might be some marks of his Prerogative, that might put distinction between the Matter of Miracles, and those that

that acted onely by vertue of his orders. There are yet some other Miracles which never were wrought, neither before the coming of *Christ*, nor since his Ascension, but onely by himself, immediately; whereof hereafter we shall see some examples.

Whatsoever thou shalt bind on Earth, shall be bound in Heaven, &c.

Let me have leave to bring on these ~~words a new Exposition, or at least~~ a Conjecture: This binding and loosing hath no relation to the persons, as if they were to be bound or loosed; nor to the things, as if *to bind* should signifie *to prohibit*; and *to loose*, should be the same *to permit*, which is the Exposition of a learned modern Author. But the next foregoing words in this Text, *I will give unto thee the keys of the Kingdom of heaven*, do give some light to these. It hath been observed, that among the Solemnities used by the *Jews*, in the creating of a Doctor of the Law, some keys were put into his hands; namely, the keys of the Archives or places where the Copies

of

of the Sacred Books vvere kept; and 'tvvas as much as to fay, that the nevv Doctor had povver henceforth publickly to read and teach. *Jefus Chrift* makes an allufion on that Ceremony, promifing St. *Peter* to make him a Doctor of the Gofpel. This hath been obferved by our Predeceffors, but vve may add thereunto vvhat follovveth.

It's knovvn vvhat the form of Books of old vvas, they vvere made after the manner of Rolls, and neceffarily tied vvith fome fmall ftring, to avoid the imbroiling of the Margents, and keep them in a good condition; vvhen any one vvas vvilling to read therein, they ufed to untie them; and vvhen a long intermiffion of reading vvas intended, they vvould again tie them. Novv the Keys promifed by *Chrift* to St. *Peter*, vvere the Keys that opens the dore to the Doctors of the Gofpel, that they might take out of it the Book, and might tie and untie it; that is to fay, that they might keep it fhut, or open it, as it fhall be convenient. The firft is done vvhen they do refufe unbelievers and unrepenting perfons the application of the Promifes contained in the Gofpel. The fecond is done upon a contrary fubject. An example of the firft in St. *Peter* himfelf, vvhen he faid to *Simon* the Magician, *Thou haft neither part nor lot in this matter,*

matter, viz. in the Doctrine of the Gospel. Then was that Book tyed, as to that Hypocrite. That which is tyed and untyed, is indeed but one and the same Book, but distinguished from it self by the difference of those two actions. That which is favour of life unto some, and favour of death to others, is but one and the same Gospel.

Of Christ's *Transfiguration; and first, of the four Orders of men that were found there.*

IN this occurrence so illustrious, there were, 1 Living men that were to die. 2 One that had been dead, and was returned to life again. 3 One that never died, and yet ascended bodily into Heaven. 4 One that was to die, and to return to life again, and bodily to ascend into Heaven.

The living persons that were to die were the three Apostles, that accompani'd our Lord.

He that had been dead, and was return'd to life again, was *Moses*.

He that had never died, and yet was bodily ascended into Heaven, was *Elijah*. He

He that was to die, and return to life, and bodily to afcend into Heaven, was *Jefus Chrift* himfelf.

That Affembly was the Epitome of the univerfal Church, confidered in divers conditions, and at feveral times.

1. The three Apoftles, that were yet fubject to perfecutions, and to death, reprefented the Church, as 'tis yet Militant.

2. He that had been dead and was returned to life, reprefented the Believers, who fhall rife at the laft day.

3. He that was afcended into Heaven, without tafting death, reprefented thofe that fhall be found alive at the laft day, and fhall not die, but fhall be changed.

4. All thefe three Orders hold of *Jefus Chrift*, who is the head of the Church, both of the living and the dead; of thofe that fhall rife, and of thofe that fhall be changed. In the perfons of thofe that have appeared at his Transfiguration, the whole Church hath appeared before him, without whom, that Affembly could not be complete, nor yet framed.

A Distinction between the three Apostles that were Spectators of the Transfiguration of our Lord.

'Tis known, that on several occurrences he made choice of them, to be the onely witnesses of them. In this occasion we do onely consider the death of the two first, *Peter* and *James*, to have been violent. All the three represented, as we said before, the Believers, who were yet subject to death. But as death is either violent or natural, and the first man that died, *viz. Abel*, died a violent death; so the wisdom of God was pleased, that of the three, who, at the Transfiguration of *Christ*, represented the Militant Church, there should be two who were to die that kind of death, as representing such as God had appointed to Martyrdom, *Joh.* 21. 19. *Act.* 12. 2.

A

A Considerable Mystery in the Apparition of Elijah and Moses.

Several reasons are given of the choice made by God of those two Prophets, to appear in that Assembly, where met those three persons that were famous by a Fast of forty days. But let us add thereunto the following observations.

The bodies of those two great Prophets had formerly been miraculously taken out of the sight of men, and miraculously they then appeared again. That of *Elijah* was taken up into Heaven; men looked for it a while, but in vain, 2 *King.* 2. 15, &c. *Moses* his body was never seen dead, for God took it out of the sight of men, and with his own hands put him into a grave, unknown to this very day. So the bodies of those two Prophets being again brought to sight, it could not be but for a very extraordinary reason, as we shall see in the following observation.

Three kinds of Witnesses, 1 *From Heaven.* 2 *From Earth.* 3 *From under the Earth.*

IN the Transfiguration of our Lord there appeared, 1 A man come from heaven, *viz. Elijah.* 2 Three men yet residing on the earth, *viz.* the three Apostles. 3 A man come out from under the earth, *viz. Moses.* And so the glory wherewith our Lord did then appear, hath had some Witnesses come from all parts of the world, *viz.* from heaven, from earth, and from under the earth, that is, the grave: Which was a prelude of *Christ*'s Exaltation, before whom all knees shall bow, of things in heaven, of things in earth, and of things under the earth.

Why among so many holy men, that were out of this World, Elijah *and* Moses *were chosen*

chosen to be present at the Transfiguration of our Lord?

'TWas needful to have one from Heaven, and one from the Grave, as we said just now. But in heaven, there were but two men in body and soul, viz. ~~Enos~~ and *Elijah*; all others that were ~~there~~ were onely in their spirits or souls. Of those two that were corporally in heaven, God sent down him that had lived the nearest to the days of *Christ*, and to whom the fore-goers of *Christ*, *John Baptist*, had the more likeness. Moreover, 'twas a common prejudice among the *Jews*, that *Elijah* was to come in person before the *Messiah* should appear. But *Elijah*, that same Prophet, whom they thought would personally come before *Christ*, came then to witness, that *Christ* was already come. 'Twas convenient that the error that was then common touching *Elijah*, should be convinc'd by *Elijah* himself, before *Christ* should go out of the world: But the time of his departing was then drawing near, when *Elijah* appeared at his Transfiguration.

As for those that were in the Grave, *Moses* had that particular to himself, that none other was ever buried by God's own

own hands; from whence it followed, that he could not be transferred nor taken out of his grave, but by the same hand that had shut him in there, and had even concealed the place; and that being brought to sight again, it was necessary for some great action, whereunto God had reserved him. But as it was to give testimony unto *Christ*, *Christ's* dignity hath so much the more appeared therein.

Elijah *came not back again into the world, till after* John Baptist *was gone out of it; and why?*

WHen *Elijah* appeared at the Transfiguration, *John Baptist* was already deceased. The wisdom of God, all, whose reasons we cannot know, would not permit that there should be two *Elijah's*, at the same time, in the world; for, *John Baptist* was also an *Elijah*: Not that they were incompatible, sith the one came, in the spirit and vertue of the other. But, as its likely, because it should not seem that the testimony given by *John Baptist* had been suggested to him by *Elijah*, as by the Master to his Disciple, and not immediately

mediately by the holy Ghost; whereas *John Baptist* was even more then a Prophet. And 'twas very important that his testimony should be attributed to the immediate calling of God, as since that of the Apostles was, *Gal.* 1. 1.

The Assembly of those that appeared at the Transfiguration of our Lord, and their distinction.

THat Assembly consisted of seven persons, *viz.* of three Disciples, of two Prophets, of the head of the Prophets, and of him that presided among them, *viz.* God the Father.

The three Disciples that were there to see & to hear; to be spectators of the glory of *Christ*, and hearers of what should be spoken there concerning him. St. *Peter* went beyond his limits, when he undertook to speak there, whereas he was there onely to hearken, and to contemplate.

The two Prophets were there as two Witnesses of the quality of *Christ Jesus*, and of the sufferings he was about to undergo. If 'twere a lawful thing to wish, I could wish to have the Discourse of those

two

two Prophets at length. How many Lights, and how great Starrs would be there discovered to our eyes? Doubtless *Moses* drevv there all the Curtains of the Tabernacle, he shevved hovv they ought to pass through the blood of the Sacrifices, to that of Christ; he displayed the Pattern he formerly had seen on the Mount, and vvhich he vvas seeing much better on that Mount, vvhere *Christ*, the truth of the Figures, vvas himself present. As to *Elijah*, his Sacrifice authorised by the miracle of the fire from heaven; several vvonders, as that of multiplying food, and the raising of a dead person, the food an Angel brought him, as the Angels served *Christ* vvhen he vvas hungry in the Wilderness; and finally, his being taken up into heaven, a type of *Christ's* Ascension, may very vvell have been the subject of the speech of that Prophet. But vvhatsoever vvas contained in the Old Testament, touching the sufferings through vvhich *Christ* vvas to enter into his glory, vvas remembred and interpreted by himself, on the very day of his Resurrection from the dead, *Luk.* 24. 27.

That Head of the Prophets spake not in the Assembly vvherein happened his Transfiguration; for the subject of it vvas the hearing of the Witnesses, that vvere speaking concerning him; and their testi-

A 2 mony

mony, which was sufficient, was for him.

But God himself spoke in that Assembly, as President, and pronounced the conclusion of it, that hence-forward, when his Son should speak, they should hearken unto him.

The voice from the midst of the Clowd.

Formerly, when God was speaking to *Moses*, the voice came from the bottom of a Clowd, *Exod.* 33. *Numb.* 11. and 12. But now, in the presence, and in the hearing of *Moses*, God spoke out of the bottom of a Clowd. The Disciples that were present at the Transfiguration of *Christ*, and to whom the voice was directed, were instructed by as glorious a means, as that whereby *Moses* formerly received his instructions, *Heb.* 2. 3.

Why no Angel appeared at the Transfiguration of our Lord.

The Angels appeared on several other occasions: Why not at such an illustrious

rious one as that was? We have seen, that that company that was on the Mountain of Transfiguration represented the Church, which confisteth of men, all redeemed unto God by the blood of the Lamb. But the Angels, although *Chrift* be also their head, belong not to the company of those he hath redeemed. The Angels are no part of that Church for which he hath suffered. And as there is but one God, and but one Mediator between God and man; so God, the Mediator, and men onely met in that Affembly, which was the Epitome of the Church.

Almoft all such as God made extraordinarily to tafte heavenly Joy, did prefently after meet with fome great fubject of forrow or fadnefs.

SO did the three Difciples, who were coming from contemplating the transfiguration of their Mafter, and hearing the two greateft Prophets fpeak, yea, and from hearing the voice of God himfelf, met prefently after with the hideous fight of a poffeffed perfon, whom Satan tore,

tore, and heard the pitiful cries of a father, who was craving mercy for his onely Son: So *Moses* coming from his conversing with God on the Mount, during forty days, and from enjoying a communion full of pleasures, much surpassing the thoughts of all men, met with the *Israelites* in a disorder, full of horror, prostituting their souls to a molten Beast; at which he grew so angry, that he broke the Tables of the Law he had in his hands, and made a great slaughter of those unhappy Idolaters. So *Christ* himself, after he had seen the heavens opened; after the holy Ghost was come down upon him in a visible form, and after, by the very voice of the Father, he was proclaimed the Son of God; presently after the same Spirit leads him into a frightful Wilderness, where he remains forty days without food, and with the onely company of wild Beasts; and also afterwards Satan doth present himself unto him, and carries him to high and dangerous places. So the Apostle St. *Paul*, having been caught up into Paradise, where he had heard unspeakable words, presently after is exposed to a messenger of Satan to be buffeted by him.

But this so strange a vicissitude, which happened to these several persons, for divers ends: To *Moses*, that he might know, that those divine and so transcendent favours

vours, did not free him from the future, of all sorrow, in the Government of the people committed to him. To *Christ*, because that by opening of the Heavens, the coming down of the holy Ghost upon him, and that glorious proclamation, tended only to strengthen and arm him against the same temptations he underwent, and which he was necessarily to undergo for sinners. To the Disciples that were present at his Transfiguration, that under pretence of that previledge, they should not think they had any Truce with Satan. To St. *Paul*, to prevent the pride he might fall into, because of so high a Revelation.

The 33 year of *Christ*, the fourth of his Ministery.

From the beginning of that year to Christ's death there are six months, which make the third and last part of the three years and a half, or of the half week of years of his Ministery.

These latter six months of Christ's Ministery were more abundant, and more illustri-
ous

ous in Miracles, then the former.

THis is manifest. Heretofore he had restored sight to such persons as had lost it, either accidentally, or by sickness: but hereafter, he will give it to such as never had it, but were born blind. Heretofore he raised bodies that were yet whole, and had not yet seen corruption; but hereafter, he will raise such as were already putrifi'd. The nearer he came to the end of his Ministery, the more he enhaunsed his Miracles, carrying them to the supreme degree. And we shall see those Miracles he wrought at his very death.

Why the Son of God refusing his Disciples to command fire to come down from Heaven on the Samaritans*, gives them a reason of it, which seemeth to be contradicted by an* *an act done since by him*, Luk. 9. 56.

THe reason of that refusal was, that the Son of man was not come to destroy mens lives: for, from thence he infers, that he ought not to suffer his Disciples to cause the *Samaritans* to die. But when St. *Peter* caused *Ananias* and *Saphira* to die, which happened since, was it not by the permission, yea, and by the commission of the Son of God, and by vertue of the power of working Miracles, he gave to that Apostle? But did not the same reason, for which he would not cause the *Samaritans* to die, avail likewise for *Ananias* and *Saphira*?

Here we must distinguish the times. Whilst *Christ* was on earth, conversing among mortal men, he would work no other acts but of mercy towards them, causing those that were a dying to live, and such as were already dead to live again. But after his Ascension into heaven, 'twas necessary he should likewise work some acts of justice, to shew, that he is at the right hand of God, and that one day he will judge the secrets of men, as he then judged the plot of *Ananias* and *Sapphira*. On earth he practised but mercy, since he is in heaven, he hath shewed a pattern of his justice.

'Twill therefore be necessary to demand here, Why God suffered Satan to cause fire to fall down from heaven on *Job*'s servants, and yet would not permit the Apostles should cause fire to come down from heaven upon those infamous *Samaritans*.

Why Christ*'s enemies, being come to ensnare him in words, withdrew for one onely word he spake to them?* Joh. 8. 3, &c.

HE had obliged them to declare, whether any of them was without sin; but the accusation of their own conscience hindred them from bragging of it. Yet, was there none impudent enough to affirm himself without sin? In all likelihood they feared the Spirit of *Christ*, who knew them all, and had even shewed that he knew what was in man's heart, *Joh.* 2. 24, 25. Had they not reason to fear, lest he should discover the sins of every one of them, note the particulars, and

and send them away laden with shame? Therefore they did wisely in withdrawing silently.

The first Temple was violated by the Jews, *who stoned therein a Prophet; and the second Temple was by the* Jews *violated, when they offered therein to stone to death the Head of the Prophets.*

Both the Temples became abominable for many reasons, but particularly for those two crimes of the same kind. The *Jews* hold, that the chiefest cause of the destruction of the first Temple, was the death of *Zechariah* the son of *Jehoiada*, whom their fathers stoned to death in the Court thereof; yet that Temple stood 1260 years after the death of *Zechariah:* What cause will they give of the destruction of the second Temple, which lasted but 40 years after the *Jews* attempted to stone therein *Jesus Christ?* Joh. 8. 59. Yea, and the ruine of that second Temple was more extreme, then that of the first, as we shall see presently. Two

In the Temple, where the Jews took up stones to stone Jesus Christ, not one stone stood on the other.

That Temple was not onely burnt, as the former, but even the place where it stood was brought to such a state, that there remained no mark of any building, no not of the very stones themselves. The History reports, that the *Romans* turned the same into a tillable or manured field, yea, and they caused the Plough to pass over it. And so not onely the Temple vanished away, but even the very pavement thereof, the stones whereof had been made use of for so horrid an attempt.

Two great wonders which were never wrought by any, but by the Son of God, and that but once, and onely towards the latter end of his Ministery; the one having immediately

diately followed after the other, and both expressed in one and the same verse of a Psalm.

THose two Miracles are, 1 The healing of the woman that had been bowed together many years, (*Luk.* 13.) 2 The fight given to one that was born blind, (*Joh.* 9.) Both these were marked before-hand, above a thousand years before, and joyned together in one and the same Psalm, and in one and the same verse, *Psal.* 146. 8. *The Lord openeth the eyes of the blind, the Lord raiseth them that are bowed down.* Moreover, each of them two happened on a Sabbath-day, as we shall see.

Two considerable Circumstances in both these Miracles, viz. one in each of them.

SOme days afore our Lord wrought those two wonders, he occasionally spoke of eighteen men on whom the Tower in *Siloam* fell, and slew them. And
soon

soon after, being to give sight to a man, who was born blind, he sent him to the Pool of *Siloam*, that the same place that had been fatal to those men, might be happy to this man.

The other Miracle, the healing of the crooked woman, went before this, and followed nearer the discourse *Jesus Christ* had made touching the eighteen men, whom the Tower in *Siloam* slew. The eighteen years of the infirmity of that woman, (*Luk.* 13. 11.) do they not bear some analogy, tending to make it a memorial of that wonderful cure, of an inveterate disease of so many years as there were men slain, whom *Jesus Christ* had a little before remembred?

These circumstances happened not by chance: and the circumstances the Evangelists have recorded thereof, can by no means be thought to be idle; the places, the times, the persons have therein such relations, as ought to be considered of. In vain shall any ask, how a disease of eighteen years hath so precisely met, after the discourse of the death of eighteen men. For Divine Providence extends and prepares so the times before-hand, that they might fall out at the very point of time he prefixed.

The

The fifth Sabbath solemnized by Christ with a Miracle.

'TIs that when he wrought that same miraculous cure, which was singular to the *Messiah*, delivering that creature whom Satan had kept bound eighteen years, (*Luk.* 13. 10, 13, 14, 15, 16.)

The sixth Sabbath solemnized by Christ with a Miracle.

'TIs that he made remarkable by a wonder unheard of till then, giving sight to a man who was blind from his birth, (*Joh.* 9. 14.)

The season of the year Christ gave the sight to that blind.

'TWas in Winter time, about the beginning of *December*, a little before the feast of the Dedication, which was celebrated about the middle of that month, (*Joh.* 10. 22.) The cures made by natural means, require favourable seasons;

sons; but miraculous acts are not subject to the time of the year. And indeed, what Spring, or what Harvest-time, could have contributed to the production of such a wonder as this?

'Twas in Winter time, when the Son of God healed that sick of the Dropsy, mentioned in the fourteenth Chapter of St. *Luke*. It was about the latter end of Winter, when he wrought the first cure of a sick of the Palsey. 'Twas in the middle of Winter, when he cured the son of a Nobleman belonging to the Court. Whosoever will observe the intervals measured in the New Testament, and marked by Interpreters, shall find, that those healings, and others the like, have happened in the Winter-season.

And as to that blind man, what might avail him what was prescribed to him, to wash in a water, which the rigor of the season might rather render it to him hurtful and dangerous in other respects.

Why Jesus Christ *never gave Almes to the Beggars he healed.*

THat blind man was poor, yea, and a beggar, (*Joh.* 9. 8.) Another blind man

man whom our Lord cured, was also reduced to beggery, (*Mar.* 10. 46.) But *Jesus Christ* gave alms, and one of the Apostles was the dispencer of it, (*Joh.* 13. 29.) But he caused no alms to be given to those poor blind men. Would it not have been a double beneficence, if when he gave them sight, he should likewise have afforded them wherewith to satisfie their hunger? But as the best actions are the most subject to detraction, *Jesus Christ* could have wanted no adversaries, who would have disputed the truth of the Miracle, saying, That it may be those beggars were never blind, but onely feigned to have been so, being hired with money: And indeed, as to him that was born blind, the *Jews* would not believe he had been so, till they were convinced it was so, (*Joh.* 9. 18, &c.) To prevent their blasphemies, *Jesus Christ* abstained from bestowing any alms on those beggars. St. *Peter* had neither gold nor silver when he caused him to walk, who was born lame, (*Act.* 3. 6.) But although that Apostle should have had wherewith to shew himself liberal to that beggar, 'tis likely his prudence would have kept him from doing it, for the cause aforesaid. This brings in the following Observation.

Several

Several of the greatest Miracles were wrought, either alternatively, or indifferently, in the behalf of the Poor and of the Rich, of the Meanest, and of the Greatest.

THe first dead man that was raised, was the son of a poor widow of *Sareptha*, and the second was the son of the rich *Shunamite*, (2 *King.* 4. 8.). The first raised by *Christ* was the son of a certain Widow, whose quality is not named in the History; and the second raised by *Christ* was son to one, who was the head of the Synagogue, and therefore illustrious among his fellow-Citizens, called *Jairus*. The first raised since the Ascension of *Christ* was the good *Tabitha*, rich in alms she gave: And the second and last that was raised since the Ascension of *Christ*, was a young man who hath no other Epithet, but remains without a title, as having none that were considerable in the world.

Among several sick folks healed by *Christ* or his Apostles, we find the son of a Lord belonging to the Court, the servant

of

of a Centurion, and the chiefest man of an Island, (*Act.* 28. 7.) Among those that honoured *Christ Jesus*, living and dead, we find *Nicodemus*, one of the chiefest of his Nation, and the rich and honorable *Joseph* of *Arimathea*.

The wisdom of God was pleased, that among those who have given testimony to *Christ*, there should be some of the rich and highly qualifi'd ones, that their testimony should even be above all suspicion of corruption or of complacency.

A Digression on the mis-rekoning of such as confound the seasons of the year, which the Evangelists have distinguished.

IN several Orthodox Churches, the custom is yet retained to read publickly certain pieces of the Scripture once yearly, each of them having a certain day appointed for that end. So the words of *Jesus Christ* contained in the tenth Chapter of St. *John*, *I am the good Shepherd*, &c. were read upon the second Sabbath day that follows that which is called *Easter*; therefore

therefore the reading of that passage is made in the Spring, and very seasonably, as a learned Divine of ours hath written, because, saith he, it is the season whereat the Shepherds and their Flocks do begin to take the field.

But it should be observed, that those words of *Jesus Christ* were uttered in Winter time, above three months before the coming of the Spring, (*Joh.* 10. 22.) so that that *Simile* was not taken by the circumstance of the time of the year. We know that every place of Scripture may be read at any time whatsoever; yet it ought to be done with prudence, chiefly in publick Exercises. And particularly it is important for us to observe the several times, wherein *Jesus Christ* spoke or acted; otherwise, we can have but a very dark and confused knowledge of the History of the Gospel, and subject to several inconveniences.

The second time the Jews offered to stone Jesus Christ in the Temple, (Joh. 10. 31.) A question on that subject.

WE read of our Lord, that two several times he expelled from the Temple

ple the Merchants, one about the time of the first Passover within his Ministery; and the other time, about the fourth and the last: The first time he onely rebuked them for making the Temple a Market-place, (*Joh.* 2.) but the other time he charged them with a crime of another nature, and which was more enormous, namely, to have made the Temple a Den of thieves. The reason of this, in my opinion, may be this:

The first time our Lord expelled these Merchants, none had, as yet, attempted to stone him in the Temple, therefore he onely termed it then a market-place: but since they had endeavoured to spill therein the blood of the righteous, that place deserved to be called a Den of Thieves, *Matth.* 21. 13. For it seems, that our Lord pointed onely at their selling and buying practised in the Temple, yet to name that Theft and Robbery, would be a great Hyperbole, should not the term imply a more enormous crime then that of trading; I say, a crime, called by its proper name, and already committed by the *Jews*: for they had truly committed an act of true Robbers in the Temple, even when they endeavoured to murther therein *Jesus Christ*, even twice. And it often happened, that God visiting the lesser iniquities, expressed not the same in the

censure,

censure, but onely remembred the greater, whereof the others are but the additions. Therefore here our Lord intended to say to them, You profane this Temple by the trading you practise therein: But was it not sufficient for you to have polluted it with murder, when you went about to stone me therein?

The *seventh and last* Sabbath which the *Son of God* solemnized by *Miracle*.

'Twas by curing the man sick of the Dropsie, mentioned in St. *Luke*, *chap.* 14.

The *Parabolical History* of Dives *and* Lazarus.

The first Observation.

WHen the Scripture speaks of one that is in hell, if hell be named, the person is not named; but if the person be named, hell is not named at all.

So the name of hell being expresly in that

that Parable, the proper name of that rich man is not expressed. But on the contrary, when the son of perdition, *Judas*, is named after his death, he is not said to be in hell, but onely that *he was gone to his own place*, *Act.* 1. 25. So we know, that there are some spirits in prison, (*1 Pet.* 3. 19.) but not one of them is named in that Scripture, when it speaks of their prison. That silence of the holy Ghost condemns the rashness of those, who do, even before-hand, appoint *Hell* for the habitation of a soul, whom God alone hath power to send into hell-fire.

The second Observation.

Three souls are here represented, one onely in the place of torment, and two other, *viz.* of *Abraham* and *Lazarus*, in the place of Rest; yet the soul of that *Dives* is not alone in hell. But those that are in that place of torment have no affection one to the other, nor none of them is comforted by the society of those that are with him. But on the contrary, such as are in Bliss, rejoyce to be there in company, even in that of the Patriarchs, and do make there an admirable consort.

The third Observation.

The soul of that *Dives* being in hell, makes no addresses to God, but onely to *Abraham*; yea, it doth not so much as pronounce the name of God; either because those that are in hell have utterly forgotten God, or because they expect no comfort from him, or else because they abhor him, and speak of him but in the ways of blaspheming. The Parable is full of wisdom.

The fourth Observation.

When *Moses* came into the world, *Abraham* was gone out of it 250 years before, therefore this Patriarch had never seen *Moses* his writings, nor the writings of any of the Prophets that followed *Moses*. But this *Abraham's* voice recommending the Scriptures, is the voice of God himself, signifying, that we are not to expect, either from the Fathers, nor from any other, to make any other addresses, but such as are afforded us by the Scriptures. And truly *Abraham* is represented here speaking as *Isaiah*, who forbidding to consult the dead, sends us to *the Law and the Testimony*, *Isa.* 8. 19, 20.

The fifth Observation.

Abraham faith, That although *Lazarus*, or any other of the dead, should rise, the living would not be the better for it. Hath not this been verifi'd in another *Lazarus*, he of *Bethany*, whom soon after our Lord raised from the dead? Not onely was it put to deliberation to send him back again to the grave, but also they procured the death of him, who had restored him to life.

Doubtless, when *Christ* uttered that Parable, he alluded to that second *Lazarus*, whom he intended to raise from the dead too, seeing for that Miracle happened few days after: and the effect of it, as to many of the chiefest amongst the *Jews*, was no other but their being hardned, which expressed here by *Abraham*. In that point the Parable is become an History, and that so much the more visibly, that even a *Lazarus* hath been raised from the dead.

The Petition of the two blind men not far from Jericho, Matth. 20. 30, &c.

ONE of the greatest wishes of the Patriarchs, Kings, and Prophets, was, to see the *Christ*. *Simeon* having seen him, was content never to see any thing else. These blind men, who made their addresses to the Son of God, ought onely to have desired the sight that they might see him; though they should never see any other object; yea, and though they should never have any eyes after they had seen him once. But most of those who have craved his assistance, have been wanting, or otherwise irregular in their demands.

Of the Stature of Zacheus.

WE know, that the measure of the body, be it great or small, neither avails nor hurts, as to man's salvation; for although the Physiognomists from thence draw their marks, both of wit and manners, yet their conjectures meet with many exceptions; chiefly, where Grace mends

mends Nature. Yet the holy History never mentions any men of an extraordinary stature, but they are noted with some bad quality; we read but of two in *Israel*, viz. *Saul*, and an eldest brother of *David*, called *Eliab*. On the contrary, among the *Canaanites* there were whole families of Gyants, and some of such high stature, that in comparison of the *Jews* of a reasonable heighth, were but very small Grashoppers, *Numb.* 13. But now, the case of man is so far from being able to add a cubit to his stature, that it will rather make him stoop; for, *a broken spirit drieth the bones*, *Prov.* 27. 22.

Why the Son of God stayed four days before he raised Lazarus from the dead?

AMong the reasons of that delay, this is very considerable; *Christ* was nigh his death; but he had promised to rise the third day, and that was incredible, it being without an example; for it had never happened, that a body, dead three days before, had returned to life. None of those on whom such a miracle had been done, had so long staid in the condition

of

of the dead, when God caused them to live again. Not the son of the widow of *Sareptha*, who was raised few hours after he yielded up the ghost; not the son of the *Shunamite*, between whose death and resurrection there past not a whole day; not the daughter of *Jairus*, lately expired when the Son of God raised her; not the young man of *Naim*, whom they were going to bury; nor yet he who was thrown into the Sepulchre of *Elijah*. For it was not the custom of *Israel* to keep dead bodies long unburied, unless they were imbalmed; and the heat of the Climate corrupted them presently, specially if they were kept above three days. But as to the young man of *Naim*, and him whom they threw into the Sepulchre of *Elisha*, neither the condition, which seems to have been but very mean, nor the silence of the History, will not suffer us to say, they were embalmed, no more then *Lazarus*, whose corpse stunck after the fourth day. Let us add thereunto, that if they had been kept to the third day, the holy Ghost would never have been silent of that circumstance, which might have served to shew the more, the greatness of the miracle; in that God should have raised some corpses that had been then so near putrifi'd.

In a word, *Christ* having foretold, that he

he would rise the third day from the dead, which as yet had never happened to any dead, he raised one that had been dead four days; to shew, that he could very well raise one the third day, since he had raised one who had been a day longer among the dead.

Why Jesus Christ *wept for* Lazarus, *and wept not for* John Baptist?

SEveral causes are alledged of the tears *Christ* shed upon Lazarus his grave; but if it was for the death of a man, whom he loved, why did he not weep for the death of such a friend, yea, of such a Prophet, who died for the truth, *viz. John Baptist?* If it was in general for the misery of mankind, which death swallows down every day; whence is it, that *Jesus Christ* wept not for the two other dead he had raised before? If he wept, because *Lazarus* was returning to the miseries incident to this life; had he not the same subject at the resurrection of the others? If he wept out of compassion towards those, who were taking on for the death of *Lazarus*, why did he not weep, when he saw

a

a poor widow, a mother, lamenting for the death of her onely son, the young man of *Naim*, whom she accompanied to the grave?

It's very certain, that *Christ* had a great tenderness for us, but he hath kept in his tears to the drawing near of his last sufferings. Therein, as well as in most of his actions, several degrees are to be observed, near one to the other, and in particular this: Before he did sweat blood, which happened the day before his death, he expressed his sorrowfulness by a much less violent demonstration, *viz.* by weeping on *Lazarus* and on *Jerusalem*. It was convenient he should shed tears, before he should shed his blood; there was but a few days difference between both. For we do not read that he ever wept before. Although his whole life was a continual series of sorrows, yet they encreased more and more, as his death was drawing nearer and nearer; and at last they united and centred altogether, caused the tears to gush out, which he had still refrained dureing his former sufferings. In a word, he was nearer to his last and more extreme sufferings, when he went towards *Lazarus* his Sepulchre, then when he heard of *John Baptist's* death.

The

The seven days immediately preceding *Christ*'s Resurrection.

'Tis observable, that according to the Scripture, the custom of the *Jews*, and the style also of the Evangelists is, that the day began at Sun-setting; and the following hours, whereof the first are those of the night, do belong to the same day, which began at the setting of the Sun, and extends it self to the following evening. According to that account, that's known to be the antientest, the Passover which our Lord celebrated, his agony in the Garden, his death, and the circumstances thereof, happened all within one and the same day. So his entry into *Jerusalem* happened not the next day after the Supper made to him in *Bethany*, although there was a night between, but within the same day. And for want of observing that rule, many take their measures ill, and the distinctions which the History affords upon that subject.

The

The first Day.

A dead man raised, and he who raised him, did eat together at one Table.

This happened in *Bethany*, *Joh.* 12. 1, &c. there *Jesus Christ* and *Lazarus* met, whom he had raised few days before. If the persons be taken notice of, 'tis one of the most remarkable Banquets that ever was; there was to be seen a man lately come from among the dead, eating with the living. The ordinary way of men is to go from the Table to the Grave, but this went from the Grave to the Table. There was likewise to be seen the Author of that wonder, which were two very admirable objects.

Mary's intention, in annointing the feet of Jesus Christ.

IT may be it went no further than to express her gratitude to him, who had given her again *Lazarus*; but Divine Providence brought out of it another Interpretation,

terpretation, although *Mary* thought not then of *Chriſt's* funerals, and that ſhe rather wiſhed him a long dwelling on earth: her piety was the cauſe that that thought is attributed to her. So the bleſſing given by *Iſaac* to *Jacob*, even when he thought to impart it to *Eſau*, is alſo imputed to the faith of that Patriarch, as if indeed his intention had been to bleſs *Jacob*, *Heb.* 11.20.

If theſe ſhould hold their peace, the ſtones would cry out, Luk. 19. 40.

THis Hyperbole became an Hiſtory ſix days after, for it was accompliſhed at *Chriſt's* death, when no body ſpeaking for him, the Rocks burſt, and 'tis very likely with a noiſe. However, the ſtones opened their mouthes, to condemn ſuch as were ſhut at a time, when they were to be opened to give glory to the Son of God.

The

The small interval of time between Christ's *turning out such as were selling in the Temple, and the vail of the Temple's being rent.*

ON the first of those seven days, next foregoing his Resurrection, he chastised those who profaned the Temple, and on the sixth day, namely, that of his death, happened the Rent of the Vail; to signifie, that the service of the Temple was abolished. But why was our Lord so angry at the profanation of a service, which was but to continue six days longer in its lawfulness?

The Question is the Answer it self. The nearer the Ceremonies of the Temple came to their end, the more religiously were they to be observed. For the death of *Christ* being represented by the Sacrifices, 'twas necessary that those Types should be handled and proposed with all reverence and holiness; but above all, when they came nearer to that perfect Sacrifice, the death of *Christ*; then were they the more holily to be displayed in the presence of their Prototype.

The

The Blind and the Creeple came to the Temple to Christ.

THose two sorts of impotent persons never entred into *David's* Palace, but were debarred ever from going into it, 2 *Sam.* 5. 8. but God gave them leave to enter into his Temple; yet none of them were ever healed therein, till the Son of God wrought that wonder there; and that onely once, some few days afore his death; and he never healed therein but blind-men and creeple: for indeed, none other presented themselves to him there.

The third time of the proclaiming of the Son of God from Heaven, by the voice of his Father.

THe first time was at his Baptism, and then God declared, that he was well-pleased in His Son.

The second, at his Transfiguration; and then God added, that they should hear his Son.

The third, after he had made his entrance into *Jerusalem*, and then promised to glorifie his Son, *Joh.* 12. 28.

The gradation in these three proclamations is visible enough, and the diversity of the times and occasions, when these happened, shews the causes of the diversity of the matters.

The Second Day.

Of the Fig-tree cursed; the defending of the common reading of that Text against some modern learned men.

THe Evangelist St. *Mark*, chap. 11. vers. 13. having said, that *Jesus Christ* found but leaves on that Fig-tree, addeth these words, *For the time of Figs was not yet*. But some learned men read otherwise, For the time of Figs was then: But the reason why they go from the common reading, and substitute other terms formally contradictory thereunto, is, say they, because at that season of the year, *viz.* about the Feast of the Passover, Figs were already ripe in *Palæstine*, considering the heat of that Climate,

mate, and that also Harvest then began.

But these men have either forgotten, or were ignorant, of the diverse kinds of that Fruit, growing at very different seasons of the year. For in Countries much less Southerly then *Judea*, there are some Fig-trees, whereof the Fruit is ripe before the Summer's Solstice, and others that bear ripe fruit but four months after; so that some do already afford nourishment to men, when the others have not yet put forth their buds. Who doubteth, but that the same may be in *Judea*? So, what is objected, that in the Spring there were some ripe Figs, cannot be said but of some kinds of that fruit, and of the latter sort of them, of which 'tis said, that the time of Figs was not yet. Therefore *Jesus Christ* met with some of those Fig-trees, the time whereof was not yet come to bear. And thus ought this to be limited, when it is said, that the time of Figs was not yet come; *viz.* of those Figs of that kind of Fig-tree, where *Jesus Christ* looked for some fruit. For in general, the Figs have more then one season.

It's observable, that those that put on an Affirmative in this Text, saying, 'Twas the time of Figs, make the Evangelist speak without reason; after he hath said, that *Christ* being come to the Fig-tree found there nothing but leaves, adds immediately

mediately after, *For the time of Figs was not yet*; and this shews the reason why *Jesus* found there no fruit. But if you read, as those Interpreters do, He found there nothing but leaves, because it was the season of Figs, What reason was that? There were but leaves, because 'twas the time of Figs; there was no fruit, because it was the time of fruit. Hath such a reading any sense at all?

Such as endeavour to introduce that Exposition, do but change one word in the Text, yea, and onely a word of one syllable in the Greek Original; for instead of one *ε* that is negative, and the consequence thereof is, that it was not the time of Figs, they put an *ε* whose consequence bears a quite contrary sense: But such a change is against all the antient Copies, without reason, yea, contrary to reason.

Some other Expositors endeavoured to save the truth of the Text, by a means that's neither necessary nor secure; for in stead of the time of Figs, they read, The *year* of Figs, which is a very much forced Exposition, and is alledged without proof. What we have distinguished touching the divers kinds, and the different seasons of that fruit, is a certain thing, grounded upon experience.

An

An Observation on the cursing of the Fig-tree.

THe Priesthood of *Aaron* and his Successors, having been newly established, 'twas further confirmed by the Miracle of a drie Rod, cut off from an Almond-tree, which in one nights time budded, bloomed, and yielded Almonds, *Numb.* 17. 8. this signified, that that Priesthood would flourish and bear fruit. But when it was about its expiration, our Lord signifi'd it by a contrary miracle; for then he caused a Tree, full of leaves, wholly to drie up in the space of one night: to signifie, that the Priesthood of the Old Testament, which was onely a Type of that of *Christ*, would henceforth be without fruit; or else in general, that the Synagogue, represented by the Emblem of the Fig-tree, was near to its destruction, *Luk.* 13. 6, &c.

A Parenthesis concerning the Trees usually planted in the Land of Canaan.

THeir fruit was accounted unclean the first three years, at the fourth, the *Israelites* offered them unto God, though they were not permitted to eat of them before the fifth, (*Levit.* 19. 23, 24, 25.) but this prohibition extended onely to the fruits of the Land of *Canaan*. Now why were the fruits of the Land of *Canaan*, the holy Land, accounted unclean, yea, during the first three years? whereas the fruits of other Countries were never taxed with any uncleanness? Would it not seem otherwise, that the holiness of the Land of *Canaan* should sanctifie the fruits coming from her? or at least, that they were not to be accounted unclean, whilst the fruits of other Countries were not so accounted?

This is full of mystery, and hath rather relation to the Men then to the Plants. That which is left as indifferent to those that are far from God, is often accounted impurity in those that are near to him; for his presence doth oblige these to a more exact holiness, *Levit.* 10. 3. So many actions were lawful to the *Israe-lites lies* in foreign Countries, which were not lawful to them in *Canaan*; and many were lawful in *Canaan*, that were not so in the Temple.

Another Digression touching the Fruits prohibited by the Law, and sanctifi'd by Christ.

THe same Law that pronounced unclean the fruits of the three first years, declared, that on the fourth they should be sanctifi'd, being offered to God. That Law had its accomplishment in *Christ*, who on the fourth year of his Ministery, having offered himself unto God, hath sanctifi'd all manner of food, abrogating all the Laws contrary thereunto.

The third Day.

If ye had faith, ye shall say to this Mountain, Be removed, &c.

COuld there be a greater Miracle then the removing of a Mountain? To stop

stop the Sun, to make it go back, and to suspend the whole order of the Heavens, that are so much above the reach of man's arm; were they not greater wonders then the removing of a Hill would be, yea, then the removing of the *Alps*, or the *Pyrenaans*?

Such a Miracle would be so much the more considerable, because it never happened; for never was a Mountain removed from its place, but by natural means, as for example, by some Earthquake, or by Gun-powder, or by the work of mans hands, which is not miraculous. The miracle would be, if without the help of such means, but by the meer word, or the meer sign of a man, a Mountain should go from its place, and should remove to some other place; but never such a wonder happened. 'Tis Therefore propounded for its rareness, yea, as being without example. And so of what the Apostle saith, *Though I have all faith, so that I can remove mountains,* 1 *Cor.* 13. 2.

[147]

The time that passed since the blood of Zecharias the son of Barachias began to be revenged, to the full vengeance thereof, Matth. 23. 35.

THe blood of that Prophet began to be revenged in *Joas* the murtherer, in the year of the world 3160, for then he finished his Reign, his diseases making him unable to sway any longer the Scepter, which for that cause was put into the hands of his son, and three years after he was killed in his own bed, 2 *Chron.* 24. 25. But from that year 3160, to *Christ*, at the year 3960, remembred that blood of *Zecharias*, it appears, that there was just 800 years, which are twenty times forty years. And from that time of *Christ's* remembring that blood, till it was fully revenged on the *Jews*, which happened at the last ruine of *Jerusalem*, there were forty years, which makes in all 840 years. But the 840 makes 12 times 70, and so from the beginning of the vengeance for that murther committed in the first Temple, to the consummation of that vengeance, which happened at the ruine of the second Temple, and with the desolation

of

of the whole Land, there were 12 times 70 years; a term like to that of the *Babylonish* Captivity, which happened 12 times 70 years after that the twelve Tribes had shared the Land of *Canaan*, as we have said in the first part of the *Harmony of the Times*.

If the ruine of the second Temple happened for revenging the blood of Zecharias, how can Christians say, that it happened for revenging the blood of Christ?

THese words are not inconsistent. If the Murtherer, who hath got the pardon of his crime, commits again another; Justice doth not onely punish him for the murther that followed the pardon, but also for the former, though pardon'd before; for the falling again of him into his crime, abolisheth the abolition of his first offence. Then two murders committed at several times times, and on several persons, are expiated by one and the same punishment. Now what is found just among men, shall it be found unjust

in

in God ? God had pardon'd the *Jews*, so that for the future their hands should be kept clean from blood: But, loe, their very streets have been full of the blood of the Prophets; and yet God did bear with them, till they put to death the Lord of glory; and yet he gave them a respite of forty years, calling them to repentance. And finally, the blood of *Christ*, called the blood of all the righteous men that had been slain, even from the time of *Abel*.

We may yet add this, that the blood of the righteous, that were before the coming of *Christ*, seems to have been fully revenged, as to the temporal pains, by the ruine of *Jerusalem*, and of the *Jewish* State. But that desolation was but the beginning of the vengeance for *Christ's* Blood, that is still on them, and on their children; witness the reproach they lie under, and the hatred of all the Nations towards them, in the dispersion they are in so many Ages since. So that what they do suffer since the ruine of the second Temple, is no more for *Zecharias* his blood, or of the rest of the righteous slain under the Old Testament; but for the blood of *Christ*, and of such Martyrs as have suffered for his sake.

The last time Christ was in the Temple. An Observation on the circumstance of that day, Matth. 24.

OF the six days that went immediately before the burying of *Christ*, he gave three to the Temple, honoring the same by his Presence, his Doctrine, and his Miracles; they were the three first days, on the last of which he went out of the Temple, never to return thither any more, and foretold the utter ruine of that building, and on the last of the three other days, he rent the vail of the Temple, which was a manifest fore-runner of the ruine he had foretold. The Interval was but of three days.

Two Observations on the Parable of the Virgins, Matth. 25.

THe *Jews* never held a Synagogue, unless the Assembly were at least
of

of Ten men: They neither used Circumcision, nor contracted Marriage, nor gave the Bill of Divorce, but in the presence of the like number of men; nor celebrated the Passover, unless ten persons should together partake of it, though it was lawful to have a greater number; whereunto even *Christ* conformed himself, when he celebrated that Sacrament. And it seems, that that Ordinance of the *Jews* was grounded on the example of *Boaz*, who being to contract mariage with *Ruth*, chose ten men of the chiefest of the Town to be witnesses thereof: And it is very likely, that from thence also came the custome of having at least ten Virgins at the Nuptial Solemnity, *Ruth* 4. 2.

The five wise Virgins seem to bring to remembrance the five daughters of *Zelophehad*, commended for their prudence, *Numb.* 27. 1, &c. Oftentimes, the words of the Scriptures, besides the matter they directly relate unto, do carry their reflexions on such as are collateral in some respect.

The fourth Day.

Christ is in Bethany; Judas treateth and agreeth with the Priests about the betraying of him.

The fifth day.

The Preparation of the Passover.

The sixth Day.

On that day, which was also the day of the Passover, Jesus Christ died.

WE have said already, that the day began with the *Jews* at the evening, and ended at the evening of the day following; according to that computation, which admits of no kind of doubt, *Jesus Christ* died within the very same day wherein he celebrated the Passover; for he did celebrate it in the evening, which was

was the beginning of the sixth day, and he died before the following evening, that is to say, before the beginning of the seventh day: the Type and the Anti-Type did meet within one and the same day; the Type or Figure in the evening, and the Anti-type or the figurated truth in the morning. For, according to the Scripture, which speaks according to the order of the Creation, the evening and the morning do signifie a whole natural day. That concurrence of the Passover, and of the death of *Christ*, happened within one and the same day, the one in the night, and the other in the day-light, doth appear wonderfully lightsome and shining; but we cause it to be eclipsed by our misreckoning, when we say, that *Christ* died onely the day following *Easter-day*.

The more the death of Christ *drew near, the less resemblance was between him, and the Types that represented him.*

WE observe this upon the occasion of the Lord's Supper, which was instituted on that day, and substituted in the place

place of the Passover. We must here consider one particular in the diversity of Figures and Sacraments, ordered to represent *Christ* at his death.

That representation was made first by the slaying of Lambs and other Victims, used under the Old Testament; but though they represented *Christ's* Death, yet they did not represent properly his Person.

In the interval of their time, *Christ* was represented by a man, *Isaac*, who was offered in Sacrifice, and in a manner recovered, as if he should have been raised from the dead; but he died not indeed, so that he rather represented *Christ's* Person then his Death.

Finally, the Bread in the Lord's Supper, and the breaking of it, do also less resemble *Christ* and his death, then such other Figures as preceded that Sacrament: For, is not a bit of bread broken, further off from the resemblance of man's body slain, then were the bodies of sacrificed Beasts? In these therefore was seen a bloodshed, yet it was not the blood of a man. In *Isaac*, a man is seen offered, but no blood shed; and in the Lord's Supper, we neither see a man's body nor blood shed.

Now this we may say on that subject, Before the death of *Christ*, it was m re

needful

needful to have it drawn and represented by Figures, that should come nearer to the outward appearance; for such Draughts and Pictures supplyed the want of the History that was not yet. But since we have the History of the death of *Christ*, and that therein he is crucifi'd before our eyes, the Sacraments being annexed to such a Picture, do rather tend to a remembrance in us of the spiritual vertue of that death, then to a new representation of all the visible circumstances therein: And so doth indeed the Lord's Supper suppose all those circumstances; but that which is thereby formally represented, is the body and the blood, as being considered in their spiritual and invisible vertue, and not in colours or features. But that spiritual vertue residing in the body and blood of *Christ*, are not represented by the figure, or by the colour of the bread and wine, but by their nutritive faculty; wherein they go beyond all other food.

D d   *The*

The Scripture never mentions the Soul of Chrift, but when it speaks of his sufferings.

MY *soul is exceeding sorrowful*. Item, *My soul is troubled*. And, *The Son of man came to give his life a ransome for many*. Yea, in the Old Teftament, *Ifa*. 53. *When thou shalt make his soul an offering for sin*. Once onely we read thus, that *He rejoyced in spirit*, Luk. 10. 21. but the spirit and the soul are not always equivalent terms ; and although they should be so here, yet it should be the sole exception that can be alleaged on our obfervation. For through the reft of the whole Scripture, the Soul of *Chrift* is never named but on occafion of his sufferings. Though he did not always suffer in the Body, yet his Soul was still sorrowful.

Twice

Twice onely the Angels appeared to Christ. *The difference of those two Apparitions. An Observation thereupon.*

IT's true, the Angels have rendred many services to *Christ*, since his coming in the flesh, but they appeared but twice visibly to him; once, after his being tempted in the Wilderness, *Matth.* 4. 11. the other time, on the Eve of his death, *Luk.* 22. 43. The first time many Angels came to him, and ministered to him; but the second time, one Angel onely appeared to him, and yet afar off, namely, from heaven. In former times a whole Army of Angels went to meet *Jacob*, (*Gen.* 32. 1, 2.) but *Christ* being in an Agony, one Angel onely appears to him, and yet doth not come near him.

All this hath been a part of the abasing of *Christ*; and the nearer he came to the last degree of his humiliation, the more did the Angels draw away from him, one onely appearing then unto him, and yet at so far a distance. Morever, in that that Angel came not out of heaven, but appeared to him in glory, whilst *Christ*

Dd 2   was

was so much humilitated, it may be seen, that then, more then at any other time before, was Christ made inferior to the Angels, *Heb.* 2. 9.

The Angels never spoke in the presence of Jesus Christ. A review of the common opinion touching that Angel that appeared to him.

'Tis an ordinary, though a rash prejudice; that that Angel was speaking to *Christ*, and uttering some comforts to him; but the History saith no such thing, but onely that that Angel appeared to *Christ* strengthning him. Some will ask, How did he strengthen him, but by speaking to him? *Answer*, The meer amicable apparition of an Angel did sufficiently shew to *Jesus Christ*, that it proceeded from God's love towards him, and that was enough to strengthen him, without a necessity of the Angels speaking to him. So did *Jesus Christ* himself appear from heaven to St. *Stephen*, and yet spoke not to him, encouraging him by his meer apparition, *Act.* 7. 55.

And when the Angels came to *Christ*
in

in the Wilderness, and ministered to him, we do not read that any of them spake to him then; when they spoke, it was still in his absence: And so they said to the women that were looking for him in the grave, *He is not here*. So spoke they to the Apostles, after *Christ* was ascended into heaven, *Act*. 1. 10. But why they never spake in his presence, and much less to himself, we may say, that thereby they have shewed, that *Christ* received no kind of instruction from them. Several Prophets have been info:med by the Angels thereunto appointed. But as to *Jesus Christ* his knowledge, he had it immediately from God; and that it might appear that the Angels did contribute nothing to it, they have always kept their silence, wheresoever he was present.

Of the twelve Legions of Angels, Matth. 26. 53.

WHy that number of twelve? Although the Interpreters give some reasons of it, our own is more natural, as being drawn from the chiefest circumstance of the matter in question. The persons that had then occasion to be afraid, were twelve in number, *viz. Jesus Christ*

Christ, and the eleven Apostles, that followed him; therefore as many men as there were, as many Legions of Angels would have come to their assistance, a Legion for each man, and yet more, had *Jesus Christ* desired it of his Father.

A Legion was of 6000 men; see what would have been the proportion of 6000 Angels to one man.

Of the Cock that gave warning to St. Peter.

Jesus Christ had said to him a little before, and to others also, *Watch and pray*; now he gives him warning by the Cock, a watchful creature, which makes it self to be heard to give warning unto men; which marketh the quarters of the night and of the day, and which alone of all Fowls doth awake to crow at midnight.

God did not give him an humane voice: He never made any Beast to speak, but to rebuke a Reprobate; it was when a she Ass rebuked *Balaam*. But such a prodigy was never used for the conversion or the amendment of a man.

Six

Six High-Priests, whom the Scripture declares to have been guilty, and a seventh who hath been more guilty then all the former.

THe six first were, 1 *Aaron*, who, since the melting of the golden Calf, murmured against *Moses*. 2 *Heli*, whose indulgence undid his sons and the people. 3 *Abiathar*, who had a hand in the conjuration of *Adonijah*, *Solomon*'s competitor. 4 *Urijah*, who, to please King *Ahaz*, built in the Temple a bastard-Altar. 5 *Serajah*, who is not accepted of the number of the Priests that persecuted *Jeremiah*. 6 *Jehoshua*, whose sons, in the *Babylonish* Captivity, maried strange women.

But the height of all the crimes that defiled that holy Order, was, when the high Typical Priest condemned the true High-Priest, namely, *Christ*. The Priesthood which *Caiaphas* exercised, ought to have justifi'd that of *Christ*; whereas the Figure hath given the lie to the Truth, and the Shadow hath endeavoured to annihilate the Body.

Barabbas.

Barabbas.

His name shews he was a *Jew*, and therefore it was so much the more important to the *Jews* to have him punished, that they might not incur the suspition of abetting a seditious person; for they were very much subject to rise against the *Romans*, their Superiors. By procuring life to such a man, they endanger their Nation, or expose it to State suspitions; but their madness depraved their judgment.

Why did God pardon many of those that procured Christ's *death, and not* Pilat's *wife, who opposed her self to that death?*

God hath set in the way of salvation many thousand *Jews*, who had crucifi'd the Lord of glory, *Act.* 2. 23, 37, &c. and 3. 14, 15. and 4. 4. And the same history rehearses, that there were a great number of Priests, whom we know were guiltier of the death of *Christ*, who

who were since brought to the obedience of Faith. Such were the effects of the goodness of God, who was willing to save them through the same blood which they had spilt, and cause their crime, the most heinous that ever could be committed, to turn to their own salvation.

But if grace was shewed to those, to the murtherers of the righteous, to those that used him as a malefactor, why not also to that person, who alone pleaded for him on this occasion, and endeavoured to deliver him? Among many Answers that may be given to that Question, 'twill suffice now to say, that *Pilat*'s wife was onely moved therein by the fear of punishment, in case her husband should condemn an innocent man; that such terror is far from the true motives of charity, and of the love of justice. Thus, among many persons that are guilty, God doth often pardon the guiltiest of all, and leaves others to the condemnation they have deserved. In both he shews, that he hath power to shew mercy or justice, notwithstanding the degrees of the offences.

Judas

Judas *his death*.

WHen a man is so notoriously wicked, that in wickedness he surmounts all other men of his time, ordinarily he becomes his own Hangman. The Scripture mentions five men, who, doubtless, were the wickedest men of their time, and all of them were their own murtherers. One *Abimelech* son of *Gideon*, who put to death seventy of his brethren. *Saul*, guilty of many notorious crimes. *Ahitophel*, a Traitor, and an abhominable Counsellor. *Zimri*, one of the Kings of *Israel*, and extremely bloody. And finally *Judas*, whose crime went beyond all the crimes that were ever committed by men.

Let us add here an observation which is indifferent. In the *Roman* Histories, and in our own experience, there are more examples of women that have murdered themselves, then of men; this is observed by such as are curious. But we add thereunto, that the contrary is found in the Scripture; for in all the holy History, there is not an example of any woman that ever killed her self: not that that sex was so long a time without giving examples of such Tragedies, but because

it

it had no relation to any important matter of the History.

Chrift *praying for thofe that crucifi'd him.*

UNder the Law, he that had unwittingly killed fome body, had liberty to retire himfelf into any of the Towns of Refuge, to avoid the wrath of the kindred of the deceafed party; and the death of the High-prieft happening, that manflayer had full liberty to return home, and there to live, without fear of being ever molefted on that accompt, *Numb.* 35. But *Chrift* himfelf procured pardon to his murtherers, praying to his Father to pardon them that crime, alledging their ignorance, *They know not what they do*.

Here a queftion may be moved; The death of the High-prieft freed the perfon that had committed man-flaughter; but if any had cafually killed the High-prieft himfelf, would that death have delivered the author of it? or would he have been neceffitated to ftay untill the death of another High-prieft? But although this be not mentioned in the Law, yet it is more likely, that the error which occafion'd the death of a High-prieft, could not be blotted

ted out but by the death of another High-priest, succeeding the former. But *Christ* having no successor in his Priesthood, his murtherers could not find their expiation, but in the death they procured to him.

The onely time when Christ *speaking to God, did not call him Father.*

IT was upon the Cross, when he cryed out, *My God, my God;* until then he had always called him Father, even at his agony in the Garden; and yet when he committed his Spirit into his hands. But that interval wherein he cried out, *My God,* is as the center of his Humiliation, He kept himself then in the common rank of the Believers, who, under the Old Testament used not, when they prayed to God, to call him their Father. So he who alone had the priviledge to call him so, did forbear it whilst he was in the depth of his abasement. We have alledged several other reasons of it, in our observations on the Symbole.

F I N I S.